Thatcher, Politics and Fantasy

The Political Culture of Gender and Nation

For my parents Sylvia and Bert Nunn

Thatcher, Politics and Fantasy

The Political Culture of Gender and Nation

Heather Nunn

Lawrence & Wishart
LONDON 2002

Lawrence and Wishart Limited
99a Wallis Road
London
E9 5LN

First published 2002

Copyright © Lawrence and Wishart 2002

British Library Cataloguing in Publication Data.
A catalogue record for this book is available from the British Library

ISBN 0 85315 962 9

Typeset in Liverpool by E-Type
Printed and bound by Bookcraft, Bath

Website address www.l-w-bks.co.uk

Contents

Acknowledgements

I have received assistance and advice on research materials from a range of institutions. The British Academy and the University of East London provided me with research bursaries. Thanks go to the British Library, the British Newspaper Library, and the Conservative Party Archives, the Bodleian Library, Oxford. The Conservative Party archivist, Dr. Martin Maw was a particularly valuable source of advice. The National Sound Archives provided invaluable recorded material and particular thanks goes to the archivist Tony Cadogan for his assistance. For information on the historical and current state of women in Parliament the 300 Group, London was very informative. The Public Information Office, House of Commons provided detailed information on women in the House of Commons and recent general elections. Thanks also to Senate House Library, University of London, Barking Reference Library and the Learning Resource Centre, University of East London. The Senior Archivist Joy Eldridge at The Mass Observation Archive, Sussex University sent useful information on public responses to the Falklands war.

I could not have completed this book without the support of many friends and colleagues. A number of people deserve warmest acknowledgement for their interest, advice and information: Dr. Caroline Bainbridge, Professor Andrew Blake, Professor Kenneth Parker, Professor Alan O'Shea and Dr. John Parham, Ruth Biressi, Miri Forster, Berni O'Dea and Kathryn White. My parents Sylvia and Bert Nunn listened with patience to my complaints and provided me with a wealth of contemporary press cuttings. Most importantly I have to thank Professor Sally Alexander who taught me how to think and write clearly and Bill Schwarz, a special friend and constant inspiration on thinking about Conservative politics. Last, but never least,

Anita Biressi deserves all my gratitude for her constant advice and support, without her this book would never have been completed.

CHAPTER ONE:

Introduction: Thatcher, Politics, Fantasy

> Fantasy, with its aggrandizing narrative appetite, appropriates and incorporates social meaning and, structuring its public narrative, forms the historically specific stories and subjectivities available – that aspect of fantasy is open to political analysis and negotiation.
>
> (Kaplan, 1986:153)

This book begins with an image, an image that, for me at least, is both evocative and disturbing. This image in many respects encapsulates what it is that I find intriguing and worthy of sustained analysis about Margaret Thatcher's political persona. In September 1988 Thatcher visited Germany, and images of her test-driving the new British-built Challenger tank appeared in newspapers and on television. Swathed in white, with a headscarf trailing behind her in the breeze, white leather gloves upon her hands, she stood upright, seemingly guiding the bulky armoured tank across barren desert-like terrain. As the tank advanced across the scrub, her scarf flowed in the slipstream and appeared to move in concert with the union jack flag raised on her right side. She gazed forward intensely, her bearing suggesting confidence; she appeared unafraid of imagined opposition, and at home with the machinery of war that carried her.

Myths of national strength and national identity are frequently accorded emotional strength and simple clarity through the imaginary reconstruction of past wars and battles. Thatcher's image of national leadership – surrounded by the latest technology of the battlefield – conjured up fantasies of imperial venture and heroic narratives of masculine courage and strength in the face of adversity, of defending one's own land alongside the righteous incursion of another's terri-

9

tory. Her speeches throughout the 1980s were replete with references to 'our' victory in World War Two, as were her numerous invocations of the wartime Prime Minister Winston Churchill, who was a model of masterful national leadership that she sought to adopt. The embedding of Thatcher within such myths gained strength with the British war against Argentina in the Falklands conflict of mid-1982. Britain's victory, personalised in the media as Thatcher's triumph over the Argentine leader General Galtieri, fuelled the Conservatives' successful 1983 electoral campaign and provided their leader with a clear symbol of her combativeness for subsequent political speeches. Clearly, then, this image of Thatcher in a tank could be read as another reference to Britain's recent military past and, specifically, as an allusion to General Montgomery's victorious tank offensive in North Africa against General Rommel's German Afrika Korps at the 1942 Battle of El Alamein. Her photo opportunity also prompts comparison with other fictionalised dramas of past heroic agency. It recalls, for example, the heat and dust spectacle of David Lean's epic *Lawrence of Arabia* (1962); and this evokes associations with the symbolic traces of Britain's empire, and a model of masculine adventure and stoic national pride – qualities resonating with the Thatcherite notion of 'enterprise culture'. But most importantly for this book, this image juxtaposes heavy-duty military weaponry with Thatcher's visible, perhaps slightly outmoded, femininity: the vaguely regal Englishwoman costumed in pure floating white. If women are conventionally excluded from the grand narratives of warfare – of the public ability to die for one's country – they are nonetheless invoked in sublime nation-symbols such as Britannia or Lady Liberty, in the wartime address to the nation as family and in notions of the pure and morally policed homeland. For some then, this image recalls the colonial portrait of Katherine Hepburn clothed in white, seated in a boat gliding down the river, centre frame in John Huston's *The African Queen* (1952) – a symbol of strong unflinching, pristine, steadfast femininity.[1] For this book, the latter comparison has particular resonance. It should be recalled that, in *The African Queen*, Hepburn's spinsterish, morally scrupulous character was played out against the backdrop of World War One. Her femininity concealed the iron will and determination to avenge those she had left behind, slaughtered by the German foe.

As my opening quotation indicates, an understanding of such symbolic fictions and their public usage is more textured when placed in historical and cultural context. To fully comprehend the aggressive assertion of leadership made in this particular photo-call, one should recall surrounding events. September 1988 was, in retrospect, a significant month for Margaret Thatcher. One can track the line from her political positioning in this month to her fall from power in November 1990. To point up the context of the above image is to emphasise why, in addition to its immediate visual resonance, it now appears so memorable. The Conservative Party had won the 1987 general election the year before, partly on the basis of their strong defence policy; this was informed by an emphasis on nuclear deterrence and an emphatic maintenance of post-war defence links with NATO and the United States, rather than on an evolving European Community. This advocating of nuclear armament as the essential component of a fortified and aggressively strong nation had been endorsed in the previous 1983 general election. The 1987 general election returned to this theme and, once again, nuclear armament was interpreted by the Conservative government as an extension of the righteous spirit of conventional warfare, epitomised by Britain's lonely stand in World War Two, and continued in the Falklands conflict. It is important to signal here how this position was fortified by Thatcher's image with the electorate as a strong leader, and her presentation as a woman aggressively warding off international threat and the dilution of the nation's identity. For a significant number of the voting public, her uncompromising stand engaged with their anxieties about strong national protection.[2]

On 20 September 1988, Thatcher made her controversial 'Bruges Speech' to the College of Europe. The speech was a veiled response to another made that month by Jacques Delors, the new French President of the European Commission. Delors had received a rapturous reception from British trade union delegates at the Trades Union Congress in Bournemouth for his call for Europe-wide collective bargaining. Shortly after, the Bruges speech carved out Thatcher's opposition to European centralisation and bureaucracy, as she demanded the preservation of each country's 'own customs, traditions and identity' against a 'European super-state' (Thatcher, 1988:260). Against the imagined abolition of national frontiers, she raised the spectre of roving crime and insecure borders: 'it is a matter of plain common sense that we cannot totally abolish frontier controls if we are also to protect our citizens from crime and stop the movement of drugs, of terrorists, and of illegal immigrants' (Thatcher: 263). She was, in this projected chaos, 'combative, solitary, righteous and outnumbered', a presentation that wed her to a beleaguered Britain and recalled modern myths of the wartime nation 'standing alone and at bay' (Foley, 1993:161).

Her speech provoked extensive media coverage and debate. It scored an existing division within the Conservative Party between those for or against greater political and monetary integration with Europe, a division that Thatcher continued to exacerbate in her latter years of leadership. This rift culminated in the resignation of the Chancellor, Nigel Lawson on 26 October 1989 and Geoffrey Howe's resignation on 1 November 1990, over differences on European policy.[3] Howe, Leader of the House and last remaining survivor of Thatcher's 1979 Cabinet, spurred Conservative dissent. In his vitriolic resignation speech on 13 November 1990 he attacked her vision of 'a continent that [was] positively teeming with ill-intentioned people, scheming, in her words, to "extinguish democracy"' (Watkins, 1991:153). The speech provided a focus for broader dissatisfaction with her leadership, including with the recent introduction of the unpopular community charge with which she had become strongly identified, and a string of lost local elections and by-elections. Following a leadership challenge and subsequent widespread Cabinet opposition, Thatcher reluctantly, indeed tearfully, resigned on 28 November 1990.

Shortly before that resignation, in September 1990, exactly two years after her appearance aboard the Challenger tank in Germany, Thatcher selected the tank again as 'the best possible equipment' to reinforce British troops in the erupting Gulf conflict with Iraq (Thatcher, 1995:825). In her final speech to her Central Office workers, she informed them she had been 'very, very thrilled' that, following the announcement of her resignation, the United States President George Bush had still called her to discuss the Gulf conflict. The conflict became a metaphor through which she indicated to her staff that she would not 'falter' from future political battle albeit as a 'backseat driver' (CPA: TS 11/90).[4] Here, most clearly, anticipated war and active engagement in conflict were, for Thatcher, a way of surmounting her (lost) political battle much closer to home; in a most fragile moment, as power was slipping from her grasp, they seemed to secure her future political relevance.

The image then, of Thatcher riding in a tank, and its immediate force, can be embellished with other 'historically specific stories' in which real and imagined political and national enmities are brought into play. As an assertion of British leadership through the most war-like of representations, this image signals for me the importance of thinking about politics beyond the official set of policies, regulations, set debates and procedures. It flags the importance of media representations as powerful cultural forms through which subjects can construct the field of meanings associated with political and national life. Crucially, it opens up, or initiates a space for thinking about the relationship between the categories of woman and nation, of political power and violence. It prompts exploration of the role certain forms of femininity and masculinity play in securing or negotiating imaginary constructions of political leadership and national identity, in which fantasies of mastery and invasion come to the fore. This relationship, and how it is brought sharply into focus through Thatcher's distinct political persona, is central to this exploration. I argue that Thatcher's gender was (and is) crucial: it informed the construction of her persona, was drawn on to vitalise her political discourse and was frequently disavowed. The common sense statement that she was a woman who was the 'best man' for the job was integral to the broader political and media articulation of her image, to the cultural representation of Thatcherite politics, and to the imagined communities and identities she was said to represent.

This book addresses her performance of grand adversarial leadership, and the ways in which political colleagues and the media negotiated her presence on the public stage. The image of Thatcher at war, as constantly embattled, appeared in a diverse range of texts which constituted her political image, and are the object of my analysis – speeches, press photos, campaign posters, radio interviews, magazine articles, political biographies. I explore how these texts present a woman encountering opposition, danger, and hostility on a number of levels: personal, party, doctrinal, civil, national, international. From the outset of her leadership she was seen to be at odds with the recent Conservative past as well as in fierce conflict with a range of oppositional political figures and beliefs. In the following chapters I illustrate how her leadership came to signify a radical engagement with the aims and objectives of Conservative politics and, more broadly, an attempted disengagement with forms of collectivist and consensual politics that held sway in post-war Britain. She was presented as being at permanent war with political stagnation, national complacency, dependency on the Welfare State, official bureaucracy and also social insurrection and international threat. This book contends that it was within this arena of conflict and always-possible violence that she flourished as a successful politician.

I argue that Margaret Thatcher was a politician who thrived on extremes; who thrived on acting upon, or appearing to act upon, the clash between civilisation and violent discontent. She often turned turbulent political events to her advantage. She bolstered her image as 'Iron Lady' (the sobriquet itself originally an intended insult by the Soviet press) through the mediation of a series of political 'battles'. The battles were captured in her phrase 'enemies without and within', which symbolically linked diverse events. These conflicts were numerous and were often interpreted in her speeches as direct assaults upon her political values. They included the military conflict with Argentina over the Falkland Islands (April 1982), and the subsequent ideological battle with advocates of unilateral nuclear disarmament in the 1983 general election campaign. Continual antagonistic relations with the trade unions were epitomised in the long and hostile dispute with the National Union of Mineworkers in the year-long strike from March 1984 to March 1985. The IRA bombing of the Conservative Party at the Grand Hotel, Brighton during the 1984 Party Conference was recast by Thatcher as a broader battle with a 'spectrum' of violence and 'calculated hostility' within the nation's borders, which united terrorists, trade unionists, criminals and 'Fascist Left' Labour opponents (Thatcher, 1984:200). In the late 1980s, as the Cold War conflict with the Soviet Union dissipated and communist power abdicated or ceased to exist in numerous Eastern European states, Thatcher focused with renewed vigour her attack upon those political opponents who supported political unification with the European Community.

Finally, her reluctant relinquishment of office in 1990 was cast as conflict. Of this moment she has recalled: 'I would fight – and, if necessary, go down fighting – for my beliefs as long as I could. Dignity did not come into it' (Thatcher, 1993:832). Correspondingly, the press presented her resignation as the result of calculated violence against her – a political betrayal or indeed assassination – and a conclusive 'battle of the sexes' in which she was fleetingly cast as victim of the 'men in suits'.[5] These narratives of conflict, I suggest, were intimately bound up with Thatcher's gender and the way it was drawn upon to both underpin and equally to challenge her political power. In the following chapters, specific texts (such as newspapers or political biographies) and the political discourses that informed them are explored for the different inflections of nation, family, ethnicity, masculinity and femininity which are played out in the presentation of Thatcher and her project to revive Britain.

The conventional association of public political power and strong leadership with masculinity and how this was reconciled with

Thatcher's femininity is addressed throughout this book. Chapter Two will illustrate how gender was fundamental to Thatcher's reception within the Conservative Party and also how she became the focus for projected fears and anxieties about the role of populist Conservative discourse. I locate the national and party political context of her rise to Conservative Party Leader and indicate her disruption of the post-war conventions of the party and more broadly of 'one nation' Conservatism. Thatcher's anomalous position as female Prime Minister was often advantageous for the Conservative Party's image in the 1980s. In some respects, the very fact she was a woman added to the Thatcherite government's projected image of radicalism and novelty. Furthermore, as revealed by former Cabinet members' memories of her premiership, her femininity added a frisson of sexuality to their engagement with her and disturbed the public school code of conduct and decorum formerly operating within the all-male preserve of the party's higher echelons. Yet, critics within her own party interpreted her as a brash outsider. Her perceived lack of decorum and her disdain for the post-war consensus were viewed, by some, as the Conservative Party's dereliction of social responsibility or the unleashing of selfish individualism within its grass roots (Gilmour, 1992). Importantly, in Chapter Two I signal how some critiques of Thatcher cast Conservatism and rational political behaviour in masculine terms. Here, femininity was latched via the figure of the 'Tory woman' to mass party political participation and to a feminised gut punitive response to crime or national decline. In this respect, Thatcher was situated with the rank and file of the party; and this location of her by critical colleagues revealed broader anxieties about Conservatism's long-held preoccupation with social chaos, and the collapse of that purportedly rational concern into irrational demands for aggressive authority and retributive government.

Within the broader public realm, Thatcher acquired an iconic status and invigorated media depictions of politics. The image of a woman tackling the hide-bound traditions of the Conservative Party and the vagaries of Whitehall's Civil Service provided a novel angle to representations of the bureaucratic, often torpid practices and policies of mainstream politics. She provoked powerful identifications that were often conveyed and played out to full advantage in media coverage of her. Loathed or loved, coverage of her was rarely dispassionate and the tendency of news discourse to personalise the political was accentuated by the Conservative Party's own promotional emphasis on their leader. She was a prominent spokesperson for the pre-eminence of 'the individual' in social engagement. She also appeared to represent a distinct personalisation of mainstream politics: her brand of Conservatism was presented as 'conviction politics' fuelled by her individual personal vision. Part of her electoral success can be attributed to the electorate's perception, sustained through favourable media coverage, that she reduced the otherwise distant and disembodied world of high politics to everyday female common sense.

It has become a commonplace that contemporary 'media culture' provides the symbols, myths and resources which help constitute the structure of everyday life and the fabric of political and social identities. Thatcher was an astute politician. She was fully aware of the political potential of the modern mass media for the advancement of both her image and her political discourse. The accounts of her highly skilled team of media and image professionals and of their careful orchestration of her public image, electoral campaigns, television performances, press and magazine interviews have contributed to her multi-media persona (Lumsden and Forbes, 1986; Cockerell, 1988). Her aggressively populist stance informed her engagement with the tabloid press, with television chat shows and 'light' radio programmes. Alongside the media focus on her leadership 'style', this embrace of the media led to debates about the emergence of a presidential form of British politics and analyses of the changing relationship between politicians and the media (Negrine, 1989; Foley, 1993; Franklin, 1994).

An emphasis on the performance of aggressively masterful political leadership will run through this book and will be one strand in the overarching concern with Thatcher's masquerade.[6] It has been argued that the mass media 'encourage secular charisma', that the compulsive interest in personality has led to a contemporary emphasis on the politician's appearance, on 'the quality of the mask' (Sennett, 1986:284-5). Thatcher's Press Secretary Bernard Ingham complemented her aggressive stance in working the media and has since reflected that contemporary government and media coexist in a 'permanent and natural state of tension'. He concluded that these relations are 'essentially cannibalistic': politicians and the media 'feed off each other' (Ingham in Franklin, 1994:14).[7] The media both produced and consumed images of Thatcher, reproducing the texts produced for them by her team of consultants, but engaging also in the construction, elaboration and revision of those images. Political opponents and critical journalists seemed to both revel in and deplore her; she was attacked and celebrated in press cartoons, her name featured in pop songs, novels, films and plays. She was famously caricatured on the satirical television programme *Spitting Image* as the cigar-smoking puppet autocrat, wearing male suit and tie and savagely beating opponents; a portrayal that captured the volatile mix of projected violence and uneasy humour that informed many images of her. This outpouring of popular cultural images and the vitriolic nature of many sketches of Thatcher prompt analysis of the disciplinary and punitive nature of her political discourse and image and their possible fascination.

To understand that fascination, Jacqueline Rose, in her provocative essay 'Margaret Thatcher and Ruth Ellis' (1988), signalled the theoretical and political importance of unpacking Thatcher's image and discourse in psychoanalytical terms. She highlighted the difficulties raised for feminist analysts in encountering a woman who had reached the 'summit of political power' but who 'embodied' the excesses of phallic mastery that had been located, in much feminist thought, as a patriarchal system of authority. Thatcher's political presence highlighted a taboo area of feminist analyses: woman's engagement with structures of political power and discourse that aggressively asserted nationhood, militarism, and state authority. Thatcher constituted a problem. Her authority seemed to derive from both her movement across gender identities, troubling the binaries of sexual difference, and also through the way she endorsed an unequal gender divide by locating women within the domestic and moral sphere and placing men as active public subjects. Her persona and political discourse provoked and tapped into others' ambivalent identifications. As a woman and as a jingoistic and disciplinary political leader she provoked idealisation often interwoven with aggression on the part of colleagues, media commentators and the electorate. But her persona also seemed to thrive upon images of violence or threat and her political discourse conjured up fantasies of a better self often achieved through another subject or group's removal.

Following Rose, this book acknowledges political culture and its representation as part of a broader system of gendered representation. This analysis of Thatcher works from assumptions made in recent feminist cultural analysis that the image of the 'woman' in Western society functions as both guarantee of stability and as destabilising problem (Rose, 1986). To analyse Thatcher's persona and its force, different psychoanalytic concepts will be drawn upon throughout this analysis: negation, disavowal, fetishism, masquerade, paranoia, the super ego. Two general critical concerns hold these concepts together. Firstly, a concern to interrogate the powerful prominent representation of the aberrant 'woman', and the political and cultural negotiation of that figure. Secondly, a concern to understand the relationship between psychic constituents of identity and the troubled ambivalent identifications of allegiance and fragmentation, guilt and exoneration, hate and love, desire and fear, that forge and fracture the imagined community in a particular historical and political moment. I draw selectively upon the work of Sigmund Freud, Julia Kristeva, Slavoj Žižek and Joan Riviere. These theorists are all drawn upon to show how particular political and social subjects are defined through negativity in a range of dominant political discourses in the 1980s.

Thatcher was a woman who operated through negativity. She produced images of exclusion, marginality and chaos. I illustrate how these conditions (both real and imaginary) and the subjects that embodied them were central to her opposing images of the stable, self-sufficient and securely bordered nation. I suggest that her authoritative persona was secured by invoking the perilous proximity of the violent transgressive other who threatened and jeopardised the Conservative voter, family or nation. In this sense Thatcher's discourse deployed structures – negation and projection – that are fundamental to social identity while pushing them to their limits. For the recognition of the other that constitutes subjectivity involves a paradoxical process in which 'the object is *in fantasy* always being destroyed' (Benjamin, 1988:38, her italics). Thatcher's absolute assertion of authority and self-certainty, her demand to have her way at whatever cost, were hyperbolic displays of aggression and omnipotence that refused any submission as weakness. Here, her ambivalent placing as woman and as masterful masculine political leader crystallised the gendered demarcations that underpin social being; demarcations that her political persona crossed but also continually reasserted for other men and women. For, the social order's fundamental dialectic is that of gendered difference. Here, the woman operates within symbolic systems of representation as a 'point of impossibility, its other face which it endlessly seeks to refuse – what might be called the vanishing point of its attempt to construct itself as a system' (Rose, 1986:219). Thatcher, as a woman, provoked divided and often deeply conflicting responses. On the one hand, her bellicose leadership seemed to symbolise the guarantee of a political power that upheld an aggressively phallic economy of control. On the other hand, as a woman, she was also read as potential point of excess or collapse of that systematic control and order.

In Chapter Three I draw upon Joan Riviere's (1929) concept of the 'masquerade' to theorise Thatcher's gender ambiguity. Riviere noted that, as professional intellectuals and public speakers, modern women were often able to combine conventional feminine interests and activities with competent professional activity 'at least as well as the average man' (Riviere, 1929:36). Riviere's analysis produced an account of the female professional's exaggerated, often compulsive performance of 'feminine' behaviour – deference to male colleagues, anxiety, flirtation, anxious enquiry about public ability – as an attempt to contain the anxiety of anticipated reprisals from father-figures after her competent intellectual performances (Riviere: 37). Riviere famously equated womanliness *per se* with the masquerade: 'The reader may ask how I define womanliness or where I draw the line between genuine womanliness and "the masquerade". My suggestion is not, however, that there is any such difference; whether radical or superficial they are the same thing' (p38). However, what is sometimes overlooked is her contrast of the masquerade as 'a primary mode of enjoyment' with the masquerade 'used more as a device for avoiding anxiety' (Riviere: 38; Fletcher, 1988: 53-4). The former position offers femininity as a reaction formation, a placatory display of passivity and receptivity as the (still troubled) acceptance of conventional femininity. The latter position offers femininity as a mask that covers up the refusal to renounce castration wishes: the desire to take, act and speak in the powerful public sphere. My analysis of Thatcher emphasises this refusal and the consequent anxiety and aggression that attend her masquerade. But I also emphasise her relish of political contestation and engagement in battle. In doing so I contend that to fully understand the operation of her masquerade, other markers of identity – those of class and of religion – must be integrated into an analysis of her (very public) gendered persona. While Riviere's concept of the masquerade is one aspect of this analysis, I develop a more general notion of masquerade as political performance and national display. Here the connotations of a female leader who postured as a war leader or a disciplinarian are interwoven with the broader playing out of fantasy in political and media representations.

Party political discourses and images appeal to political subjects collectively but also as individuals; they attempt to articulate desires and fears about contemporary and future life, register nostalgia about the past and reassure that bad or traumatic events in the nation's recent past do not recur. In this book these hopes and fears are located specifically in the post-war crisis of British social democracy. Recent social theory has marked this as the socio-political moment when collective traditions, customs and values were increasingly overturned (Jenkins, 1987; Kavanagh, 1987; Hall, 1988; Hall and Jacques, 1989; Mercer, 1990). The globalisation of the economy and the growing network of multinational corporations that marked rapid technological and industrial change partly resulted in the collapse of British heavy industries and the destabilisation of working communities (Harvey, 1980:Ch.8; Hutton, 1995). Furthermore, in the post-war years Britain's national sense of identity finally lost its old imperial markers. Meanwhile, consumer culture promised adventure, growth and transformation of self-identity but also gave rise to individual or collective feelings of longing, frustration and exclusion. Both left and right wing political discourses attempted to tap into, explain, and harness these senses of fragmentation and of change and to mobilise new ideological constituencies that married the changing times.

One of the central theorists of the crisis of British social democracy and its relationship to the moment of Thatcherism was Stuart Hall. In a series of influential papers throughout the 1980s, Hall analysed how Thatcherism, as the articulation of distinct economic, political, cultural and racial discourses, sustained hegemonic authority through three successive general elections. He charted the conditions of Thatcherism's emergence from the late 1960s. These conditions included the failures of the Wilson and Heath governments, the longer deterioration of Britain's economic position, and the increasing difficulty of sustaining economically and ideologically the universal commitments of the post-war Welfare State. Added to these factors was the potent political 'interpellation' of the 'race issue' into the sense of fragmentation in 'British civil and political life' (Hall et al, 1978:306; Hall and Jacques, 1983; Hall, 1988). The term 'authoritarian populism'[8] was coined to capture Thatcherism's fractured, inconsistent but nonetheless powerful mobilisation of authoritarian and disciplinary discourses in conjunction with populist appeals to the individual consumer-voter and self-sustaining family.

Following Thatcher's third general election victory in 1987, Stuart Hall (1988) stressed the importance of analytical engagement with the role of image and desire in political identification. He urged left wing political analysts to consider the strategic importance of the 'symbolic majority' in the success or not of a political party and underlined that political allegiance was partly based on projection. Voters identify with particular constructions of the future aligned with a certain political party. Political discourses latch material considerations to particular imaginary identities: 'People make identifications symboli-

cally: through social imagery, in their political imaginati
themselves" as one sort of person or another. They
future" within this scenario or that' (Hall, 1988:33).

He highlighted the ambivalent and contradictory nature of political
identification, and argued that there are no 'natural' blocs of Labour
or Conservative voters. Thatcherism appealed to conflicting social
identities such as 'mother', 'working woman', 'home owner',
'concerned parent', 'law-abiding citizen', 'proud Britisher', 'responsible father', 'tax payer' and 'entrepreneur'. These identities were
addressed at different political moments and united in constituencies
that crossed class allegiances.[9] This book examines how conflict was
central to consolidation of these Thatcherite subjects and their
enemies: the miners, Marxists, 'loony Lefties', trade unionists, unruly
children, hooligans, muggers, and 'trendy' teachers that littered
Thatcher's speeches. Representations of conflict between these
enemies and 'individuals' or 'families' fighting for their values and
identity addressed contemporary fears about unemployment, children's education, the power of trade unions, the closure of coal mines,
violent crime, the ability of Britain to trade effectively abroad and to
defend itself from military attack. Chapter Four focuses on the importance of 'the family' and 'the child' in Thatcher's discourse and the
imaginary battle of the responsible parent against progressive education, politically motivated teachers and the libertarian legacy of the
'permissive 1960s'. Here I chart the links between Thatcher and New
Right endorsement of social authoritarianism, morality and the 'traditional' nuclear family. I analyse the idealisation of the family and its
crucial role in political fantasies of harmony, self-sufficiency and
material comfort. Focusing specifically on the child as a repository of
adult hopes and fears, I argue that Thatcher envisaged a 'privatisation'
of the child that symbolised a broader extraction of Thatcherite
subjects from the dependency of the Welfare State and into consumer
self-sufficiency. I illustrate how adult fears about the undisciplined or
politically indoctrinated child tapped into and stirred up unconscious
anxieties about subjective fragmentation and desires for authority and
control.

In dialogue with Hall, Jacqueline Rose (1988) provocatively underlined the importance of fantasy to an understanding of political
imagery and discourse in general and, most specifically, to the operation of Conservative discourse and the powerful role of Thatcher
within that operation. Correspondingly, this analysis is informed by
the contention that fantasy – as a realm of psychic division, conflict,

multiple identification and desire – enhances an understanding of the political and cultural realms. Two related aspects of fantasy are held as central here. Firstly, fantasy is understood as 'a script' – a scenario of 'organised scenes' – which offers the dramatisation of desire and the possibility of a range of roles for each subject, a range of possible identifications (Laplanche and Pontalis, 1973: 318). Secondly, fantasy is understood as a protective function that provides the subject with a mode of defence. Fantasy enables the re-elaboration of desires; it enables a partial recognition of repressed memories. Consequently, it is also the locus of a fierce defensiveness and facilitates such defence processes as negation or projection (Laplanche and Pontalis: 318).[10] Fantasy is the precondition of our gendered and sexual selves – as a realm of conflict and division – it 'frames our contemporary social and political worlds from the start' (Elliott, 1996:2). Moreover, fantasies of authority, community, and nation bind us into and make meaningful our collective life. Freud indicated that fantasy operates at conscious, subconscious and unconscious levels: as a term it encapsulates the processes of narrative and visual representation in daydream, fiction, and romance. Fantasy here can be seen as a stepping out of, and back into, the social world, and, crucially, as an active creation, which shapes and is shaped by that world.

I demonstrate how Thatcherite discourses addressed the trauma of instability that characterises contemporary British times; they offered visions of a strong Britain and of strong British subjects. I explore how Thatcher's 'family romance' provided a model for social aspiration and how Thatcher's persona often involved the maintenance of a tenuous equipoise between masculine and feminine positions. Her persona was contradictory; it moved across the spectrum of highly conventional gender roles, from a celebration of herself as 'housewife' managing the nation's budget, to an engagement with a pre-existent repertoire of cultural idioms of powerful or disciplinary British womanhood: the nanny, matron, governess, or warrior-queen (Warner, 1985:51-2). Her success within a male-dominated high political sphere was partly dependent on her ability to inhabit particular feminine positions while often simultaneously disavowing her femininity (Brunt, 1987:23). Her presentation as 'Iron Lady' or 'barrier of steel' between 'the people' and the violent 'others' of her nation involved the repudiation of femininity and its concomitant vulnerabilities in favour of the most hyper-phallic of roles (Rose, 1988:65). Crucially, I highlight Thatcher's positioning in relation to images of social chaos and violent unrest, which, I suggest, rehearsed a range of aggressive and submissive fantasy scenarios in which she or her loyal subjects faced a host of malefactors, oppressive state structures, or potential emasculating dependencies. Furthermore, I shall demonstrate the process of nostalgia in her speeches, wherein can be seen the compulsive repetition of past glories or visions of a better bygone age – the Victorian era, World War Two, the 'traditional' family – run as defence/defiance against the present.

Broader issues of imagined communal identity are also under investigation, for the 'scapegoat mechanism' on which Thatcher thrived is crucial to the social symbolic bond and how a community binds, secures and regulates itself (Rose, 1988:74). Chapter Five explores the 1983 general election campaign. On the back of the 1982 Falklands conflict, the 1983 campaign was fought most centrally on the issue of defence policy. This chapter explores the Conservative Party's support of nuclear armament as a prerequisite of national survival and as an aggressive symbol of national strength. I analyse the ways in which Thatcher, as 'war leader', was set up as the barrier to impending chaos and social disarray and as the embodiment and supporter of legitimate force and state control. Oppositions between freedom and thraldom, liberation and restraint, were central to Thatcherite discourse. I investigate the placing of her persona, and by implication Thatcherite Britain, on the cusp of these oppositions, and how this dialectic was played out in the Conservative and pro-Thatcher press. An analysis of the varied political and media accounts of social chaos emanating from or turned against her leads, in this chapter, to an interrogation of the 'cultural super-ego' and its ambivalent relationship with the nation-state's identity (Parker, 1997:115).

This interpretation of Thatcher is crucial here. At her first Conservative Party Conference as leader, she stressed that the 'first duty' of her government was 'to uphold the law'. She warned that 'to bob, weave and duck round that duty' was to encourage 'the governed' to do exactly the same and 'then nothing [would] be safe, not home, not liberty, not life itself' (Thatcher, 1975:28).[11] Alongside a self-presentation as national conscience and moral barometer, she proclaimed herself to be advocate of the freedom of the market and the individual and the lessening of state control over private and public life. She also endorsed the strengthening of police power, was committed to maintaining nuclear weaponry and was personally in favour of the return of capital punishment. She conjured up images of communist state violence and oppression and then displaced the connotations of ideological compulsion and physical coercion onto political opponents within the British nation. Her vision of a powerful British nation engaged with modern hopes of control, comfort and civilisation and fears of social discontent. The super-ego provides one way of understanding how Thatcher's imaginary power was consolidated through an ambivalent laying bare of illegitimate violence, and a counter-investment in the extreme violence of the state and the law. Freud likened the super-ego to 'a garrison in a conquered city': a metaphor that attempted to capture its role in containing revolutionary forces and its engagement in aggressive surveillance and control (Freud, 1930:316). My argument suggests that by examining Thatcher's extreme persona one can start to consider the violence and aggression that underpin the modern British nation.

References

1. I am indebted to students on my 1999 'Media, Gender and Ethnicity' course at King Alfred's College, Winchester who spoke fluently about their responses to a screening of television footage of this event. The imagery was brought into the class in response to a mature student who had recalled this image as the one which had stopped her in her tracks as a Conservative voter, when she thought Thatcher 'had gone too far'.
2. A MORI poll in 1987 found that between 25 and 30 per cent of the voters considered defence as the important single concern. This was a high figure for the post-war period as a whole and among all voters defence was behind only unemployment, education and housing in importance (MORI poll in *The Sunday Times*, 4 January 1987).
3. For a succinct account of the disputes with the Conservative Party over Monetary and European policy from 1989-1990, see Derbyshire and Derbyshire's *Politics in Britain* (1990:208-217).
4. CPA refers to the Conservative Party Archives at the Bodleian Library, Oxford. Folders will be referred to by their initials and catalogue numbers. Refer to archive list at back for key and full details.
5. See for example coverage in *The Times, Independent, Guardian, Daily Mail*, and *Daily Telegraph*, 23.11.90.
6. In this book the concept of 'masquerade' is drawn from Joan Riviere's account in 'Womanliness as a Masquerade' (1929) but also the term is used more broadly to analyse specific examples of gendered political performance.
7. Margaret Thatcher appointed Bernard Ingham in November 1979. Beforehand he was a journalist and then, from 1967, press officer with Barbara Castle, Eric Varley and Tony Benn. Assessments of Ingham often state his intuitive rapport with Thatcher. Some cast him as her Rasputin-

figure, others note the considerable expansion of his status and power by the latter years of Thatcher's premiership when she appointed him to the head of the entire Government Information Services (Thomson, 1989: 222; Young, 1989:165-6; Harris, 1990:170).

8. See Stuart Hall's 'The Great Moving Right Show' in S. Hall and M. Jacques (eds), (1983:19-39).

9. For critiques of Hall see B. Jessop et al (1988) and P. Hirst (1989:11-35).

10. My understanding of fantasy here is dependent on a number of texts: Freud's essays 'Family Romances' (1909), 'A Child is Being Beaten' (1919), 'A Note upon the "Mystic Writing-Pad" ' (1924); and J. Laplanche and J.-B. Pontalis' entry on 'Phantasy (or Fantasy)' in *The Language of Psychoanalysis* (1973).

11. This statement is taken from Margaret Thatcher's first speech to the Conservative Party Conference as leader (10.10.75) in Blackpool. Thatcher posed the choice Britain faced between a reinvigorated Conservatism committed to capitalism and liberating the talents of the British people, and economic and social decay under the Labour government.

CHAPTER TWO:

Tory Woman

A woman at the top: politics and gender

Gender is one of the recurrent references by which political power has been conceived, legitimated, and criticised.

(Scott, 1988:48)

On 11 February 1975, following recent defeat in the 1974 general elections,[1] the Conservative Party ousted Edward Heath and elected Margaret Thatcher as its new leader in opposition.[2] In that process she became the first woman to lead a political party in Britain. Four years later, on 3 May 1979, she became Britain's first female Prime Minister, defeating James Callaghan's Labour Party with a majority of forty-four per cent of the vote. She won a further two general election victories in 1983 and 1987 in which the Conservatives maintained almost the same percentage of the vote that they had achieved in 1979.[3] Thatcher remained in office until her reluctant resignation on 28 November 1990, by which time she was the longest serving Prime Minister of the twentieth century. She nostalgically recalled this period in her memoirs as 'eleven years, six months and twenty-four days ... [in] the well-lit world of public life' (Thatcher, 1995:465).

Thatcher's image thrived on surrounding chaos. The ideological quandary and divided loyalties that characterised the Conservative Party in 1975 enabled her unexpected rise to power. In the face of the failure of senior candidates Keith Joseph and Edward du Cann to stand against Edward Heath, the way stood open for Thatcher.[4] Many established colleagues interpreted her success against Heath in the first ballot of the leadership challenge as the fleeting reward of an outsider's reckless bravery (Gamble, 1988:91). Her precocious break with Heath

enabled her to defeat his loyal followers William Whitelaw, Jim Prior
and Geoffrey Howe with 146 votes in the second ballot. The *Daily
Telegraph,* anticipating the favourable coverage of Thatcher throughout the 1980s, headlined an editorial on her challenge: 'Consider her
Courage' (Gamble, 1988: 91).

Margaret Thatcher is now such a familiar figure on the political
landscape that it is hard to recapture the shocked reactions produced
by her sudden accession to the top of her party. The Conservative
Party's response, particularly within the Cabinet, was one of disbelief
and disorientation mixed with the expectation that she was merely a
contingent and temporary figure. Her success was construed as a vote
against Heath rather than *for* her (Critchley, 1985:121; Young and
Sloman, 1986:30; Gamble, 1988:93). Thatcher's political past had not
suggested her rapid rise to leadership. This route to political power was
marked by her gender and her promotion to leader appeared to established Conservatives to be all the more shocking because she was a
woman. She had become President of the Oxford University
Conservative Association in her last year of study at Somerville
College (1943-47). (Oxford itself had been a chance opportunity for
young Margaret Roberts when a preferred candidate dropped out.) In
her role as president she gained experience in electioneering and had
made valuable contacts, but her gender excluded her from the Oxford
Union and denied her the contacts and debating skills that oiled the
route for aspiring male predecessors such as Harold Macmillan and
Edward Heath. Her first jobs as research chemist for a plastics factory
and for J. Lyons, testing cake-fillings and ice cream, did not chime with
the professions that marked out Conservative eligibility. Nor did she
possess the inherited propertied background that eased a path to politics in the Conservative Party. In interviews she recalled how her father
scraped up her fees to Oxford when she failed to gain a scholarship
(Murray, 1978:24). She acknowledged that financial restraint alone had
halted her consideration of a career in politics until the 1946 rise in
politician's pay from £600 to £1,000 (Murray, 1978:42). She recalled: 'I
couldn't have done a proper job as an MP on £9 a week ... I had no
private income or trade union to back me. I just didn't think of being a
Member of Parliament' (Wapshott and Brock, 1983:44). Before the pay
rise Thatcher considered she would adopt the role of most women in
the Conservative Party, she viewed 'politics in terms of voluntary part-
time activity, on a local level' (Wapshott and Brock: 44).

In 1948, when Margaret Roberts was first proposed as candidate for
the Dartford constituency, the Conservative Chairman considered

women unsuitable for 'very tough industrial areas'. She was still adopted and unsuccessfully stood against the Labour candidate in the 1950 general election (Wapshott and Brock: 52). In the mid-1950s, after six months final pupillage as the sole woman lawyer in tax chambers, she was told her place was terminated as the chambers were contracting. Her former pupil master suspected that, as tax was 'a male domain', Thatcher was victim of prejudice against a female lawyer (Murray, 1978:59). At her next tenancy she was welcomed with the comment that a single rather than a married working woman would have been preferred (Wapshott and Brock, 1983:61). Her marriage to wealthy factory owner Denis Thatcher in 1951 enabled her to study for the Bar and to take a 'respectable' route into mainstream Conservative politics. Married, she could afford the accoutrements of political life: the secretary, home in London and nanny for her young children. Escorting an old school friend around the House of Commons Thatcher acknowledged that her ability to be a politician rested upon 'Denis's money' (Wapshott and Brock, 1983:59). These first-hand memories of restricted finances and career exemplify Thatcher's tendency to make public stories of her personal past and to signal, but ultimately deny, the hindrance made to her political progress by her gender, class or by institutionalised prejudice. Instead her memories often legitimated, through self-example, a moral economy in which the enterprising individual's hard work and self-sufficiency earned the right breaks to success.

She entered Parliament in the October 1959 general election through a safe seat in Finchley, North London. Her first government post came in October 1960 as Parliamentary Secretary for the Ministry of Pensions and National Insurance. In 1963 Macmillan resigned during the Conservative Party Conference at Blackpool and Alec Douglas-Home became Prime Minister, and the following October Thatcher became his opposition spokesman on Pensions. In October 1965 she moved to a Shadow post in Housing and Land and in November 1968 to Transport, followed by a move to Education one year later. When Edward Heath defeated Harold Wilson's Labour Party in June 1970, he gave Thatcher her first Cabinet position as Secretary of State for Education and Science. Fleetingly, under Heath's Shadow Cabinet of 1974, she had responsibility for Environment and then as spokesman for Treasury. Importantly then, she served under three Conservative Prime Ministers, in a variety of junior and senior posts, an apprenticeship with diverse experience for a fairly young ambitious female politician. Throughout these early years Thatcher

appeared to toe the party line. She only indicated radical tendencies in
her Vice Chairmanship of the Centre for Policy Studies, a think-tank
for right-wing revisionists formed in May 1974, and in an admiration
for Enoch Powell, a vociferous detractor of Heath during the early
1970s.[5] Thatcher was a competent but undistinguished politician
marginal to the inner circle of distinguished Conservative politicians.
To a number of Conservatives she did not provide the long-term
authority, vision or broader populist appeal to unite the party and
accumulate larger electoral support.

'A distrust of the unknown'

As Thatcher's leadership commenced the Conservative Party were
embroiled in debates about change and modernisation. Historically,
Conservatives had upheld gradual cautious change in contrast to
violent revolution or radical disengagement from past practice
(O'Gorman, 1986). Toryism evolved in response to the threat of the
French Revolution and its successor Conservatism inherited the fear
of ideological and unruly populist fervour.[6] Throughout the late eigh-
teenth and nineteenth centuries, Conservatives claimed that deference
to monarchy, rank, religion and the proper ordering of the sexes was
their instinctive and natural bulwark against mass dissent and social
disorder. In contrast to the image of a rational, ordered, internally
disciplined Conservative high politics, revolutionary dissent was cast
as irrational, unruly, crude, monstrous and often implicitly feminine
(Colley, 1992:253). In the early twentieth century Conservatism was
remodelled to engage with the seemingly similar dangers posed by the
emerging Labour Party and also the Liberal governments, for it was
feared that all forms of collectivist action would 'lead to the despotism
of the mass over the propertied' (Ball, 1995:32).

Conservatism was widely held to be a matter of innate temperament rather than ideology. Lord Hugh Cecil's philosophical tract on
Conservatism (1912) contended that 'natural conservatism is a
tendency of the human mind'. Conservatism was 'a disposition averse
to change' that relied on an organic and empathetic 'faculty in men to
adapt to their surroundings'. It was permeated by 'a distrust of the
unknown' and a valuation of the familiar (Cecil in Ball, 1995:127).
Cautious change and adaptation to circumstance exemplified the
emotional bedrock that secured political rationality. Society was, from
this viewpoint, a living organism and to engineer society in any seemingly mechanical or ideological way was to ignore the ever present
dangers of human fallibility: greed, fear, ignorance, envy, superstition

(Ball, 1995:30). Quintin Hogg's *The Conservative Case* (1959) presented Conservatism as 'a universal spirit opposed to restless and reckless change' (Hogg, 1959:16). In his presentation Conservatism was inherently gendered:

> [Conservatism] is as old as the Garden of Eden, where it has been suggested that Adam represented the Conservative qualities of content-ment and stability whilst Eve was overeager for novelty and liable to be led away by seductive and dangerous slogans such as 'Eat More Fruit' or 'Free Fig Leaves for All'.
>
> (Hogg: 16)

Critical Conservative ministers viewed Thatcher as the embodiment of radical and destructive change and cited as evidence her doctrinaire approach, lack of Cabinet experience and emphasis on principled governing over pragmatic practice (Pym, 1984; Prior, 1986; Gilmour, 1992). Her novel persona became the focus for projected anxieties about femininity, grass roots members and about punitive authoritar-ian traits of populist Conservative discourse which seemed to threaten high Tory decorum.

To critics, Thatcher exacerbated divisions within society and more specifically the party and thereby challenged the 'one-nation' Conservatism of key post-war figures: Churchill, Eden, Macmillan, Butler, Douglas-Home and Heath.[7] Social reform was one route to uniting the nation. In the 1950s this broad reformist tenet led to a Conservative acceptance of state intervention, where necessary, to remedy social want and to create the basis for popular consent. Thatcher's emphasis on freeing the economy from state intervention and her repeated desire to 'roll back the state', appeared to oppose the consensus that dominated the post-war politics of the party (Skidelsky, 1988; Holmes, 1989; Gilmour, 1992). In 1946, following electoral defeat to the Labour Party, Quintin Hogg attempted to reformulate Conservatism. He made the 'Conservative case' for grad-ual reform harnessed to 'the *mystique* of a traditional authority' in which Church, Crown and preservation of property would continue to prevent revolutionary bloodshed (Hogg, 1959:31). At the outset of Thatcher's leadership, Ian Gilmour also captured this 'one-nation' philosophy against the imagined backdrop of a volatile electorate: 'The preservation of freedom is a complex business. But if people are not to be seduced by other attractions, they must at least feel loyalty to the state'. He warned that 'homilies to cherish competition and warnings against interference with market forces will not engender loyalty' and hinted at social insurrection if people were left to 'wait for impersonal forces to overcome disaster' (Gilmour, 1977:118). Thatcher was charged with the formation of abstract plans for society rather than the formation of judgements based on experience and circumstance. This would lead, warned critics, to the misguided destruction of traditional institutions and the Conservative identity established through them.

In her first visit to the United States as party leader, in 1975, Thatcher challenged her predecessors. She asked her audience, The Institute of Socio-Economic Studies, 'What lessons have we learned from the last thirty years?' and answered that 'the pursuit of equality' was 'a mirage'. Strongly signalling the tone of her new leadership, Thatcher added that 'equality of opportunity' was the 'desirable' edict the Conservatives should follow. This included 'the right to be unequal and the freedom to be different' (Thatcher, 1975a:16). Thatcher suggested justice and 'rights' had become weapons for social insurrection and a means to financially drain the tax-paying citizen. Conjuring up images of social dissent she warned that 'a powerful and vocal lobby pressing for greater equality' opposed 'ordinary people'. Such groups would swell in numbers and, undemocratic in nature, would press 'politicians and institutions' and clamour for 'redress' (Thatcher, 1975a:13). She warned that 'promotion of greater equality' went 'hand in hand' with the continued 'extension of the Welfare State and state control over people's lives' (Thatcher: 3, 7). Her defence of the 'right' to want larger incomes and material goods showed little sense of the guilt exhibited by a number of her political predecessors. She argued that the last thirty years had seen government cave in to the 'envy' of the 'egalitarian' that resented 'those who were better off' and to social reformers fuelled by 'bourgeois guilt'. She now stood against those who attempted to 'impose on others a programme of impoverishment' through high taxation to feed the 'aims of the State' and a bureaucratic and soulless form of charity that obviated individual responsibility (pp6-7). Thatcher claimed she was not so much 'rejecting the social advances of recent decades' as 'reviving a sober and constructive interest in the noble ideals of personal responsibility' (p3). She noted that there was 'far less general desire for equality (as opposed to equity) in Britain today than is claimed' and suggested 'in some respects the concepts of social responsibility had turned sour' (p7, p3). At the risk of greater unemployment and increased social inequality, she declared it was necessary to release individual and social energies by linking reward to effort, risk and wealth creation (Foley, 1993:66). Thatcher's desire for change clashed with the prevailing Conservative emphasis on administration of the existing order, her self-presentation as a 'conviction politician' with the sense of politics as assessment and calculation, and her confrontational stance with the pragmatic emphasis on moderation of the opposition.

While ostensibly these factors marked the division between 'true Conservatism' and Thatcherism, both shared, differently inflected, a fantasy of social chaos and insurrection as the justification for their approach. 'One-nation' Conservatives often veiled their visions of violent popular dissent in oblique references to the people's dissatisfaction if government were not meeting their needs. Thatcher's cautions were overtly apocalyptic. 'I feel', she warned party and nation in early 1975, 'there are times when we have lost our vision of the future'. 'We know', she added ominously, 'that where there is no vision, the people must surely perish' (Thatcher cited in *The Times*, 21 February 1975). Thatcher was both disturbing and exciting for party members and political observers because she rendered explicit the fearful fascination with social chaos that hovers on the edge of the Conservative imagination. What is more, she promised a revolution inspired within the party and appeared to revel in anticipated battle with a host of enemies and dissenters. 'I am the Cabinet rebel', she remarked on more than one occasion and, at a party in Downing Street, she stood on a chair and announced herself 'the rebel head of an establishment government' (Harris, 1990: 93). Thatcher's 'favoured role was that of beleaguered enlightenment facing dark forces' and her persona was from the start dependent upon the presence of threat (Foley, 1993:72; Riddell, 1991). As Labour MP Peter Shore noted:

> It's almost as if she thought of herself as being one of a small band of pioneers and conspirators that found themselves in a kind of minority, an exposed position in Whitehall and Westminster ... [who] had to stick together ... to get the great machinery of state to be responsive to their new and radical approach.
>
> (Shore in Young and Sloman, 1986:53-4)

Trepidation about Thatcher's leadership revealed Conservative MP's fear about the erosion of institutionally embedded power relations. These anxieties were often articulated as a woman's challenge to upper-class masculine propriety.

The 'wets'

> I tend to look at things more logically than do my colleagues. They come eventually [to my point of view] because there aren't any other ways to go.
>
> (Thatcher in McFadyean and Renn, 1984:102)

Historically, the Conservative Party granted high office to those of inherited wealth and property, prestigious private education, and who were in possession of the influential fraternal links of Oxford, Cambridge, the City, Inns of Court and the higher reaches of the military or Church of England (Butler and Pinto-Duschinsky, 1980). The Conservative Party's electoral hegemony in the twentieth century has partly been due to its close, seemingly 'natural', interaction with Britain's powerful institutions (Gamble, 1974; Johnson, 1985). Here it is important to signal the significance of Thatcher's 'political style' because one of its distinctive features was an antipathy towards assumed institutional power and political deference (Kavanagh, 1987:246-280; King, 1988; Foley, 1993). Thatcher's antipathy was expressed through an anti-intellectualism that challenged the second order institutions such as the Church of England, the BBC and universities which were filled, as she saw it, with over-educated liberals. But she avoided overt criticism of the main iconic institutions of the British state: Parliament, the House of Lords, the Monarchy and the judiciary and she frequently lauded the armed forces.

It was widely rumoured that Thatcher dominated her Cabinet, rode roughshod over high-ranking Whitehall civil servants and many MPs. Gendered imagery informed the interpretation of this authoritarian approach. Her control of government has been described as a peculiarly female implementation of Machiavellian 'fear' which induced the well-brought-up Englishman to quail before her 'formidable female personality': 'torn between the desire to strike and the desire to sulk, not knowing what an appropriate response would be' (King, 1988:58). Marina Warner noted the way Thatcher's power was established and negotiated through familiar cultural idioms of British womanhood. Warner argued that the identification of Thatcher with the 'nanny' or 'governess' tapped into 'an enormous source of female power: the right of prohibition' which was drawn upon to strengthen as well as attack her persona (Warner, 1985:52).

Male politicians known to oppose Thatcher's style were popularly captured in cartoons and newspaper sketches as recalcitrant schoolboys receiving a beating from Thatcher or as unwilling patients shrinking from Matron's medicine. Politicians such as Norman St John-Stevas, Ian Gilmour, Peter Carrington, Jim Prior and Francis Pym represented a more detached deliberative, laconic style of political engagement. Thatcher reinterpreted this as emasculation and dubbed them 'the wets' to signify their political and implicitly sexual impotence. Entering Thatcher's private discourse early in her leadership, 'wet' was scrawled in the margins of policy papers submitted to her and used to denounce the caution of 'one-nation' politicians.[8] It became public coinage in 1980 when she was under Cabinet attack for a wave of public spending cuts, rising unemployment, collapsing businesses and an economic recession (Young, 1989:198; Thatcher, 1993:54-5).[9] She used the image of effete masculinity, of 'waverers and fainthearts' to distinguish her bravery, discipline and innate national leadership under which Britain 'belonged to the courageous, not the timid' (Thatcher cited in *The Times*, 8 September 1978). She claimed that the 'wets' lacked rigour and, unable boldly to declare their opposition, were instead prone to 'the indecent obscurity of leaks to the *Guardian*' (Thatcher, 1993:52).

The 'wets' criticised Thatcher's hectoring style as contravention of a mannered political propriety underpinned by long-held assumptions about upper-class masculine power (King, 1988:57). Jim Prior, a rival for Heath's place in 1975, described Thatcher's confrontational approach as 'a personal and political anathema' that offended his sense of masculine propriety (Holmes, 1989:6). Her antagonistic style contrasted with his own reconciliatory Conservatism, it undermined his 'overriding' political desire 'to work with the grain of society, to plane down the causes of conflict' (Prior, 1986:260). Similarly, Trevor Russel and Ian Gilmour anticipated Thatcher's grip on the party to be short-lived, her leadership being 'an aberration', a 'brief ... unfortunate ... interlude' before proper authority was restored (Russel, 1978:167; Harris, 1988:32).

What must also be signalled here is the denigration of the narrow and parochial that accompanied such criticisms of Thatcher. When she campaigned against Edward Heath for leadership of the party, supporters of Heath insinuated that she was privileged and out of touch with everyday life. Rivals from the Labour front bench swiftly joined the fray. Denis Healey famously dubbed her 'La Passionara of Privilege' (Wapshott and Brock, 1983:129). Anxieties about Thatcher's gender and the relation between her gender and her class underpinned these debates. Outside the upper echelons of senior Conservatives and

Tory grandees she was cast as the unpolished woman of provincial England: a role she was to relish as spokeswoman for common sense values.

The Tory woman

Significantly, those for and against Thatcher frequently expressed their opinion of her in gendered terms. One stereotype that was brought to the fore was that of the 'Tory woman' whose symbolic power and imaginative place within Conservative history had a legacy bound up with the democratisation of the party. The expectations of the 'Tory woman' and her political engagement with the party were the template against which Thatcher's behaviour was measured, and aspects of that stereotype were drawn upon to represent her as a strident woman who offended boundaries of mannered political decorum.[10] Since the inception of the Primrose League[11] in the latter part of the nineteenth century, the involvement of large assemblies of voluntary female activists had been wedded to the creation of a mass popular base of Conservative voters (Pugh, 1985). Before their independent vote, women had oiled the Conservative Party machine at grass roots level, registered voters, canvassed, distributed propaganda, raised funds, promoted and extended both middle and working class votes (Campbell, 1987:5-33). The Primrose League promoted Conservatism through the active and unashamed engagement with popular political publicity, a practice in which women eschewed mainstream party political involvement but were the tireless 'upholders and promoters' of Conservative Party principles from the active margins of political power (Campbell: 6, 27). No British party has benefited so consistently from women's political support as the Conservatives, indeed they currently constitute around fifty-five to sixty percent of the party membership and are the mainstay of supportive activity at constituency level (Lovenduski & Randall, 1993:61; Whiteley, Seyd and Richardson, 1994). As Beatrix Campbell observed, 'women's role in the party' has long been 'associated with the self-denying qualities of femininity which support the power of others' (Campbell, 1987:270).

Thatcher directly eschewed such self-effacing feminine qualities, although at the outset of her leadership the media and, less openly, colleagues often branded Thatcher as another 'Tory woman', a humorous but also contemptuous image which implied trivial, amateur or non-rational political involvement. In his sketch of Conservative back-bench life under Thatcher, Julian Critchley notes:

'"Tory women" ... conjures up pictures of tweedy women with cut-glass voices towed by Labradors, comfortable middle-aged bodies in unspeakable hats who sit cheerfully knitting through the rowdiest of debates and cheerful girls brandishing handcuffs at the rostrum' (Critchley, 1985:43). The symbolism of such humorous denigration is significant, because the 'Tory woman' presented here is not dignified or decorous. She is positioned outside the sphere of public debate, knitting at the margins and, most importantly, represents an unthinking, light-hearted delight in retributive punishment. The 'Tory woman' is frequently a symbolic vehicle of aggression, born of a female sense of vulnerability to crime: 'It is, I suppose, as "hangers and floggers", stridently demanding the return of rod and rope, that "Tory women" are thought to come into their own' (Critchley: 44). A feminised triviality and superficial vanity are projected onto them, they are captured 'enveloped in clouds of blue tulle' sipping endless 'cups of milky Nescafé' as they campaign on 'mean streets' (p44). Furthermore they take on the shape of the gullible mass at the annual Party Conference where 'several thousand of them' are 'flattered, cajoled and exhorted' by the Cabinet whose indifferent performances nonetheless 'are invariably rewarded by a standing ovation' (p44). Any considered answer to crime is, according to Critchley, 'not easy' to convey to this 'emotionally charged mass' (p44). He recalls that Thatcher's 1959 election to Parliament summoned up comparisons with the 'Tory woman' amongst Conservative colleagues, one proclaiming that Thatcher was like the Chairman of his Woman's Advisory Committee 'writ horribly large' (p32). Thatcher's style was abrasive and doctrinaire but significantly this was interpreted as evidence of the parochial and the suburban: of Thatcher belonging to a class and a gender unaccustomed to the broad sweep of political power. The fear was that the party under Thatcher would fail to acquire populist appeal and would relinquish power by retiring behind a 'privet hedge' to indulge in 'a world of narrow class interests and selfish concerns' (Gilmour in Gamble, 1988: 93, 139).[12]

The 'Tory woman' then foregrounds an anxiety about the mass intrinsic to the Conservative political imaginary, but this chaotic emotional group are at the heart of the Conservative Party itself. Several objects of fear and disdain intersect in this much-maligned figure. She represents the feminisation and domestication of political life and is an emblem of the suburb or heartland of middle England, both of which are central to the Conservative vote but which do not match the pace and competitive edge of high political life. In addition she represents the adulation of mass party gatherings. Their less calculating, often overt advocacy of punitive law and order disrupts mannered political discourse whilst simultaneously laying bare the veiled violence of many Conservative calls for retributive state punishment. Transposed on to the figure of Thatcher, this disdain and fear of 'the Tory woman' indicates anxiety about a woman at the top of the political hierarchy who was perceived to unsettle the proper focus and agenda of Conservatism. Furthermore, they reveal a fear that the boundaries of proper political discourse and action will be tainted by insular concerns explicitly marked as private and domestic. These humorous asides or veiled warnings about Thatcher reveal a defence against and anger with the powerful female entering and finally leading government and, through those responses, suggest that the most fundamental images of gendered difference underpin the way in which an institution's limits are defined. Crucially such comments also indicate an association of women with hatred and violence. The 'Tory woman' is an object of fantasy: the figure who articulates too loudly and explicitly the limits of Conservative ideology – the right of the State to punish fully by beating or taking a life for a life. But this is also the figure upon which the politician depends for the footwork and the mass support. Conservative women are addressed by their political leaders as the defenders of moral, sexual and social mores and as central to a political philosophy that idealises the 'traditional' family (Gardiner, 1983). But if this identity provides a limited recognition of women's lives, aspirations and fears, it also encourages that they articulate desires and fears through the register of concerns allotted them by their political 'betters'.

'There are still not many of us who have made the grade as men'

Mainstream political power has, until recently, been conventionally associated with men, and Thatcher's singularity as a Conservative politician, let alone as a party leader or Prime Minister, arose out of the historical exclusion of women from high political office. Despite achieving legislative eligibility for nomination and election to the House of Commons in 1918,[13] women MPs have constituted a marginal group. Indeed, for the sixty-one years up to 1979, they had composed less than five per cent of elected members of British Parliament (Public Information Office, House of Commons: 1995). Despite Thatcher's success that year, it is salutary to note that of 206 women standing for Parliament only 19 were elected (2.9 per cent of the elected members of Parliament).[14]

When the House of Commons was first televised (in November 1989) it provided the shocking spectacle of male political power. A few splashes of colour among the 'sea of suits' signified the token presence of the few female MPs (*Guardian* 2, 5 May 1995:5). In any photograph of the British government throughout the 1980s, Thatcher stood out resplendent in bright colour against a backdrop of black-or-grey suited men. Against this uniform backdrop, Thatcher signified novelty and uniqueness and this singularity was sustained by the lack of women in her Cabinet. Thatcher only ever included one woman in her Cabinet, Baroness Janet Young, who briefly served as Leader of the House of Lords. Furthermore Thatcher patently refused to see gender as a hindrance to political office. In an interview for Thames Television News in early January 1981 she declared that nothing more could be done to change the law to prevent gender discrimination. 'After all', she added, 'I don't think there's been a great deal of discrimination against women for years' (Thatcher in Tusscher, 1986:77). Interviewed on Radio 4's *Woman's Hour* in December 1986, she declared herself ignorant of the Conservative Party's poor record compared to other parties with the lowest number of prospective women candidates. She argued against positive discrimination or even strong influence over constituency choice and implied that male colleagues were the mark of standard to which women candidates should aspire: 'I don't want to get to a position when we have women just because they are women. We want to have women because they are able and as well equipped as men and sometimes better' (NSA: B2075).[15] As Prime Minister, Thatcher cited the first woman to exercise power in the House of Commons, the Conservative MP Lady Nancy Astor, as evidence of the progressiveness of the party and, in doing so, when it suited her, placed Conservatism in the legacy of the suffragette movement.[16] She brandished Astor to female audiences as evidence of women's long-held ability to participate in the political realm if they were able and willing and thereby dismissed the relevance of gender, and of feminism, to Parliamentary participation. She told the 58th Conservative Women's National Conference that:

> It was a Conservative, Nancy Astor, who was the first woman to take a seat in Parliament and who did so with great style and confidence – proving that a woman does not have to be masculine to succeed in a man's world. It was the Conservatives who extended the vote to all

refused to acknowledge discrimination but actively encouraged it through her policies.

women in the Equal Franchise Act, 60 years ago. And, dare I say it – it was a Conservative who became Britain's first woman Prime Minister.

(CPA: TS 229/88)[17]

But, in 1919, the year Astor entered Parliament, the young Winston Churchill recorded his discomfort with the female politician in terms that presented women's Parliamentary presence as a seizure and a violation of masculine space. 'I find', Churchill stated, 'a woman's intrusion into the House of Commons as embarrassing as if she burst into my bathroom when I had nothing with which to defend myself, not even a sponge' (Coote and Pattullo, 1990:265). Astor recorded her first six months in Parliament as 'sheer hell' and ostracism: 'Men whom I had known for years would not speak to me if they passed me in the corridor' (Miles, 1988:276; Coote and Pattullo: 265).

In the early 1960s, when Thatcher gained experience in her first ministerial post in Harold Macmillan's government, the perception of Parliament as masculine territory did not appear to have changed. It was observed that MPs, now 'mostly very ordinary people' none the less still 'assume[d] the heightened manner' of a male only 'club – the affectation of an older, more confident generation' (Sampson in Coote and Pattullo: 257). Thatcher's peer, the newly elected MP Mark Bonham-Carter, noted with some relish on entering the House that the esoteric rituals and rules bred 'a sense of anxiety and inferiority' amongst politicians not hardened by the conventions and cruelties of the boy's public school (Coote and Pattullo: 257). The location of political acumen in gender and class-exclusive terms informed colleagues' early assessment of Thatcher as she began her political career. Recalling Thatcher's first appointment as his junior at the Ministry of Pensions, John Boyd-Carpenter captured the gendered exclusivity of that club and revealed implicit assumptions about the insouciant Prime Minister Harold Macmillan and about aspiring female politicians:[18]

> I thought quite frankly, when Harold Macmillan appointed her that it was just a little bit of a gimmick on his part. Here was a good-looking young woman and he was obviously, I thought, trying to brighten up the image of his government.

(Young, 1989:47)

When interviewed by the *Daily Telegraph* in late 1966 about the lack of female peers, Thatcher placed this absence firmly upon the inadequacy of female candidates: 'The trouble is that there are still not many of us who have made the grade as men. Therefore we stand out more conspicuously' (Thatcher, *Daily Telegraph*, 6 May 1966). Over twenty years later as Conservative Party leader, other aspiring female MPs still stood charged of reticence. Interviewed by Roy Plomley on Radio 4's *Desert Island Discs*[19] Thatcher acknowledged that, in 1978, there were still only 'twenty five or six' women in the House of Commons. To her this was 'absurd', but she added, 'so many of them ought to come forward, to offer themselves as candidates' (NSA: P1261). Such comments revealed Thatcher's 'absolute adherence' to the appearance of unthreatening femininity even as she was 'engaged in a flight from it' and from the place her party primarily afforded women (Abse, 1989:253).

'This one is different': the styling of exceptional womanhood

An awareness of being a woman in a masculinist political culture informed Thatcher's autobiographical narratives of her 'path to power'.[20] Amidst her understanding of the high political arena as neutral, a space of power in which women could operate once legal barriers to their participation had been removed, was the recognition that she had to operate in a political culture designated naturally male. A career in the Conservative Party and within Parliament involved the negotiation and disavowal of Thatcher's female status (Warner, 1985; Rose, 1988). In some cases her gender was deployed to benign effect as in the image of Thatcher as 'housewife', managing the nation's budget, used from 1975. At other times it was flatly cancelled out. One year after becoming Prime Minister, her comment to the *Daily Mirror* encapsulated a frequent defensive strategy throughout her years in power. When asked how being a woman informed her political identity Thatcher curtly retorted, 'I don't notice I'm a woman. I regard myself as the Prime Minister' (*Daily Mirror*, 1 March 1980).

In political speeches, photo opportunities or media interviews, Thatcher's persona was continually projected as one intimately bound up with both fortitude and fortification. Stories of physical endurance as well as of mental strength abound. These stories, told by Thatcher herself and her media observers, often had a gendered inflection: they indicated strength, resilience, meticulous preparation and a certain defensive aggression as the byword of the ambitious (watchful) political woman. Readers of biographies and magazine articles were continually informed that Thatcher only needed four hours sleep, exhausted all about her on walkabouts or political campaigns, cultivated backbenchers with 'manic energy' (Young, 1989:119), tirelessly researched, memorised detail and mastered any political brief.[21] Breathlessly, journalists have described interviews with Thatcher as 'frantic'. They spoke of 'wilting' before her 'colossal energy' as she 'positively hungers for work, any work' (Peters, 1978:10). William Whitelaw, while Thatcher's Deputy Leader of the Opposition in the late 1970s, spoke with admiration of her ability to 'run a home, work at the Commons from early morning to late at night, and spend hours and hours writing speeches'. He concluded: 'She's got twice as much stamina [as any man]. She could quite easily kill me in a day with the amount she's able to do' (Murray, 1978: 143). Such descriptions portray Thatcher as exceptional rather than an everyday or normal woman; they mark her as different, even inhuman in her capacity and ambition. Furthermore, they frequently contain an undertow of sexual anxiety or frisson of desire on the part of male and female commentators, as in Edwina Currie's account of a typical ministerial encounter with Thatcher:

> The Prime Minister turned to me with a challenge, asking me to explain ... the reallocation of NHS resources ... She has a powerful blue-eyed look that has turned strong men to stone. You stop whatever else you are doing, and start thinking fast. This lady prefers it straight ... You know you have scored when she nods, satisfied, and turns away to make someone else tremble. Just as she did, however, she gave me a sharp look ... 'Really'? she said, interested. Then she floored me completely.
>
> (Currie, 1989:230)[22]

Such anecdotes are numerous, most stress the experience of intellectual and public humiliation, for Thatcher frequently played out her competence and strength before an audience. Biographers and journalists often spoke of her mental strength as courage in adversity. The meticulous biographer, Hugo Young, defined Thatcher's 'inexhaustible psychic energy' as a 'desire to dominate' and 'a passion to decide', alongside a 'conviction that she alone could bring the necessary wisdom and understanding to whatever issue on the agenda at the time' (Young, 1989:547-8). It was frequently noted that her 'political vision' resulted in an intractable obstinacy, a domination of her male Cabinet and disruption of its system of 'gentlemanly' debate (Harris, 1988:81). Her stamina and success became the model for a form of corporate feminism in which an individualistic ethos of high achievement and financial success glossed over structural inequalities

↳ just because she flourished in government doesn't mean women in general did too.

(Benton, 1986; Loach, 1987).[23] But her political performance was frequently judged against other men and in masculine terms: ' ... at the despatch box ... she was ... a first-class performer, always cool, consistent, steady and strong. She could handle interruptions, ribald jests and barracking as well as any man' (Harris, 1988:81). Her 'determination' and 'readiness to fight' were judged ingredients of a 'tough colleague' and 'formidable opponent'. These attributes were discussed amongst male MPs in the camaraderie of the House of Commons smoking-room and led Conservative colleague Iain Macleod to conclude that in comparison with other women MPs: 'This one is different' (Harris: 82). She was, he added, 'Quite exceptionally able. A first class brain' (Wapshott and Brock, 1983:85). Reasoned, calculating, tough political behaviour was coded as masculine and assumed as the preserve of men, Thatcher's 'difference' from other female politicians was underwritten by a common sense barrier between the sexes which was already incorporated into a whole range of formal and informal rules, practices and customs.[24] → acting like a man gather by in government.

Heath and Thatcher: the modern man and the modernising woman

> It's no good dreaming about U-turns. There are none available.
>
> (Thatcher in the *Observer*, 3 August 1980)

Until the mid-1960s the Conservative Party was dominated by 'a narrow, upper-class, public school educated elite', with 'organisational control vested in a mysteriously opaque clique of grandee power brokers' (Derbyshire and Derbyshire, 1990:38). Nepotism was rife. Just over a third of the eighty-five members of Macmillan's 1958 government were related to the Prime Minister by marriage (Derbyshire and Derbyshire: 38). When Macmillan resigned from office due to ill health in October 1963, the Foreign Secretary, Lord Alec Douglas-Home, was adopted as party leader in an informal process of preferment. In Douglas-Home's 1963 Cabinet, eighty-seven per cent of its members had a public school education and their leader was an Eton-educated Scottish aristocrat.[25] In the early 1960s, party officials increasingly acknowledged the narrow social background of the party's higher ranks and the disparity between government and the broader social make-up of party members. They urged a democratisation of the party's power structure and an update of its image (Seyd, 1975; Derbyshire and Derbyshire, 1990:38).

In 1965, Edward Heath was the first Conservative leader to be elected by a ballot of the Parliamentary party following changes to the party rules implemented by the outgoing premier Douglas-Home. To many young Conservatives, Heath's relatively lowly background (grammar school and Oxford University-educated son of a Kent carpenter) signified the party's transformation to a modernising, meritocratic system. Heath's succession to leadership paved the way for Thatcher, and later her similar lower-middle-class background became an integral element of her populist image. Competition was Heath's watchword. Heath anticipated Thatcher in presenting his leadership as the route to a more radical market-oriented approach. Restraint and control of government and union power were captured in the Conservative's phrase 'a quiet revolution' (Clarke, 1996:330). He gave space to party thinkers who challenged the Welfare State's ethos of universal provision in favour of selective benefits, he endorsed businessmen and entrepreneurs as society's leaders and promised a curb on trade union power (Behrens, 1980; Holmes, 1982).

Heath's years in office from 1970-74 were blighted by major conflicts with trade unionists and by prolonged periods of industrial unrest following legislative reforms designed to prevent unofficial stoppages. During 1971-2 a series of one-day strikes were called to oppose the new Industrial Relations Act and there was a major dock strike in mid-1972. Against a deeply unstable economic backdrop (oil prices quadrupled in late 1973 after the Arab-Israeli war and the onset of world recession resulted in sharply rising unemployment figures and mounting inflation) Heath came under vociferous and sustained attack from detractors within his party. It was alleged that he had reneged over nationalisation and intervention in industry by bailing out the Upper Clyde shipyards and injecting funds into Rolls Royce when it fell into financial difficulties. He failed to curb union power, introduced an incomes policy halfway through the period of government and presided over the declaration of five states of emergency over the three and a half years in office (Behrens, 1980:31-7). Heath's inability to settle on a hard-line approach to policy, Labour opponents and trade unions was reduced to the motif of the 'u-turn' following his fall from power in 1975. As a new Prime Minister the 'u-turn' became a sign of weakness and lack of conviction against which Thatcher measured her own agenda of political reform.[26]

Heath is significant for his role in the popular mythology that surrounds Thatcher's succession and also as a hesitant and imperfect figure of authoritative masculine leadership against which Thatcher's iconic status was forged. In the late 1970s Thatcher's admirers frequently regaled the press with soundbites on Heath's 'capacity for surrender' (*Guardian*, 21 October 1978). Heath, through his background and particularly his managerial discourse, signified the tenuous and ambivalent entrance of middle-class masculinity into the corridors of Westminster. Along with his rival Harold Wilson he legitimated the high political absorption of a set of professional competencies which had been important to the consolidation of middle-class masculinity in the 1950s and 1960s.[27] But Heath still clung to the older aristocratic style of easy political authority. His strangulated vowels, love of sailing, frequenting of gentleman's clubs, dining with paternal patrons like Macmillan, and distant aloof manner revealed the apprehensive masquerade of an aspirant gentleman-politician.

A better tomorrow

In a Monday Club pamphlet written in the late 1960s, Conservative MP John Biggs-Davison revealed the imagery of subterfuge and violation that wove through much New Right polemic on national disintegration. He warned that 'under the creeping socialism of a generation' the nation had 'been stripped well nigh naked of our monetary, military and moral defences'. He added that 'the threat to our kinsfolk and partners overseas' was 'matched by the threat to domestic economy' and the impending 'social disorder' (Young, 1989:59). Biggs-Davison declared that the Conservative Party had to cast off their 'degeneracy and materialism' and commence the 'almost superhuman labour of national rescue and revival' (Young: 60). Heath's political image, against this imagined dissolute backdrop, was that of a forceful leader remedying Britain's industrial rather than moral backwardness (linked to Britain under Labour). But unlike Thatcher, for whom New Right ethics were provocative and who wedded fiscal defence to moral revival in her political discourse, Heath studiously avoided the adoption of a morally vigilant tone.

In 1970, in competition with the Labour leader Harold Wilson, Heath's concern was to convey his party as the modernising party with long-term goals for economic expansion and a radical vision for industry. The 1970 general election, which brought Heath to power and Thatcher into the Cabinet, was fought upon the Conservative Party manifesto, *A Better Tomorrow: the Conservative Programme for the Next Five Years* (1970). Heath's election pledges borrowed the tropes of Harold Wilson's Labour government (1964-70) and drew heavily on scientific and rationalistic metaphors to suggest that the Conservatives would herald a new technocratic era in which politics was about problem-solving and managerial thought. Heath's valued repertoire of skills latched middle-class manliness onto political authority and radically contrasted with the effete and otherworldly personae of his predecessors Macmillan and Douglas-Home. Involvement in production, design, accountancy and insurance had been central to the formation of modern middle-class masculinity since Britain's advanced industrialisation (Davidoff and Hall, 1987). Heath drew upon these quite specific forms of knowledge and skill as they had been refashioned in the post war years to meet the demands of mid-twentieth century technology and finance. He presented politics as risk assessment, planning, calculation, dealing with capital and investment and thereby underlined his modernisation of the party and his relevance to modern Britain.

Set alongside this highly functional (and masculine) language of management, transaction, business, execution and initiative were the campaign posters, which drew on imagery of the family to address the voter on the street. Heath was a middle-aged unmarried man. Consequently, the respectability that marriage and often children conventionally confer upon the politician had to be carefully implied. One poster encapsulated the hallowed status of the mother and child in political iconography. Under the slogan 'For a Better Tomorrow Vote Conservative', it depicted a woman cradling a young child in her arms in a sentimentalised image of maternal absorption (CPPA: GE 1970). In a second campaign poster, linked to the first by the same slogan, the mother and child were replaced by the stolid masculine presence of Edward Heath (CPPA: GE 1970). Unlike the absorption in each other of the mother and child, Heath, in the manner of sincere and powerful leaders, gazed out of the poster's frame at the prospective voter, looking out for, protecting, those unable to protect themselves. The poster indicated that Heath, as leader of the Conservative Party, husbanded and fathered the future.

The image of mother and child was a ready expression of simplicity and purity as well as hope for the society to come. As I will argue in a later chapter, the mother and child were reconfigured under Thatcher into an image of the privatised family and child. The image of Prime Minister as father of the nation and protector of women and children had a lot of work to do since Heath possessed neither wife nor child of his own. Nor was his style one of compassion and concern: on the contrary Heath was strongly associated with insensitivity, emotional detachment and curt incivility.[28] The grass roots disdained him as detached 'cold fish', while his bachelor status provoked guarded commentary and nervous anxiety on the part of party spokesmen. This anxiety was exacerbated by Labour rival Harold Wilson's projection as the homely family man. In advance of the election campaign, Wilson had been televised at home with his wife Mary and Labrador Paddy, and claimed that marriage and family were 'an essential release, relief and inspiration in trying to do the job one has to do' (Cockerell, 1988:146).[29]

Attempts to shore up Heath's heterosexuality were present from his appointment as Conservative Party leader. Shortly after his election to the Tory leadership in July 1965, Heath had invited TV cameras to film him sailing in the South of France. Conservative Central Office, keen to demonstrate his potential as family man, suggested that he be filmed romping with the children of his host. Once again, in the 1970 election campaign, TV camera crews were invited to film Heath sailing. Media advisers, keen to counter his remote bachelor image, arranged for him to be filmed on his yacht *Morning Cloud* in the company of a young woman he had never met. This led to the press's speculative questions on whether romance was in the air to which Heath responded with the irritated reply that the young woman was 'only the cook' (Cockerell, 1988:120,157). Again, in Heath's final election campaign of October 1974, Sara Morrison, a Party Vice-Chairman and wife of a Conservative MP, travelled at his side throughout the campaign as a substitute for the supportive wife (Cockerell: 157, 212).

As can be seen from this account of Heath's political subjectivity and how it was projected to sell his party to the electorate, male politicians are also judged against gender roles and constituted through the social conventions of 'acceptable' masculinity. If Heath was projected as a 'moderniser' his electoral image involved little cultural modernisation. The posters indicate the Conservative leader's assumption of a 'proper' way of life and of Heath's firm place within 'the culture of respectability and patriarchy' (Campbell, 1987:99; Gamble, 1988:198). Such paternal authority carries with it a range of implicit value judgements that are brought to bear upon any prominent male politician concerning his virility, respectability and responsibility. It also bears upon the aspiring female politician who lays claim to rigorous political authority and strength.

Some biographers of Thatcher have contrasted her 'emotional' zest for politics and her bedrock of 'real' experience as mother and wife with the bachelor status and cool detachment of her predecessor Heath (Gardiner, 1975; Junor, 1983; Thomson, 1989). This link between femininity, emotion and conventional family status can be a convenient (sometimes facile) way for authors (and politicians) to underwrite a woman's authority. Nonetheless what is signalled in such comparisons between Thatcher and Heath is that she succeeded where Heath failed: using her gender and her personal life to infuse political rhetoric with the common touch. In interviews she underlined that the people she liked best were 'down-to-earth people'. She preferred 'men who call spades spades' and who didn't 'talk in convoluted jargon'. 'Jargon', she informed journalist Pauline Peters, was 'often used to cloak ignorance rather than act as an elucidation of issues' (Thatcher in Peters, 1978:10). Furthermore, one could suggest that her femininity gave her a form of amnesty, a certain leeway in speaking about civil, social and domestic life. Indeed by August 1978, three years into her leadership of the party, the *Sunday Times* profile of Thatcher, noted the 'uncanny ease' with which she slid 'between her roles as potential Prime Minister and superwife' (Peters, 1978:10). Thatcher spoke from a self-proclaimed position of authority and knowledge as a woman and mother as she interwove images of family, childhood, moral vision and desire for material goods with a hard-line approach to the Welfare State and economic renewal. Heath's failure to fulfil the image of the modernising-yet-conservatively-respectable leader left a space into which Thatcher stepped.

Significantly, Heath's persona distanced him from female party workers who often expressed concerns about civil society within the framework of personal values that had been conventionally assigned them by the party (Behrens, 1980:35-6).[30] In contrast to the rationalistic managerial tone of high office, party members and activists articulated their concerns and desires through the domestic and the local. Emphasis was placed on the protection of the family, fear of violence, respect for the local neighbourhood as a model of the nation (Campbell, 1987:101-2). The clash between Heath's instrumental managerial rationality and the party members' emphasis on the private sphere, personal protection and betterment reveal tensions generated by a mass electorate. The disparity between the language of the Conservative's 1970 manifesto and the campaign posters mentioned above signals Heath's failure to hold together connotations of authority and of the 'everyday'. In contrast, the 1980 booklet *Going Places, Women in the Conservative Party*, produced by the Conservative Political Centre, praised Heath for his recognition of the role of party women as upholders of moral values and defenders of family and social order (CPC: 1980). *Going Places* suggested that Conservative women act as the 'voice of realism' operating on the ground and articulating economical and political decisions through the everyday economies of 'the housewife' (Coote and Patullo, 1990:190). The 'family' and the domestic realm are set up in Conservative discourse as the responsibility of Conservative women. They are the place to which the (implicitly male) politician returns and are presented as the source of his emotional empathy and connection with everyday party concerns.

Thatcher's persona successfully contrasted with that of Heath. She offered forceful authority alongside the promise that she was particularly attuned as a woman to ordinary concerns, fears and desires. It has been argued that 'the overdetermined attributes of ordinary housewife, refined lady and warrior queen', were familiarly British constructions of femininity drawn upon by Thatcher to dramatise her authority in accessible terms and to render her alleged common sense and empathy with 'the people' credible and persuasive (Brunt, 1987:24). These aspects of her masquerade may have provided cover for a savage and divisive politics (Warner, 1985:Ch3; Brunt, 1987:24). Indeed, Ros Brunt suggests that Thatcher's frequently chauvinistic political discourse would have appeared more explicitly class-bound or racially prejudiced if spoken by the patrician Edward Heath or other New Right politicians such as Thatcher's mentor Keith Joseph. Certainly, interviews with Tory women revealed that the Thatcherite emphasis on morality, family values and the restoration of law and order was interpreted by many as a specifically female clear-sighted acknowledgement of everyday personal frustrations, discontents and disappointments (Campbell, 1987; Coote and Patullo, 1990:187-98). Furthermore, Thatcher's explicit criticism of feminism and her appeal for renewed 'traditional' family and moral values carried different overtones for Conservative women if expressed by a male Conservative when they appeared to smack of 'the prejudices of the public bar' (Campbell, 1987:176; Coote & Patullo, 1990:Ch12).

Throughout Heath's leadership a split between an emergent populist moral Conservatism and an emergent liberal economic Conservatism was left unresolved. Thatcher healed that split, rhetorically at least. When Thatcher became leader of the Conservative Party in 1975 she replaced a man who had failed to deliver, as promised, a party clearly differentiated from its opponents. Heath's exclusion from Thatcher's first Shadow Cabinet signalled that a deep rift had opened in the higher ranks of Conservative leadership (Gamble, 1988:84). Heath became a brooding figure on Thatcher's backbenches who, in a manner unprecedented for a former Conservative leader, publicly denounced many of the policies she endorsed or adopted and, for a while after his fall, fuelled half-hearted debate about his restoration.[31]

What politics and media interpretation of political leaders and events produce are not only powerful images but also forms of memory which adapt to present socio-political events and desires. Popular memory of the Heath government between 1970 and 1974 is of a government shot through with failure, incompetence and of a Prime Minister unable to impose authority. The authoritarian prescriptions endorsed throughout the Thatcher years and the fantasies of moral purpose and clarity of economic and political vision that Thatcher embodied and purveyed have shaped this memory of Heath. Heath can be read as a transitional figure. His ambivalent class status and his attempt to build a modern Conservatism, while holding onto past methods, can be interpreted through a certain decline of deference within the party: a waning of established structures of authority and a tremulous recognition of the potential of a more populist address. The anxiety about Heath's bachelor status revealed that cultural images of authority depend upon the negotiation of gendered and sexual assumptions about impotence and castration which weave through ideas and judgements about political competence.

In popular memory Heath's premiership ended with Britain's lights going out. Train drivers and electricity power workers who refused to work overtime supported prolonged industrial action by the National Union of Mineworkers (NUM) in late 1973 and early 1974. Factory and power station coal stocks were drastically reduced; images of the nation in darkness appeared in the national press. Such images inform individual as well as collective myths of the past, for I remember, quite clearly, as a child sitting excitedly with my brothers by candlelight as our electric lights went out. On 7 February 1974, in response to an NUM declaration of an impending all-out strike, Edward Heath announced that a general election would be held on 28 February to seek renewal of his mandate. Heath's unsuccessful campaign ran under the slogan: 'Who Governs Britain?' (Derbyshire and Derbyshire, 1990:42). This slogan, itself, a question not an answer, inadvertently underscored Heath's questionable authority.

Thatcher's conservatism

> Thatcherism is a self-addressed valentine card or a hymn in the key of
> me ... when they swot upon Thatcher the 'ism' they will find nothing
> but a one-woman band playing 'I Did It My Way'.
>
> (*Daily Mirror*, 1 March 1984 in McFadyean and Renn, 1984:128)

> She is inclined to strike attitudes, to shoot from the hip. Her admirers
> believe that she is the grit in the oyster; a necessary, if unwelcome chal-
> lenge to the complacency which is the concomitant of power. She insists
> upon being taken at face value. As the leader of the party of the right she
> has substituted populism for deference.
>
> (Critchley, 1985:126)

It is central to my understanding of Thatcher to examine the ways in
which she was placed as both liminal and central to her party, as traditional and also modern in her ideological concerns, as libertarian and
as advocate of discipline and authority in her vision of the economy
and the state. Thatcher's ability to hold these oppositions together in
her public image and discourse was formidable. She was able to shape
these contradictory couplets into an apparently coherent populist
address. She gave these oppositions the appearance of a common
sense, which seemed to cut through the obfuscation of hostile politicians, Whitehall mandarins and state bureaucrats in order to speak
directly to 'the people' (O'Shea, 1984).

One way to understand the appeal of populist Conservatism is
through its imaginary location at the centre of national life and as the
motor of a national-political consensus. The Conservative Party has
been particularly adept throughout the late nineteenth and the twentieth centuries in securing this consensus by resurrecting and
re-working resonant historical and symbolic moments in the national
culture (Heywood, 1992; Green, 1995; Schwarz, 1998). In the nineteenth century the Conservative Party evolved to a mass democratic
party. A crucial element of that evolution was the mobilisation of
patriotism as a core element of Conservatism that united the classes.
The maintenance of an 'ancient' constitution, the defence of property
and the popular patriotic support of the British Isles were conceived
as ideals which wed the party to and sustained the imperial nation
(Ball, 1995:10; see also Schwarz, 1996). In the mid-twentieth century,
post-war philosophies of Conservatism were testament to the continuing investment in the Crown and Church as pillars of the

constitution as the party adapted to the loss of Empire and contraction of Britain's industrial influence (Hogg, 1959; Gilmour, 1977). In the late 1940s, the Conservative Party adapted to the ethos of the Welfare State with its emphasis on state institutional responsibility for the people. But this adaptation did not completely displace the Conservative idealisation of an essential British, or often English, temperament wherein a love of freedom and democracy was rooted deep in the 'blood and soil' of the land. Bill Schwarz has suggested that a vital dimension of popular twentieth century Conservatism has been the ability to conflate its rhetorical evocations of 'old England' – 'a pastoral or neighbourly pre-modern world' – with broader imaginative cultural projections of the national community (Schwarz, 1998:133). Conservatism's 'systematic appeal to a providential past' taps into 'an imagined loss' which accompanies the dislocation of modern identity, and this ability may explain Conservatism's political prominence in the twentieth century (Schwarz, 1998:133). Thatcher was not unique in her adoption of evocative and nostalgic strategies of political self-construction and address. She represented a fresh bid for a revived and popular Conservatism, but she gave the enmities which often galvanise popular politics and the authoritarian undercurrent of strong national leadership a fresh and accentuated volatility.

Thatcherism then is understood here as a populist political project intimately bound to and given symbolic coherence by Thatcher's style of leadership. Thatcherism arose within a specific political and cultural context and out of a set of economic and social constraints that give specificity to the sense of national loss and dislocation signalled above. Economic factors included the long-term structural decline of the British economy, domestic inflation, crisis in government and local finances and the advent of a global recession in the 1970s. The 'precipitate decline' of the 'Fordist system of mass-production and consumption in the advanced industrial nation-states' and the growing network of multinational corporations signalled rapid technological and industrial change (McGuigan, 1996:51). This shift partly resulted in the collapse of local British heavy industries and the destabilisation of working communities, causing widespread unemployment and, through media-circulated vistas of empty factories and long 'dole' queues, spawned powerful visual motifs of national decline and impotence throughout the late 1970s and into the 1980s. Thatcherism constituted a radical departure from favoured post-war economic models and a movement into a monetarist or free market approach to the economy (Keegan, 1984; Minford, 1988).[32]

What is significant for this analysis is the way Thatcher interpreted and legitimated economic changes through a set of moral and ethical codes and latched anxieties about money, taxation and unemployment onto broader evocations of national loss and disintegration. Importantly, economic and class analyses of Thatcher discuss the domestic and global context in which Thatcherism evolved. They also indicate the relevance of Thatcher's specific constituency of voters, including the aspirant 'middle class' of 'shopkeepers, foremen, and the small self-employed businessmen – the petit bourgeois' for whom Thatcher's values of thrift, self-responsibility and economic independence specifically appealed (Kavanagh, 1987:299-300). Alongside this her irreverence for high political protocol found approval among sections of the lower-middle and upper-working classes for whom she embodied a 'strong and bloody-minded' survivalist mentality essential for 'a rough old world' (Worsthorne cited in Foley, 1993: 73). Conservative voters identify strongly with socially aspirant ideals – independence, property, and financial security – and it is these that have often drawn the working and middle classes to Conservatism (Whiteley, Seyd and Richardson, 1994:47). However, since Disraeli's conception of 'one-nation' Conservatism, the party has disavowed the relevance of class and, for long periods of the twentieth century, has attempted to unite the electorate and their party with other identifications through visions of a strong, protected, prosperous nation (Heywood, 1992:72-3; Ball, 1995; Green, 1995: 59-119). Throughout the late 1970s and 1980s Thatcher articulated the concerns and ideals as well as the fears, resentments and prejudices of sections of the electorate who perceived their status, values or property, wealth and respectability to be under threat. But she denied the relevance or even existence of class and claimed to speak for the reinvigorated moral responsibility of the individual, family and nation.

In July 1979, two months after winning the general election, Thatcher outlined her moral agenda at Cambridge University in a lecture entitled 'The Renewal of Britain'. Here she mapped out the failure of the past few years of government which had promoted the 'moral fallacy' that 'conscience' could 'be collectivised' through 'the wanton expansion of the state's responsibilities' (Thatcher, 1979:86-7). Thatcher fused corporeal, fiscal and moral motifs to produce an image of social corruption: 'heavy taxation had lowered fiscal morality', the 'malignant tumour of the black economy had grown' (Thatcher: 87). Against this backdrop she claimed that:

> The extent of our decline compared with other countries may show up most clearly in economic statistics. But that does not mean that the remedy lies only in economics. The economics will come right if the spirit and the determination are there. The mission of this Government is much more than the promotion of economic progress. It is to renew the spirit and the solidarity of the nation.
>
> (Thatcher: 89)[33]

The discourse of conservative populism: Powell and Thatcher

> Dissatisfaction with politics runs too deep both here and abroad. People have come to doubt the future of the democratic system and its institutions. They distrust the politicians and have little faith in the future.
> (Thatcher, 1968:271)

Thatcher's leadership marked a break with consensus politics and this break was often wedded to a broader opposition to 'the permissive society' that symbolised, in Thatcherite discourse, Britain's drift into political and moral decline. Here, I want to signal the importance of the highly controversial Conservative figure, Enoch Powell. Edward Heath's premiership enabled Thatcher's contrasting presentation of strong leadership combined with highly conventional images of 'the housewife' and family values. Enoch Powell, the most prominent far right-wing politician of post-war Conservatism, was also a significant predecessor of Thatcher (Utley, 1968; Schoen, 1977; Gamble, 1988; Smith, 1994). There are a number of issues that, for this analysis, indicate the relevance of Powell as forerunner to Thatcher. In setting these out I want to focus on a particular year, 1968, and in particular two speeches made by Powell and Thatcher that year.

The political moment is crucial here. In popular political mythology 1968 is a highly charged motif. Student protests in May 1968 have become emblematic of a counter culture and the radical social and political liberalisation of the 'permissive society'. By 1968, however, the 'permissive society' had already become a potent negative symbol of 'sexual relaxation, of loose moral standards, of disrespect for all that was traditional and good' (Weeks, 1981:249). It was drawn upon by reactionary right-wing groups to articulate 'a sense of crisis around social changes' and indicated an emergent support for defensive

'authoritarian moral solutions' (Weeks: 249). In this moment Enoch
Powell gave his polemical and still controversial Birmingham speech
on national decline and disintegration that refracted a broader sense of
social malaise through the issue of race relations. The cross-class
appeal of his address, particularly the vociferous working-class
support of Powell from the London dockers and meat porters' march
to Parliament and the country-wide demonstrations, revealed the
potential for populist extension of the Conservative vote (Smith,
1994:172). Furthermore, the timing of Powell's speech in the midst of
changing and unsettled versions of acceptable national and social identity offered an alternative to the discourse of consensus. His
denunciations of the post-war consensus alongside his association of
the Labour Party with a distended, undemocratic and oppressive state
provided motifs for Thatcher.

Powell was ideologically a political outsider. In the 1950s to mid-
1960s, as Conservative MP for Wolverhampton South-West, he
became the principal critic of excessive bureaucratic government and
state intervention. In 1958, he resigned as a Treasury minister from
Macmillan's government (along with Peter Thorneycroft and Nigel
Birch), in protest at a Cabinet decision to increase public spending by
£50 million against the Treasury's advice (Boxer, 1996:31). He returned
to front bench responsibilities in 1964 when the Conservative Party
was defeated in the general election, and became spokesman for
defence under the new leadership of Edward Heath the following
year.[34] He shot to public prominence and was alienated from Heath's
Shadow Cabinet after his speech on immigration and race relations at
the Birmingham Conservative Political Centre on 20 April 1968. Here
he famously conjured up the imaginary vulnerability of white national
identity through the examination of 'ordinary' voters' anxieties and
fears.[35] The speech won him extensive media coverage and widespread
public support. 'Headlines in the *Sun* and the *London Evening
Standard* read: "Immigration: the Powell Explosion" and "Race:
Powell's Bombshell"' (Smith, 1994:160). In his own words, the speech
'provoked a political furore without precedent since the end of the
war' (Powell in Nairn, 1977:256). Thousands of people from all over
the country and across class, party and regional divisions wrote to
Powell to express their solidarity.[36]

The speech produced a reservoir of volatile imagery that appeared
to speak directly to voters' concerns and used besieged white ethnicity as a motif for national dissolution. Some critics have powerfully
argued that racial discourses provided the hegemonic basis for the

imaginary set of exclusions and the parameters of intolerance that were drawn upon by Conservatives in the late 1970s and 1980s (Hall et al, 1978; Gilroy, 1987). Powell attacked and linked prevailing economic policies, race policies, welfare benefits for the 'undeserving poor', unrestricted entrance for all post-colonial British subjects and oppressive state bureaucracy (Kavanagh, 1987:57). Crucially, in doing so, his speech located division and dissent at the heart of the nation and identified a range of alien others who threatened the coherence of the British people. Edward Heath dismissed Powell from the Shadow Cabinet and there was broad disapproval amongst Conservative MPs of his potential exacerbation of racial tension (Schoen, 1977:33-6). However, he promoted a powerful register of insiders and outsiders, which was extended and authorised by Thatcher as party leader. Powell fractured the consensus. 'For a brief period he was the most popular politician in the land' and he mobilised 'mass fears' to 'attack elite attitudes' (Kavanagh, 1987:57).

Images of persecution and of evil are central to Powell's Birmingham speech. He began his speech by declaring that 'the supreme function of statesmanship is to provide against preventable evils' (Powell, 1968:161). The speech hinged upon a fantasy of the black invader, an alien of 'marked physical difference, especially colour' whose otherness hindered 'integration' into the British population (Powell, 1968:167). Furthermore, 'integration' signified the 'dangerous delusion' that the assimilation of immigrants into Britain enabled a homogenous national identity. In fact, Powell claimed, integration obscured the black subject's preservation of 'racial and religious differences' which would increasingly, aided by legislation, lay claim to privileges the white citizen did not possess (Powell: 168). Powell presented the Labour government's stand on race as censorial, oppressive, 'dangerous and divisive' (Powell: 168). Furthermore, he placed himself outside high office and on the side of the people, indeed as the mouthpiece of the 'ordinary working man' and 'white' female old-age pensioner who communicated to him their frightened isolation, abuse and fear at the hands of immigrants. Of the elderly female constituent, confined to her home in a street full of immigrants, he declared:

> She is becoming afraid to go out. Windows are broken. She finds excreta pushed through her letterbox. When she goes to the shops, she is followed by children, charming, wide-grinning piccaninnies. They cannot speak English, but one word they know. 'Racialist', they chant.

When the new race relations Bill is passed, this woman is convinced she will go to prison. And is she so wrong? I begin to wonder.

(Powell, 1968:167)

In his speeches Powell frequently drew upon corporeal metaphors to locate his ostracised man or woman of the street in the physical running of the nation and its economy. He spoke of the 'collective will of the nation' and located it in the 'consumer', the 'savers and investors' who 'use[d] their eyes and brains' to organise resources effectively. These economically energised people were the synapse in the 'complex nerve system of the market': they activated the economy through the expression of their 'wishes', 'needs and expectations' (Powell, 1969:4). In his Birmingham speech, Powell represented the nation in a state of impending collapse. Abject imagery of bodily waste and broken windows implied that the borders of the nation and the private boundaries which separate 'ordinary, decent, sensible people' from the nightmare of offensive abuse had virtually broken down (Powell, 1968: 166).

In November 1968, Powell informed the London Rotary Club gathering at Eastbourne that his Birmingham speech six months before had: 'revealed a deep and dangerous gulf in the nation'. He signalled, as he saw it, the narcissistic delusion and isolation of 'a tiny majority with a monopoly hold upon the channels of communication'. They seemed 'determined ... not to face realities' and hence were rent apart from 'the overwhelming majority of people throughout the country' (Powell, in Smith, 1994:153; see also Nairn, 1977:275). Powell's grand oratorical style, lent weight no doubt by his early years as a Professor of Greek at the University of Sydney,[37] fused an apocalyptic prospect of an abandoned England with a familiar idiom of 'everyday' disenchantment and frustration with the elite offices of public life. As a 'classic populist strategy', this assault upon central aspects of post-war policy revealed the possibilities of a reformulated Conservatism translated into a national-popular mode of address (Kavanagh: 57; Gamble, 1988:71; Smith, 1994:6-7).[38]

Later the same year, at the Conservative Party Conference, Thatcher made what is arguably her first key speech, 'What's Wrong with Politics', to the Conservative Political Centre (Wapshott and Brock, 1983; Gamble, 1988:81).[39] This speech can be read as her first public (careful) criticism of prevailing Conservative philosophy and as an intimation of her more overt populism as party leader. Here Thatcher, albeit less controversially, drew upon Powell's language of personal vision, political separation from mainstream government and alliance with 'the people'. Like Powell, she associated consensus with the Conservative 'appeasement' of competing pressure groups and the taint of socialist collectivism which represented for her the loss of Britain's clear direction. She also spoke of the electorate's alienation from the government and of its need for greater recognition and independence. In 'What's Wrong With Politics', Thatcher denounced consensus politics. She did so by proclaiming her speech as the expression of the people's discontent: 'People have come to doubt the future of the democratic system and its institutions. They distrust the politicians and have little faith in the future' (Thatcher, 1968: 271). While Powell took on the role of organic intellectual translating 'ordinary' fears, Thatcher claimed to assess a 'deep' popular 'dissatisfaction with politics both here and abroad' (Thatcher: 271). Powell had stressed the politician's use of story and powerful imagery to convey prosaic fears. He suggested that 'the greatest task of the statesman' was 'to offer his people good myths and save them from harmful ones' (Powell in Gamble, 1988:69). Thatcher similarly presented her speech as everyday and also mythic: an attempt to 'retest old assumptions and to seek new ideas' in 'the spirit' of the mythic encounter between the wisdom-seeking soldier of fortune and 'the Sphinx' (Thatcher: 273).

She promoted family values, the freedom and natural justice of the market and the citizen's right and obligation to care for him or herself with only a minimal welfare safety net. Her attack on state bureaucracy closely followed a speech Powell made in 1964 when he attacked government information gathering. His attack culminated in a listing of census questions in which the citizen was 'managed and controlled, planned and organised, with material distilled by experts' (Powell, 1969:62). Thatcher castigated official bureaucracy as the enemy of individuality and freedom. Government intervention had been passed to officials and bureaucrats who distanced the people from the processes that controlled their lives and rendered government increasingly remote (Thatcher, 1968:274). In a *tour de force* she outlined the standard course of a citizen's life in modern bureaucracy as a passage through a list of twenty-two possible areas of documentation from birth certificate to death grant (Thatcher: 279). The 'people' were presented as 'swamped' and isolated; government and industry had 'become bewitched with the idea of size': 'everything has become so big, so organised, so standardised and governmentalised that there is no room for the individual, his talents, his requirements or his wishes' (p279). Against this backdrop of alienation, she redefined 'consensus' as undemocratic:

> There are dangers in consensus; it could be an attempt to satisfy people holding no particular views about anything. It seems more important to have a philosophy and policy which, because they are good, appeal to sufficient people to secure a majority.
>
> (p281)

She did not offer an alternative collective identification, but an atomised form of 'responsibility and independence' for the people, an identity which would extract them from dependency on MP or government 'to solve their problems'. Importantly, for later chapters, this speech indicated Thatcher's ability to hold together two forms of potential identification. Firstly, 'danger' and 'dependency' linked consensus to powerlessness, passivity and loss of control. She suggested that one unforeseen result of mass franchise and the party political structure was the electoral promise that a party, once elected, would carry out all the promises made in their manifesto (p272). This system led to suspicion and disdain on the part of voters and rejection of politicians if promises were not fulfilled. Importantly, Thatcher posited an alternative ethos in which the promise of strong leadership and a broad set of values were in the true spirit of democratic government. Consequently, she promised 'an alternative' autonomy, control and activity: 'The Conservative creed has never offered a life of ease without effort'. Democracy, added Thatcher, was not for the dependent but for the already independent, self-supporting individual: 'Self-government is for those men and women who have learned to govern themselves' (p281).

References

1. There were two general elections in 1974. The narrow result of the first in February made the second contest inevitable. The Labour Party, under Harold Wilson, defeated Edward Heath's governing Conservative Party (1970-74) but with a narrow majority – Labour 301 seats, Conservative 297, Liberal 14, others 23 – and in the second contest in October, Wilson secured his majority, but only by three seats overall.
2. In the second ballot, Thatcher defeated her major contender William Whitelaw by 146 votes to 79; Geoffrey Howe and Jim Prior had 19 votes.
3. In 1983 the Conservative vote stood at 42 per cent and in the 1987 general election at 43 per cent.

4. Keith Joseph, within a week of putting himself up as a candidate for leadership, destroyed his credibility in one speech at Birmingham in which he criticised the number of births to mothers of working-class children (Young, 1989:93). This speech will be discussed in chapter four. Edward du Cann was Chairman of the backbench 1922 Committee, loathed Heath and appeared to anti-Heathites to be a viable candidate. He suddenly pulled out of the contest declaring his wife's opposition as a cause (Young, 1989:95).

5. Founded by Keith Joseph, the Centre for Policy Studies became the focus for radical right-wing thinkers who favoured a free market economy.

6. The term 'Conservative' was widely used by the party's leaders and supporters after 1830 when Tories lost the support of the reigning monarch King William IV and, sent into opposition, moved from a self-identity as the Crown's 'governing men' to a sense of themselves as a Parliament party. 'Tory' continues to be used as a more colloquial expression by supporters and opponents although it can imply an instinctive and uncompromising strand of Conservatism (Ball, 1995:3-4).

7. Benjamin Disraeli, British Prime Minister in 1868 and again from 1874-80, developed the notion of 'one nation' against a background of industrial growth, economic inequality and, in sections of Europe, revolutionary upheaval. He attempted to adapt the Conservative Party to the major extension of franchise in the 1860s and to create the institutional framework for a modern political party. His appeal for social reform and a conservative acceptance of hierarchy and duty was an attempt to avoid divisions between rich and poor.

8. Hugo Young notes the first sighting of the term in his notebooks in the summer of 1976 when Jim Prior told him he had been accused by Thatcher of 'wetness' for not wanting to reduce the trade unions to impotence (Young, 1989:198).

9. Those inner Cabinet members who harboured serious reservations were Jim Prior (Employment), Peter Walker (Agriculture), Ian Gilmour (Lord Privy Seal), Lord Carrington (Foreign Secretary), Norman St John Stevas (Leader of the House of Commons).

10. Even thorough critics and biographers replicate the stereotype of the 'Tory woman' without reflection. For example, Wapshott and Brock discuss an impressive and factual performance of Thatcher's during her leadership campaign when she first addressed the Parliamentary Press Gallery. They suggest that her impressive engagement with reporters revealed that 'she was far more than the cliché Tory woman' (Wapshott and Brock, 1983:129).

11. The Primrose League was conceived as a memorial to Disraeli, the

Conservative leader who equated patriotism with Conservatism through the ideal of 'one nation' in which values of tradition, national identity and responsibility supplanted old divisions of class (Blake, 1985). The Primrose League was formed in 1883 by Randolph Churchill, its aim to energise Toryism through an alliance between the working class and the aristocracy who formed the paternalist leadership of the party. As Beatrix Campbell suggests, in the formation of the Ladies Grand Council of the Primrose League, it 'institutionalised the rites of the great Tory hostesses, the women who exercised political power by proxy' (Campbell, 1987:8).

12. Once Thatcher had consolidated her leadership, just prior to the general election in May 1979, her gender and middle-class suburban background were drawn upon by Conservative party menbers as evidence of the party's radical revision. The Shadow Leader of the House, Norman St John-Stevas, was interviewed on BBC2's *On the Record* (24 March 1979). He informed interviewer Robert McKenzie that it was hoped that the number of people 'repelled' by Thatcher being a woman would be cancelled out by those 'attracted to her because she is the first woman' contending to be Prime Minister. He continued by stressing that Thatcher's gender was 'a very good thing for the Conservative Party' as it exemplified 'a most dramatic and radical issue which we have solved' (CPA:PPB 79).

13. On 23 October 1918, the House of Commons passed a motion (by 274 votes to 25) proposed by Herbert Samuel 'that ... it is desirable that a Bill should be passed forthwith making women eligible as Members of Parliament'. Lord Robert Cecil, a government minister, introduced the *Parliament (Qualification of Women) Bill* on 31 October and it was passed with little opposition within three weeks. It received Royal Assent on 21 November 1918, on the day that Parliament was dissolved for the forthcoming general election (Public Information Office, House of Commons, 1995:3).

14. Of these 19 MPs, 8 were Conservative ministers and 11 were members of the Labour Party.

15. NSA refers to the National Sound Archive, British Library. The key and full source references are listed in the Archive Source List.

16. In these references to Lady Astor, Thatcher often sustained the popular myth that the campaign for women's suffrage culminated in the election of a Conservative as first woman MP. In fact, the first woman to be elected to the House of Commons was Ireland's Countess Markiewicz in 1918. Markiewicz, a suffragette and revolutionary republican, was imprisoned in Holloway Prison and, had she wished to, could not take up her seat.

17. See also Thatcher's Pankhurst Lecture' to The 300 Group (CPA: TS 7/90).

18. For a first-hand account of Macmillan's style and its projection to the public read his press secretary Harold Evans's *Downing Street Diary 1957-63* (1981) and also Michael Cockerell's *Live From Number 10* (1988:75-95).

19. A popular once-a-week radio programme in which a famous person selects the eight pieces of music they would take with them if marooned on a desert island.

20. This phrase forms the title of Thatcher's memoirs *The Path to Power* (1995).

21. Typical of this account is the entry in Tricia Murray's early biography *Margaret Thatcher* (1978) written before Thatcher became Prime Minister. Murray interviewed Thatcher's son Mark who praised her 'legendary' 'powers of endurance': 'She's got a constitution like an elephant! She works phenomenal hours. She's the lady who never sleeps. When the heat is really on, she gets about for hours ... There are lookers and doers and she's the original doer' (Murray, 1978:65).

22. Edwina Curry was appointed Parliament Under-Secretary of State for Health on 10 September 1986. She resigned on 16 December 1988 in the aftermath of a public panic which followed her interview with ITN in which she gave advice on the potential of salmonella poisoning from the consumption of raw or partially cooked eggs.

23. See for example, Gail Sheehy's article 'What Makes Maggie Run' in *New Woman*, August 1989 and Ros Miles's celebration of 'woman power' in *Women and Power* (1985).

24. For discussion of the masculinised network of power relations in the Labour movement see Cynthia Cockburn (1987) and Barbara Rogers (1988) on men-only institutions.

25. In the 1990s, under John Major's leadership, the Conservative Party presented itself as a 'classless' party with a leader from humble origins. However, 62 per cent of Conservative MPs returned in the 1992 general election were private school educated, compared with 15 per cent of Labour MPs (Adonis and Pollard, 1997:113). In the early 1990s the great majority of party members were educated in state schools, with only about one quarter going to private schools (Whiteley, Seyd and Richardson, 1994:43-4).

26. Commentators looking for early signs of Thatcher's resolve as Prime Minister return to her much quoted declaration at the 1980 Conservative Party Conference: 'To those waiting with bated breath for that favourite media catch-phrase, the U-Turn, I have only one thing to say. You turn if you want to. The Lady's not for turning'.

27. Before the 1964 election, in one of his motivated 'New Britain' speeches, Harold Wilson had declared: 'Ability must be the test, and ability is not

measured by upper-class accents' (Pimlott, 1993:307; Adonis and Pollard, 1997:103).

28. Robert Behrens has revealed how criticisms of Heath's leadership style in this period highlight his adoption of 'an artificial manner, haughtily stiff or exuberantly bland' (Behrens, 1980:31).

29. In television interviews such as *The Prime Minister and Mrs Wilson at Home* (25 July 1969) Wilson underscored the contract between his family life and the bachelor Heath (Cockerell, 1988:146).

30. In recent quantitative and qualitative surveys (1990-92) of Conservative grassroots ratings of Conservative leading politicians, Conservative Party members ranked 'honesty', 'firmness' and 'conviction' as top leadership qualities. Out of a list of 21 prominent Conservative politicians, Heath scored the lowest percentage of support (41 per cent). Thatcher achieved the second highest (78 per cent) just under the Prime Minister John Major (80 per cent). The survey found that Heath evoked 'considerable dislike' (Whiteley, Seyd and Richardson, 1994:60-1).

31. During mid- to late- 1978, with a general election looming on the horizon, there were a series of articles in the broadsheet press discussing the possibility of Heath's return and Thatcher's removal from leadership. In the editorial 'Two kinds of Toryism', the *Observer* (9 July:6) discussed how the relationship between Heath and Thatcher would 'never be cordial this side of the grave, much less this side of the election' and reflected upon possible damage to Thatcher. By November 1978, an editorial in the *Guardian* epitomised a broader press perspective that Heath's attack on the free market philosophy of Thatcher's camp was powerful but he was bereft of allies within his party (*Guardian*, 21 October 1978:6).

32. In bolstering an image of self-determination, Thatcher was explicitly set against the various 'U-turns' between free market and managed economy made by the Conservatives under Heath's government (1970-74) (Cole, 1987:8-11).

33. The Swinton Lecture at the Conservative Political Centre Summer School, Cambridge University, 6 July 1979.

34. See Chapter 15 'The Age of Powell and Benn' in Richard Johnson's *The Politics of Recession* (1985) for a fascinating comparison of Enoch Powell and Labour Party maverick Tony Benn.

35. Powell's speech in April 1968 was timed to coincide with new race relations policy which aimed to offer equal opportunity for black British citizens in housing and employment. This speech became known as the 'Rivers of Blood' speech due to the comparison Powell made between himself and the ancient Roman who saw the Tiber foam with the blood of the civil strife.

36. In a poll by Gallup in April 1968, one per cent of respondents wanted Powell as the next leader of the Conservative Party. In May 1968, after the speech, this rose to 24 per cent. Powell received 105,000 letters of support in the first week after the speech and up to two thirds of people questioned by pollsters stated their agreement with Powell's speech (Gamble, 1988:79). See also Chapter Two of D. Schoen's *Enoch Powell and the Powellites* (1977:33-39).

37. Powell came from a lower-middle-class background, his parents were elementary school teachers, he went to a Birmingham grammar school and then Cambridge University. He was only 26 years old when he became a professor of Greek at the University of Sydney (Nairn, 1977:260).

38. For a discursive analysis of the black immigrant as 'post-colonial symptom' in Powell's speeches see Anna Marie Smith (1994:129-182).

39. Here I am indebted to Wapshott and Brock's (1983) biography of Thatcher for pointing up this speech. I draw on the full text of the speech published in their appendix.

CHAPTER THREE:

Masquerade

In the discussions which have circulated around [Thatcher and political leadership], what it is to be a 'real' woman and a 'real' man has
been a prominent theme, reflected in two paradoxical and common
judgements: that 'she isn't really a woman', and that she is the best
man in the country'.

(Webster, 1990:1)

In the preceding chapter I discussed how Thatcher's gender marked
her journey to the centre of the political arena. Sceptics or rivals interpreted Thatcher's ascent to party leadership as a feminine intrusion
upon a masculine space that was exemplified by her adversarial political discourse and defiance of established forms of political decorum
and post-war Conservative philosophy. This encroachment engen-
dered worries on the part of rivals that she would split the party and
possibly the nation, leading to a break down in democracy. Fear or
indeed reluctant admiration of Thatcher stemmed from concerns
about the chaotic or emotional dangers of femininity. Colleagues'
anxiety about Thatcher's accession also revealed disdain for the
retributive or jingoistic elements within the grass roots of the party
and within the electorate more generally. Thatcher's clear affinity with
the rank and file and her self-positioning with 'the people' was
described as 'physical and emotional compulsion' (Foley, 1993:69). In
a *Guardian* article, 'Fighter with a golden tongue' (26 November
1990), this mass appeal is sketched as a horribly alluring spectacle:

> Mrs Thatcher – a lady in a petal hat made queen – genuinely loved her
> party, breathed in and out with it, and shared its hates and loves, espe-
> cially its instincts for class war, for which members of a higher social class
> felt fastidious distaste. It was not nice to watch but it was authentic.
>
> (Foley, 1993:69)

Descriptions such as this underline the mutual association of spectacle, femininity, the party mass and potential violence in some fantasies of public life and of Thatcher's overdetermined relation to that *mise-en-scène*. Such criticism implied that to understand Thatcher was to contemplate the almost visceral instincts of the Conservative rank and file, the militant prejudices of the lower middle classes. Her alleged anti-intellectualism and her manner and tone were interpreted as 'an artificial condescending hauteur' that concealed an alarming ability to touch the base political passions (Benton, 1987:14). In *Mrs Thatcher's Revolution* (1987:86), Peter Jenkins claimed that Thatcher had inherited her father's political interests but no intellectual curiosity of her own. The complexity of politics was stripped to 'a neat set of prejudices, like a twin-set and court shoes, with which to pursue her ambition into politics'.

'Instinct' was the word frequently drawn upon by biographers and journalists trying to articulate the seemingly mysterious, unknowable, non-intellectual or non-rational quality of Thatcher's political outlook. This fed the myth that she was outside the rules and conventions that mould a party politician. It also echoed Thatcher's self-professed ability to use her private feelings to modulate politics to everyday life. Thatcher's speeches swung from idealisation to condemnation of sections of the public; she spoke of 'ordinary' desires to work hard and get on under one's own steam; and not to feel guilty if this separated one from those less successful or able or willing to make that leap. The nation she desired was full of 'men' or 'people' who seized the historical moment and, through sheer will, hard work and imagination, branded it with their vision. Thatcher's own background and political path to power were cast as the exemplary model of this narrative of transcendent mastery.

Femininity and masculinity were integral elements of Thatcher's political persona, but I have already indicated her deep ambivalence about her gender. Her flight from femininity was underlined as she informed journalists that her gender was irrelevant to her progress to power and that her political identity was as politician *not* woman. This refusal of femininity was typical. On *Desert Island Discs* in February 1978, Roy Plomley asked Thatcher about 'problems because of her sex' which had led to the previously all-male Carlton Club bending their membership rules for her. Her tetchy retort revealed a reluctance to acknowledge her gender: 'I didn't join the Carlton Club as a woman, but as Leader of the Opposition' (NSA: P1261). When Conservative colleague Patrick Cosgrave suggested to Thatcher that a private opinion poll be conducted to ascertain her relevance for women voters his proposal was firmly rejected. He recalled, 'My draft idea for a poll depended upon an emphasis upon her sexual identity'. Therefore 'She turned the scheme down flat' (Cosgrave in Abse, 1989:253).

In this chapter I will interpret Thatcher's ambivalence about gender through the concept of 'masquerade'. The emphasis will be on her recognition of the privileged relationship between masculinity, power and the public world of political activity. Thatcher's published memories of her childhood and the role of her father and (largely absent) mother in her political formation will be drawn upon to interpret this recognition of political power, its performance and the textual traces of unconscious anxiety, conflict and aggression. I will explore Thatcher's memories as an act of commemoration and testimony to her father's influence and as a process of dissociation from her mother and her role. These memories did not just describe Thatcher's past but placed her present political identity quite specifically in relation to it. She drew frequently upon recollections of her childhood to infuse her political message with a personal authority. In 1980 she told the *Sunday Times* that 'deep' in the people's 'instincts' they knew the rightness of what she said and did and she was certain too: 'because that is the way I was brought up. I'm eternally grateful for the way I was brought up in a small town. We knew everyone, we knew what people felt' (Benton, 1987:14).

Her past became an incontrovertible 'fact' with which to counter any association with 'Tory' privilege and the alleged delusions and fantasies of collectivism which, she claimed, gave Labour's socialism its flimsy base. Thatcher's masquerade was also deeply implicated in concepts of respectability and moral accountability that derived partly from her Methodist upbringing and that were made central to her political identity. The religious dimension of Thatcher's discourse and the reverential descriptions of her father are relevant here. Thatcher was a Methodist until her marriage to Denis in the early 1950s initiated the gradual movement to High Anglicanism. However her Methodist background and her father Alfred Roberts forged the link between Thatcherite politics and the triumph of the Conservative individual. Religion was adapted to a political message, for the God who sanctioned Thatcher's politics, embodied in the image of Alfred Roberts's paternal perfection, acknowledged no difference between spiritual and material well-being. She claimed of her leadership that: 'Economics are the method; the object is to change the soul' (Thatcher in McFadyean and Renn, 1984:31).

Manner and appearance: the problem of femininity

Thatcher's political memoir *The Path to Power* (1995) is the second of
two volumes and is presented as the key to her inner life, the training
and values that informed her later political philosophy. This text and
the preceding account of premiership – *The Downing Street Years*
(1993) – are significant for their extensive circulation and promotion
in the media and their construction as definitive self-authored retro-
spectives on a prominent political career.[1] In *The Path to Power*,
Thatcher suggests that the politician who refused to alter 'manner and
appearance' to enhance their public persona may wish to 'sound grit-
tily honourable' but would in fact 'betray a lack of seriousness about
winning power' (Thatcher, 1995:294-5). She illustrates how her self-
fashioning as a new Conservative leader hinged upon the problem of
her femininity and how this was accommodated with the conventionally masculine associations of powerful political authority. She recalls
the process of grooming undertaken to produce a professional look
for TV and the advice by image adviser Gordon Reece that jewellery
near the face was ill advised. The House of Commons, she
commented, 'was – and still is – a very masculine place'. This mani-
fested itself in 'the sheer volume of noise' which had shocked Thatcher
as a new MP entering the House (Thatcher: 108). As 'a woman striv-
ing for dominance in this noisy, boisterous, masculine world' she was,
as leader, professionally trained to lower the timbre of her voice
(p284).[2] A deeper voice provided strength to combat the 'curious deep
braying' of the House but, of equal importance for her, she avoided
the 'grating' connotations of female 'shrieking' (p285, p295).

The account of her first public performances as Leader of the
Opposition reveals how her new position inspired misogyny and also
romantic admiration. As new leader, her first entrance into the
Chamber to hear Prime Minister Harold Wilson make a statement was
accompanied by 'much male chauvinist hilarity – "Give us a kiss,
Maggie", etc.' (p284). The memory of her first appearance before the
1922 Committee signals her 'easier' relationship with 'the wider
Parliamentary Party' through recollection of boisterous applause and
more provocatively by 'an unsigned Valentine card' which joined the
mass of Valentines and roses sent to Thatcher's Chelsea home (p285).
These recollections of an initial public encounter between a woman
leader, colleagues and Conservative rank and file present Thatcher as
troubled and nervous but also anxious to learn and mould herself as a
competent professional politician. She acknowledges that as 'a woman
in industry, at the Bar and indeed in Tory constituency politics' she

had, 'in different ways', been 'made to feel small' (p108-9). But, she claims, the House of Commons recognised as 'equals' those who earned respect through 'sincerity, logic and technical mastery of a subject' (p109).

Thatcher's defensiveness about her femininity and the responses it provoked, her acceptance of high public office as the manipulation of self-image and the significance of her gendered persona have all been underlined. Joan Riviere's 'Womanliness as a Masquerade', first published in 1929, is relevant here. Riviere was concerned with the analysis of a certain type of 'modern' woman who seemed to hover ambivalently between conventionally recognised masculine and feminine subject positions. Riviere's analysis sets out the features of fully developed heterosexual womanhood – passivity, deference, relinquishment of power, maternal identification – defined within a psychoanalytic framework[3] and illustrated with anecdotal social observation of female acquaintances' behaviour. Riviere's career woman seemed 'to fulfil every criterion of feminine development': excellent wife, capable housewife, nurturing as a mother, friend or colleague, a centre of sociable activity and interested in her appearance. Yet the difficulty lay in the fact that, although she was also able to 'fulfil the duties of [her] profession at least as well as the average man', this ability carried with it the psychic burden of extreme anxiety (Riviere, 1929:35). Her analysis centred on an exemplary case study of an intellectual woman who, engaged in work of 'a propagandist nature', was called on to publicly speak, debate and instruct her predominantly male colleagues. However, her performances were frequently followed by acute anxiety in which direct and indirect reassurance was sought from male colleagues through overt demonstrations of deferential femininity. Riviere was concerned with the sharp contradiction between the competence and seeming ease of the woman's public performance and the juxtaposition of her anxious overdetermined feminine vulnerability and acquiescence. Riviere linked the woman's compulsive behaviour to her wish to hide the possession of masculine attributes conventionally associated with her public displays of intellectual skill. To cover up for her unconscious rivalry with her father, and the theft of masculinity this entailed, the woman dissembled as fully feminine, thus 'guiltless and innocent', thereby escaping retribution. Riviere concluded: 'Womanliness therefore could be assumed and worn as a mask, both to hide the possession of masculinity and to avert the reprisals if she was found to possess it' (Riviere: 38).

The conventionally feminine woman, then, is characterised by an acceptance that: 'I must not take, I must not even ask; it must be *given* to me' (Riviere: 43). Masquerade constitutes a refusal to accept and take on fully the myths of femininity – deference, humility and self-abnegation – plus a powerful investment in taking on and displaying certain myths of masculinity – aggressive confidence, public eloquence, mastery of knowledge. Three issues need to be stressed before returning to Margaret Thatcher in relation to her masquerade. Firstly, acute anxiety accompanies the masquerade, the anxiety of subterfuge and the watchfulness of the perpetrator who fears discovery of her 'crime'. Secondly, the masquerade reveals the potential for a critical distance from the attributes of femininity: the adoption of overtly feminine traits can then be read as manipulation and/or mockery rather than conventional accommodation to social demands.[4] Thirdly, the masquerade is always inevitably social and political: it is a public performance that requires an audience and involves the acquisition of power and authority that are institutionally endorsed.

Fear and control are held together in the masquerading woman's self-positioning within the public world. In Thatcher's recollections this template is mapped onto a fraught international and volatile domestic political scene. In *The Path to Power*, Thatcher located the initial consolidation of her authority as party leader in late 1975 and early 1976, following a tour of the United States. Her recollections depend on a number of themes: plotting, dangerous, East European dictators, volatile Western nations, sceptical or ineffectual Conservative colleagues. On the tour she was given prominent press coverage as stateswoman meeting 'leading political figures ... on something approaching equal terms' (Thatcher, 1995:357). The United States is recalled as a traumatised and fractured nation – 'in the wake of the fall of Vietnam' and Watergate (p357). Thatcher claims that *schadenfreude* fuelled America's fascination with Britain's 'precipitous decline' and deflected their fears of political and national fragmentation. The environment she reconstructs then is hostile and voyeuristic. In this arena, she powerfully portrayed the revival of Britain under a future Conservative government led by her. Her speeches wed her political vision to the abandonment of 'socialist policies'. To the National Press Club in Washington she predicted a political sea change evident in signs of the people's readiness to 'make a tough choice, to follow the harder road' that would reinvigorate the British 'spirit of adventure' and conquer the present 'British sickness' (p359-

60). Thatcher claims her performance across the Atlantic and widespread media coverage forced her Conservative colleagues' re-evaluation of her. Previously they had regarded her 'accession to leadership as an irritating but temporary fluke', but were outfaced by her serious treatment by 'some of the most powerful figures in the world' (p360). In January 1976, at Kensington Town Hall, her speech concentrated on defence and was fuelled by a virulent attack upon 'the Soviet menace' (p361). Against the prevailing political emphasis on *détente* she described Russia as a 'dictatorship of patient, far-sighted men' who were rapidly acquiring 'the foremost naval and military power in the world'.[5] 'World dominance', she warned, was the Russian goal (p361-2).

This scene of her new-found prestige is captured through imagery of magnitude: her identity as Conservative leader is confirmed through the 'most powerful' politicians 'in the world'. Thatcher's juxtaposition of doubting Conservative colleagues and 'patient, far-sighted' conspiratorial Russian men bent on world domination is revealing. The Russians as an explicit enemy were fabricated as supremely competent and capable of long premeditated attack.[6] Such an enemy enabled Thatcher to underline her strong military stance to international onlookers. The immense scale of the threat reveals fear and danger as essential components of her nascent image of authority. Furthermore, the Russian enemy was also an object of her displaced anxiety about underhand plotting against her by colleagues closer to home. In Thatcher's account, her acquisition of political authority dovetails with the 'revival of Western morale and defence preparedness' and with her adoption of an intended insult by the offended Russians (p364). Thatcher relished what she saw as the 'grotesque misjudgement' of the Red Army newspaper *Red Star*. The *Red Star* coined the intended insult 'Iron Lady'. She acknowledges her seizure of this identity: 'I quickly saw that they had put me on a pedestal as their strongest European opponent. They never did me a greater favour' (p362). Soon after, she opened a dinner speech to her Finchley constituency with the following self-dramatisation:

> Ladies and gentleman, I stand before you tonight, in my Red Star chiffon evening gown, my face softly made-up and my fair hair gently waved – the Iron Lady of the western world, a cold war Warrior, an Amazon Philistine, even a Peking plotter.
>
> Well, am I any of these things ... Yes, I am an Iron Lady – after all it wasn't a bad thing to be an Iron Duke. Yes, if that's how you wish to

interpret my defence of values and freedoms fundamental to our way of life.

(Thatcher in Webster 1990:83)

This performance is exemplary of Thatcher's resourcefulness, her ability to take on an insult and translate it into a sign of political triumph. Her speech holds together a general contempt for those who have attacked her femininity – as 'Amazon Philistine' or 'Iron Lady' – and a reassuring display of her conventionally womanly attributes: the chiffon evening gown, the understated makeup and gently waved hair of a discreet femininity. At the same time she affirms the models of masculine military strength which she claims as her own: 'Yes I am an Iron Lady – after all it wasn't a bad thing to be an Iron Duke'. Here mimicry and mockery are interwoven. Thatcher treats both her femininity and masculinity as a '"game", as something *not real*, as a "joke"' (Riviere, 1929:39). But there is a sense in which Thatcher differs from Riviere's analysand who ingratiates herself with male authority and defers (or appears to defer) to their assessment of her. Rather, Thatcher's references to her feminine appearance seem excessive and at odds with her almost militaristic persona.[7] On one level then, this strategy both covers up an anxiety about being placed in the limelight as an aberrant aggressive woman and also contests uncritical acceptance of male claims to power. But on another level her performance could be read as a pleasurable ironic play on gender rather than the anxiety-ridden compensatory gesture set out by Riviere (Doane, 1991:38).

Riviere locates the masquerading woman's fear of retribution as symptomatic of her desire to take the place of men, most specifically her father. The rivalry with the father is not over the mother as in the Oedipal trajectory, but for his active role in public discourse: 'as a user of signs rather than a sign-object, an item of exchange' (Butler, 1990:51). The audience and the public nature of this speech are crucial to Thatcher's ambivalent role, as is her humour. She presents herself first as *object* of the gaze – 'Ladies and gentleman, I stand before you tonight' – but then as a *subject* who can engage in political exchange and ultimately designate the true meaning of her words – 'if that's how you wish to interpret my defence of values and freedoms'. Thatcher's words are interspersed with the audience's laughter, she plays up to their mirth and indicates to absent enemies that they can, if they want, interpret her political message through mockery but the last laugh is hers (NSA: LP36969).[8] There appears to be an act of defiance directed not only at the Russians but also at the conventional expectations of femininity to which she was expected to adhere. Thatcher recalled that, immediately after adopting the nickname, she visited the British Army on the Rhine where she was photographed in a tank. She declares this image 'did me no harm at all at home either' (Thatcher, 1995:362).

In an interview with Radio 4's *Woman's Hour* in 1986, Thatcher admitted revelling in the vitriolic abuse and verbal battle of politics. She recalled her early performances as a young woman in the 1950 general election when she stood for the Conservative Party in Dartford: 'I was always good at questions, there was some marvellous heckling, heckling always helps' (NSA: B2075). Such attacks were for Thatcher a mark of authentic 'electioneering', being challenged in the open, 'from the back of a lorry in market places'. Such contestation was evidence of her political and personal aptitude for adversarial politics: 'and back came the heckling, back came the shouting and the blood began to pulse through one's being ... ' (NSA: B2075). This bellicose political performance seemingly involved, for Thatcher, the converse of masquerade: a display of implicitly masculine prowess rather than a disguise of that ability. She acknowledged that like many women seeking political office alongside her in the 1950s and 1960s she found herself in 'a tangled web' where the expectations of society for a married woman and mother hindered career success. She implied that she alone, as other women could have done, got herself on the shortlist and added, 'Once you're on the shortlist you're on your own' (NSA: B2075).

Thatcher appears in her accounts to be very knowing about the ability to manufacture a distance from one's feelings of vulnerability and from the sense of social powerlessness that can accompany public performance, particularly for a woman in a predominantly male sphere. She told *Woman's Hour* that in her early political speeches she was 'always nervous', always 'frightened to death' every time she went on a platform. Speaking then as a Prime Minister of seven and a half years she was still nervous each time she spoke in the House of Commons; this was a hazard of the job, whatever the gender of the minister. But she claimed that 'years of training, years of experience, years of preparation' had enabled her to 'lose' herself (NSA: B2075). Crucially she compared high politics to the national spectacle of a sporting event:

> Believe you me, if I go to Wimbledon or the Cup Final I know exactly
> how those people feel when they walk out onto the pitch or onto the

court: nervous, frightened to death until the game starts and they lose themselves in the game.

(NSA: B2075)

Here performativity was aligned with the mastery of vulnerability and also a detachment from physical fear, an absorption in the playing out of a role before an audience and the competitive battle that politics entailed. Thatcher's depiction of the competent politician suggests a kind of presupposed complicity between politician and voter or fellow MP and an acknowledgement of performance in which the political masquerade overrides the potential objectification of Thatcher as woman. Being a politician necessitated the offering up of self as combative, absorbed, skilful and fearless. She acknowledges contemporary politics as the desire on the part of the electorate for a show. Speaking to Pete Murray on Radio 1's *Late Show* in March 1982, she recalled her childhood fascination with the media, gazing at Hollywood films and sitting as a family listening to national events on the radio. But on her later role as politician, she stressed, 'It is very important that we don't just become spectators' (NSA: LP40788).

In her memoirs, Thatcher suggests that a politician's public image is partly imposed upon him (sic) by the media, this defines him and screens him off from his audience: 'Once a politician is given a public image by the media, it is almost impossible for him to shed it. At every important stage of his career it steps between him and the public' (Thatcher, 1995:470). She indicates a contemporary political environment in which the media are 'viewed as important political actors in their own right' (McNair, 1995:45). The increasing engagement with advertising, public relations and marketing on the part of political parties in the post-war years led to definitions of politics as a process of simulation: 'a world where the image, more interesting than the original, has itself become the original' (Boorstin, 1962:204). Alongside this the media, especially popular broadcasting and press, frequently interpret politics through a news-making process of personalisation which translates social and political events into individual causes and responses. Of this practice, Thatcher noted, 'people seem to see and hear not the man himself but the invented personality to which he has been reduced' (Thatcher, 1995:470). She adds that her public image was not necessarily a 'disadvantageous one': 'I was "the Iron Lady", "Battling Maggie", "Attila the Hen" (Thatcher: 470). These epithets provided her with a deceptively powerful armour: 'these generally gave opponents the impression I was a hard nut to crack, I was glad to be so portrayed even though no real person could be so single-mindedly tough' (p470).

The trope of the masquerade deepens the sense of gender as enactment. Beatrix Campbell has noted of Thatcher's public performances that her body language was 'womanly' but also somewhat stilted:

> as she speaks into the glass screens scrolling up her speeches at party conferences, she tilts her head in that gesture which is placatory but superior, her stride is stiff from the waist down, she makes her point in the nuanced tilt of her shoulders and her bosom.
>
> (Campbell, 1987:242)

In *The Path to Power* (1995) Thatcher reservedly admired former Conservative Prime Minister Harold Macmillan's skill of acquiring an elusive public face: 'Macmillan ... cultivated a languorous and almost antediluvian style which was not – and was not intended to be – sufficiently convincing to conceal the shrewdness behind it. He was a man of masks' (Thatcher, 1995:91). She characterises her difference from Macmillan in gendered terms, allocating to him a faintly disparaged femininity: 'It is clear to me now that Macmillan was a more complex and sensitive figure than he appeared; but appearance did seem to account for a great deal' (p118). To Thatcher, Macmillan's dissimulation was effete, 'ornate' and otherworldly and hence the opposite of her pragmatic and no-nonsense stance: 'Things look different from the perspective of Grantham than from that of Stockton' (Thatcher: 118).

Personal history and public life: memories of Alfred Roberts

> The child furnishes the landscape: books are read, images invested with her own meaning ... People tell their stories to the child, about other places, other childhoods; or they keep their secrets; and using them both, the child adds other detail.
>
> (Steedman, 1986:98)

Born in October 1925, Thatcher's formative years of political training were under her father, the Alderman Alfred Roberts. Accounts of Alfred Roberts's influence upon Thatcher as politician are numerous. He is frequently presented as her route to power, knowledge and mobility and the source of her conviction politics. Integral to this presentation of her father is Thatcher's own narrative of her austere, self-sufficient family home and fledgling political activity with her father in the 1930s. The defensiveness, anxiety and ambiguous adoption of masculine and feminine attributes highlighted by Riviere provide a starting point for interpreting Thatcher's persona, but the weaving of personal history and public life are also crucial here. In her speeches and interviews, Thatcher's accounts of Thatcherism and its values were often accompanied by references to a secure and symbolically usable past. Often, an iconographic past is given clarity through an individual's story. The 'unity' of the exemplary subject is refracted through the personal time of biography, historical and political events. Margaret Thatcher's biography, in particular her Grantham upbringing, inform popular understanding of Thatcherism. Thatcher continually rehearsed the account of her early life to authenticate her political beliefs – the portrayal of a 'conventional' family life became a template for the reconstruction of a stable nation. The traces of a defensive and protective lower-middle-class identity can be found in these Grantham memories. Economic self-sufficiency and precarious respectability inform Thatcher's (public) self-image and reveal both class and gender as components of her masquerade.

Prior to becoming Prime Minister, Thatcher was asked which other person she would have desired to be. The choice was uncharacteristically romantic: Anna of *Anna and the King of Siam* (Abse, 1989:64). Graham Little underlined the gendered and imperialist connotations of this fantasy:

> Politics and personal life come together in this fantasy of being consort to a King and at the same time a kind of Queen Victoria, bringing British civilisation to a backward people ... Mrs Thatcher's choice of Anna as a model is a useful condensation of her adult politics which combine femininity and a mission to civilise what she regards as an unruly world.
>
> (Little in Abse: 64)

Anna is both a romantic and a political figure in this fiction. Anna, the forthright English governess, stands out amongst the chattering Siamese women and children. She is bigger, taller, blunter and more vociferous; she brings English values to civilise and tame the King's barbarism. Anna is *with* the women but not *of* them – her place enables greater mobility around the spaces of power. Furthermore, Anna is given an ambivalent role: to the King 'she is not quite wife and not quite mother but as intimate as both' (Abse: 64). Little suggests that such fantasy 'point[s] to the relationship the young Margaret might have believed she had with her father' (Little in Abse: 64). The intense wish for glamour, power and adoration expressed in stories of kings and queens or consorts finds its early roots in the infantile fantasies of origins and of parents which are retraced in adult recollections of their past and their childhood ambitions (Freud, 1908). Prior to knowledge of 'the sexual determinants of procreation', the child draws upon a social world in which power is defined through class and visible wealth (Freud: 229). Thatcher's desire to be Anna can be read as the child's desire for freedom from her parents' social status and simultaneously as revenge upon them for their power over her. She recalls in her memoir meeting adults of higher social standing than her parents who influenced her dreams of the future: Reverend Skinner and his wife, Lord Brownlow and the 1935 Conservative candidate for Grantham, Sir Victor Warrender (Thatcher, 1995:9, 20-21). She draws upon these encounters to explain how she developed fantasies of an exciting adult life to come. In Freud's 'Family Romances' (1908) the child's knowledge of procreation brings with it a recognition that the mother appears to be fixed but paternity is uncertain and the child contents itself with exalting the father as a model of authority and possible escape. In Thatcher's public memories it is her father, not her mother, who afforded access to these figures and formed her determination to succeed.

Biographies of Thatcher inevitably dwell upon her humble provincial beginnings and chart her rise to success. The exemplary woman they depict is often placed in a masculine lineage that echoes and affirms Thatcher's own reverential memories. In such accounts Thatcher's father often appears as she herself cast him, resembling 'a childhood fantasy of an Old Testament prophet' or wise man of regal bearing (Webster, 1990:6). Biographer Robert Harris praises Roberts as an 'impressive man, six feet three inches with curly blond hair which had turned white when he was still young'. He emphasises his 'bright blue eyes' with 'piercing gaze' accentuated by thick-lensed spectacles (Harris, 1988:59). For Harris, the intellectual shadow Alfred Roberts cast upon his daughter and the intimacy of their relationship was of greater importance than even his physical bearing: 'She was not only a daughter, but pupil, protégée and potential *alter ego*, the offspring who could and would achieve the greater, wider life which circumstances and accident of birth had denied him' (Harris: 59). Thatcher's sister recalled their 'severe' and ambitious father: 'To know Margaret, you have to know him' (Harris: 59). It is frequently claimed that Thatcher's politics was 'guided by an inner mechanism', a 'deep-rooted conviction' acquired from her father and Grantham childhood (Wapshott and Brock, 1983:22). Her leadership of Britain has been described as 'a voyage around her father' – 'Britain is currently being administered by him' (Wapshott in Webster, 1990:7). In such accounts Alfred Roberts was 'the epitome of values which were the strength of provincial England' and these had 'a profound and lasting influence on his daughter's thinking' (Money, 1975:43). Hugo Young's biography echoes Thatcher's own account of Roberts's grocer's shop as a civic and political centre, beginning with the claim: 'Margaret Thatcher was born to be a politician. Her lineage and formation allowed few other possibilities' (Young, 1989:3). Thatcher was 'reared' in an atmosphere 'infused' with politics and a political life of 'service and of power' was the only one offered to her 'as a model superior' to that of her father's shop-keeping (Young: 3).

In *The Path to Power*, Thatcher's father appears as mentor, intellectual companion and central influence on her politics and character. He is constructed as 'the subject who is supposed to know' for he is the pivotal point of guidance, the one in whom trust is placed and from whom reward is received (Lacan 1973:230-5). While Alfred Roberts worked in the downstairs shop, the home was the predominantly female space where mother, sister and maternal grandmother were located. As a self-educated man his avid desire to improve himself is wed to Thatcher's worldly interests:

> the main interest which my father and I shared while I was a girl was a thirst for knowledge about politics and public affairs. I suspect we were better informed than many families. We read the *Daily Telegraph* every day, *The Methodist Recorder*, *Picture Post* and *John O'London's Weekly* ... Occasionally we read *The Times*.
>
> (Thatcher, 1995:22)

Thatcher's narrative of 'serious' reading and of public library visits with her father can be read for social and psychic connotations. The 'thirst for knowledge' marks her difference from 'many families' and also from her own mother: 'Each week my father would take two books out of the library, a "serious" book for himself (and me) and a novel for my mother' (Thatcher: 28). Her place as his consort allowed a greater mobility around the spaces of power. Thatcher stresses the continual companionship with her father on visits to the wider social and political world of university extension lectures, political meetings,

court and local council. A list of his positions of authority is brandished as tribute to his public influence. Roberts's public roles were
phenomenal and indicate a zealous (perhaps obsessional) attachment
to civic duty. He was lay preacher, school governor, local JP, Council
committee member, enthusiastic Rotarian, director of the Grantham
Building Society and of the local Trustee Savings Bank, Alderman and
Mayor of Grantham (Money, 1975:37; Thatcher: 21). Roberts was the
son of a shoemaker. He desired to be a teacher but his background and
poor schooling thwarted this ambition (Money, 1975:36-7). Voluntary
membership of local office provided him with a powerful stake in his
surroundings. As a lay preacher he patrolled the local area handing on
his knowledge of Methodist doctrine. His constant procurement of
position points to a desire to underpin his authority and lay claim to
the locale, but also to the continual and frustrating deferral of that
desire: no new directorship or committee was ever enough. His identity and his daughter's memory of that identity are intimately bound
up with upholding and reasserting that public status.

The form of paternal authority in which Thatcher invested so heavily depends upon an accrual of public power intimately bound up with
'display' (Heath, 1986: 55). For men to live up to the impossible
demands of (appearing to have) having the phallus they engage in the
rituals and symbolism of public power. Class is relevant here for it
hinders or enhances male access to rank and status. In *The Path to
Power*, three of the five photographs of Alfred Roberts depict him
formally posed in institutional settings. As President of the Rotary
Club in 1936, he is seen on the dais above the tables of dining guests.
In dinner jacket and bow tie he stands in the centre of a row of dignitaries, bolt upright 'next to Lord Brownlow', beneath the national flag
of Britain and of the United States. Positioned thus he symbolises
masculine rank and status. Thatcher adds 'my mother is four to his
right' (Thatcher, 1995: between 82-3). Two other photographs capture
him again in formal pose as Mayor of Grantham, in the magisterial
robes and chain of office. In one he towers above his wife and two
daughters: a condensation of institutional and paternal authority. In
the other photograph he stands on the steps of Grantham town hall
surrounded by male dignitaries in the robes of local office and
uniformed senior military men who take the salute from the post-war
RAF parade.[9] Surrounded by the full apparel of public office and military rank, Roberts is frozen within these ritualised scenes, exhibiting a
grandeur that Thatcher claims as his legacy to her. Recalling his death
in early 1970 just before her first Cabinet post, she states:

He never knew that I would become a Cabinet minister, and I am sure
that he never imagined I would eventually become Prime Minister. He
would have wanted these things for me because politics was so much a
part of his life and because I was so much his daughter.

(Thatcher, 1995:163)

In this account of her father no glimpse of the spontaneous, the private
or domestic is allowed. This is a flawless upright identity firmly bound
to the public sphere. As imaginary father, Roberts instilled in his
daughter a sense of lawfulness and submission to social customs. She
states that the Rotary Club motto 'Service Above Self' was engraved
on his heart (Thatcher: 16).

On winning the 1979 election Thatcher laid claim to her father's
values, declaring them as the basis of her first electoral campaign: 'He
brought me up to believe all the things I do believe and they are the
values on which I have fought the election ... I owe almost everything
to my father' (Webster 1990:6). She locates her proudest moment in
1949 as Dartford's new Conservative representative when she spoke
alongside her father at her adoption meeting. In *The Path to Power* the
dutiful daughter replays this scene and thus foregrounds her debt to
the imaginary father while supplanting him. Biographical accounts of
Thatcher as Alfred Roberts's substitute or *alter ego* inadvertently
signal ambivalence in her identification with him. Her drive to be like
him conceals the sadistic wish to replace him and to exceed his authority. The masquerading woman fantasises that she will deprive the
father of his phallic power:

> he becomes powerless (her gentle husband), but she still guards herself
> from attack by wearing towards him the mask of womanly subservience
> and under that screen, performing many of his masculine functions
> herself – 'for him' – (her practical ability and management).
>
> (Riviere, 1929:42)

Roberts was a prominent local man; Thatcher became the national
politician. But, in that first public speech alongside him, she presented
herself as appropriately feminine, urging 'the Government [to] do
what any good housewife would do if money was short' (Thatcher,
1995:65). Her father told her adoption audience that his family had
always been Liberal, but his daughter's Conservatism now stood for
old Liberalism. Appositely, Riviere suggests that the father's sanction
of the daughter's phallic power and his acknowledgement of her abil-

ity renders her safe. Riviere adds: 'Little as he may know it, to her the man has admitted defeat' (1929:43).

Beatrice Roberts

In Thatcher's accounts of her childhood and in the numerous biographies that repeat that story, her mother Beatrice Roberts remains a shadowy figure bound by the limited geography of home and Methodist church.[10] Her life revolved around the family business and domestic chores; excursions into the public domain were limited to Wednesday sewing meetings and Sunday church. She figures as object of family demand and of obstruction: she fulfils basic needs but identification with her signifies thwarted desire. The Roberts's house is constructed as the base of Thatcher's economical and political worldview; a place sober, 'practical, serious and intensely religious' (Thatcher, 1995:5). Furthermore, the house stood on the cusp of Georgian, genteel North Parade and the low, two-storey terraces of Albion Street (Raban, 1989:25). In view of Methodist Chapel, Roman Catholic Church, Blue Boar Inn, Infant School, town house and terrace: 'the social cartography of this bit of Grantham' was clearly mapped (Raban: 27).

Thatcher constructs a maternal identification bound up with the sheer drudgery of endless baking, cleaning, ironing, dressmaking, washing and stocktaking (Thatcher: 12). Beatrice Roberts's knowledge imparted to her daughter is of domestic secrets: 'how to iron a man's shirt', to 'press embroidery', to 'finish' linen with candle wax, to wash mahogany with vinegar (p12). Her mother's life symbolises a feminine self-effacement and sacrifice to the endless maintenance of others' lives:

> She had been a great rock of family stability. She managed the household, stepped in to run the shop when necessary, entertained, supported my father in his public life and, as Mayoress, did a great deal of voluntary social work for the church, displayed a series of practical domestic talents such as dressmaking and was never heard to complain. Like many people who live for others, she made possible all that her husband and daughters did. Her life had not been an easy one.
>
> (p106)

Thatcher acknowledged to biographer Patricia Murray that her home life was 'strict' and serious. Centred on the Methodist church and its dictates, she had 'drummed' into her that: 'Everything had to be clean

and systematic. We were Methodists and Methodist meant method'
(Thatcher in Murray, 1978:17). The demarcations of a respectable,
conscientious identity were mapped out closely by her father, but
their practical maintenance and the self-abnegation this entailed were
part of her mother's limited power: 'We were taught what was right
and wrong in very considerable detail. There were certain things that
you just didn't do and that was that. Duty was very, very strongly
ingrained into us' (Thatcher in Murray: 17).

A detailed and strict regime had been the hallmark of Methodism
since its inception in the seventeenth century. Itinerant preaching in
the open air, thrift, sobriety, self-education, self-control and hard
work marked out the parameters of a managed and orderly identity
embedded in the 'magnificent consistency' of a predestined ascetic life
(Weber, 1904-5:104; Halevy, 1971). For Thatcher's family Methodism
offered a sense of purposefulness within their community under the
watchful eye of God. But also, in Thatcher's narrative, a sense of isolation attended this systematic self-control and sense of self as emblem
of a greater morality. She has acknowledged that it was 'difficult' as a
child to be different from her friends, 'to have different pocket money,
or to do different things on a Sunday. However it was very much the
teaching my father followed throughout his own life' (Thatcher in
Murray, 1978:17). This difference not only set her apart but also
presaged her future adoption of moral authority. Alfred Roberts's
fundamental antagonism to frivolous or sensuous pursuits throughout
the week and particularly in observance of the Sabbath was the exemplary model adhered to by his daughters. If this marked her as
'serious' and 'different' from her schoolgirl peers, then the frivolous
and sensuous bore the imprint of a forbidden desire. In an interview
with Kenneth Harris she admitted: 'I would have liked some things to
be different ... On Saturday nights some of the girls at my school
would go to dances or parties. It sounded nice. But my sister and I
didn't go dancing' (Harris, 1988:69).

In contrast to the frugality, self-restraint and sacrifice of her
mother, the promise of an alternative femininity is sketched on a trip
to London with family friends. Thatcher retraces her early identification with the heroine of the stage musical *The Desert Song* on a visit
to the capital city. London is captured as excess, bustle, exotic, noise,
chance encounter, 'electricity':

> London was overwhelming: King's Cross itself was a giant bustling
> cavern; the rest of the capital had all the dazzle of a commercial and

imperial capital. For the first time in my life I saw people from foreign countries, some in the native dress of India and Africa. The sheer volume of traffic and of pedestrians was exhilarating ... London's buildings were impressive ... they had a dark imposing magnificence which constantly reminded me I was at the centre of the world.

(Thatcher, 1995:10)

The fantasised superiority of a declining imperialist Britain meets and is supplanted by the emotional roller coaster of modern urban life, the crowd and then the spectacle and romance of melodrama which revealed to the young Margaret 'how sweet life could be':

But the high point was ... Sigmund Romberg's famous musical *The Desert Song*. For three hours I lived in another world, swept away as was the heroine by the daring Red Shadow – so much so that I bought the score and played it at home, perhaps too often.

(Thatcher: 10)

Against the backdrop of a regulated home life in which a musical score was played 'too often', Thatcher recalls her enchantment with the white beribboned dresses of the Catholic girls seen as they passed on their way to Church. This fascination was also of the forbidden because to the Grantham Methodists, the confirmation dresses signified 'the first steps to Rome' (p8). She conjures up the spectatorial pleasures of Hollywood cinema that promised 'a realm of the imagination' beyond Grantham and a set of powerful role models: 'the four-handkerchief weepies like Barbara Stanwyck in *Stella Dallas*, Ingrid Bergman in anything ... I rejoiced to see Soviet communism laughed out of court when Garbo, a stern Commissar, was seduced by a lady's hat in *Ninotchka*' (p14).

For 'a young girl living in a small provincial town', cinema in the 1930s offered an imaginary escape, the lure of celebrity and the promise of adult life to come:

You see cinemas were so different in the thirties, they had large restaurants and some of them had brightly lit cinema organs which changed colours from blues to pinks to greens as the organ rose from the orchestra pit. The organist himself would generally be accepted as one of the personalities of the town in which he played ... to us going out was viewed as a great treat in your life.

(Thatcher in Murray, 1978:18).

As with many girls, Margaret Roberts used the cinema as an escape from parental supervision and as a relief from the repetition and work of family life. The lush splendour of the picture palace and the sensuous, immediate and transgressive pleasures of the films are drawn upon in Thatcher's recollections to articulate both a desire for and the impossibility of transcendence. The erotic feminised pleasures of 'dramatic form, human emotion, sex appeal, spectacle and style' are recalled as transcending the inwardness of provincial Grantham (Thatcher, 1995:15).[11] In contrast, Thatcher claims her parents stressed 'reality' over 'romance', worthwhile work over 'passive' entertainment (Thatcher: 15). But these romantic longings are set apart from the diligent adult daughter, are located in the past and form the part of Thatcher's childhood she has left behind (p15). Speaking as a grown woman, Thatcher attempts to rationalise these fantasies as 'a life which doesn't really exist for anyone'; she claims they have no bearing on her adult status: 'No one I know of has a glamorous life – I don't think it exists' (Thatcher in Murray, 1978:25-6).

Thatcher's childhood was situated in a community touched by the war, national insecurity, economic and industrial decline. In the 1930s Grantham was a small market town in the heart of the Lincolnshire countryside. The main industry was mechanical and agricultural engineering (Murray, 1978:13-14). Thatcher recalls the Depression, the surrounding poverty of northern towns dependent on heavy industry and impoverished agricultural communities. She deploys now familiar images of the 1930s to describe passing on the way to school: 'the long queue waiting at the Labour exchange, seeking work or claiming the dole' (Thatcher, 1995:23). Self-sufficiency, morality and the work ethic are the explicit themes of this recollection and were central to Thatcher's attacks upon the Welfare State throughout the 1980s. She claims that the unemployed 'were determined to make sacrifices', that the 'spirit of self-reliance and independence was very strong' even among the poorest of the East Midlands communities and quiet charity held these communities together (Thatcher: 23-4). This is a narrative of 'precarious respectability' (p6) and of fine social divisions: 'The real distinction in the town was between those who drew salaries ... for "white collar" employment and those who did not, with the latter being more prone to unemployment' (p23). Thatcher describes her 'poor' tenuous-middle-class community and hints at the thin line between respectability and the abyss: 'They lived on a knife-edge and feared that ... if they relaxed their standards of thrift and diligence, they might be plunged into debt and poverty' (p6). This precariousness often made the Roberts's 'otherwise good' neighbours 'hard and unforgiving' (p6).

The acquisition of respectability is central here. The repression and conscious self-sacrifice of upholding a respectable veneer are associated with Beatrice Roberts's domestic femininity. She is associated with the hard grind of maintaining family appearances and with servicing the clean and proper family. Thatcher's recollection of her mother's death is through metaphors of woman as rock, stability, sacrifice, support and silence (p106-7). Bound to the Methodist ethic of purposeful activity in which 'waste of time' is 'the deadliest of sins ... worthy of absolute moral condemnation' (Weber, 1904-5:157), Beatrice Roberts's religion fused with the conventional demands of the 1930s housewife to define her identity, and its worth, through diligent domestic labour. A school friend of Margaret Roberts captured the way Beatrice was defined by others through her children's neat appearance: 'Margaret always looked immaculate at school. Her mother who was a poppet and very shy took a great deal of pride in making sure her two children were well turned out' (Murray, 1978:31). Thatcher remembers her mother as 'always intensely practical': 'She was very proud of her home and everything in it was as shiny as a new pin' (Murray: 27). Thatcher's self-distancing from her mother and her frequent, well-recorded reluctance to dwell upon her in interviews reveals how Beatrice has become the signifier of a femininity that is 'joyless, stultifying and repressive' (Webster 1990:14). In a 1985 interview with Miriam Stoppard for *Woman to Woman* (Yorkshire TV) Thatcher inadvertently brought her frustration with her mother into focus:

> And the other thing is you – ah my goodness me – you never buy anything you can't afford to buy, never, but you live according to your means. Many, many's the time I can remember my mother saying, when I said, oh my friends have got more, 'Well, we're not situated like that'. Or when you went out to buy something, and you were actually going to have new covers for the settee ... that ... was a great expenditure and a great event. So you went to choose them, and you chose something lovely, really light, with flowers on. My mother: 'That's not serviceable.' And how I longed for the time when I could buy things that were 'not serviceable'.
>
> (Thatcher in Webster, 1990:14)

She has admitted moments of childhood rebellion against her family's frugality: 'One kicked against it. Of course one kicked against it. They [her friends] had more things than we did. Of course one kicked against it' (Murray: 18; Webster: 15). In wartime this 'ethos of frugality was almost an obsession' and Thatcher recalls her mother belittled by another woman whose thrift with tacking cottons exceeded her own:

> Clothes were never a problem for us. My mother had been a professional seamstress and made most of what we wore ... in the sales at Grantham and Nottingham we could get the best-quality fabric at reduced prices. So we got excellent value for money ... Even my mother and I were taken aback by one of her friends, who told us that she never threw away her tacking cottons but re-used them: 'I consider it my duty to do so,' she said. After that, so did we. We were not Methodists for nothing.
>
> (Thatcher, 1995:13)

Accounts of Thatcher's dogged hard work, attention to detail and her phenomenal stamina are numerous, perhaps revealing her upbringing – 'idleness is a sin' – and the need as a woman in politics to prove one's worth. Interwoven with this are historically rooted memories of potential poverty and unemployment and of a respectable façade always under threat if standards are dropped. Thatcher's Methodism is crucial here. It has been argued that Methodism promotes ambivalent identifications. On the one hand it offers the ego the conscious certainty of a sober industrious career and a corresponding 'powerful inner compulsion' to constrain and order one's life in the 'rational pursuit of salvation' (Bocock, 1992:252; see also Weber, 1904-5:105-112). On the other hand it promotes in the individual a permanent state of 'unsettledness' (Bocock: 252). The uncertainty of oneself as elect is ever present but consciously denied and accompanied by a 'relentless drive' to attain certainty of grace (Bocock: 253). The Methodist is caught up in a tourniquet of reassurance and doubt and bound to a vigilant self-surveillance for signs of weakness or failure (Bocock: 253; Thompson, 1963:44). Intense worldly activity is the Methodist means to self-confidence. Thatcher was told by her father that she must always lead: 'Make up your own mind what you are going to do and persuade people to go your way' (Thatcher in Gardiner, 1975:20). Such leadership entailed 'a systematic self-control which at every moment [stood] before the inexorable alternative, chosen or damned' (Weber, 1904-5:115).

Thatcher's stern maternal grandmother Phoebe Stephenson, who lived with them until Margaret was ten, oversaw the family home: 'she was very, very Victorian and very, very strict. I think my parents probably insisted on some of the rules because they didn't want to offend her' (Thatcher in Murray, 1978:17). Her formidable grandmother warned her that 'Cleanliness was next to Godliness' (Thatcher in Murray: 17). In 'black sateen beaded dress', her grandmother would ascend to young Margaret's bedroom on 'warm summer nights', and make her 'flesh creep with old wives' tales' of earwigs crawling under the skin to form carbuncles (Thatcher, 1995:16). Thatcher's mother and grandmother are associated with the house, its precarious respectability and the invisible hard work to keep up appearances. Together they are a condensed symbol of a bounded but frightening maternity, of retribution for idleness and the horror of social disrepute.

In keeping with the masquerade, Thatcher has used domesticity as a weapon and perceived herself intellectually superior to other women while also being a highly proficient cook and diligent housewife. She has wielded her housewifery as evidence of her supreme ability to juggle home and work and has delighted in women's magazines and interviews in giving advice to women on the need to place motherhood and the home foremost. Early in her party leadership, numerous photographs of Thatcher attending to Denis and son Mark at the breakfast table appeared in the press. In biographies they appear as a crucial sign of Thatcher's private self. This idealisation of the housewife then procured Thatcher a 'lavish return'[12] in the form of public recognition of her supreme competence. However, between the lines there is an unconscious resentment and self-distancing from maternal domesticity. Late in her career, as tales of her son's notorious business affairs became a constant feature of media coverage, Thatcher worried that she would 'just go down in history as Mark's mother' (Halloran and Hollingsworth, 1995:16).

Beatrice Roberts worked within the dictates of good mothering and supportive partnership that were on offer to married women in the inter-war years, but for her daughter this embodied a constrained future. Thatcher has publicly dismissed her mother as 'a bit of a Martha' and declared that 'I loved my mother dearly, but after I was fifteen we had nothing more to say to each other. It wasn't her fault. She was weighed down by the home' (Thatcher in Webster, 1990:20). In the years of Thatcher's childhood, upward mobility for women was limited and rarely financially lucrative. Thus origins and destiny seemed inextricably fixed. Masculinity became equated with the wider public realm. For Thatcher to succeed in that public realm it appears that her mother was 'relegated to limbo, no relations with her [were] possible' (Riviere, 1929:43). Beatrice Roberts was the sign of a possible future that was feared. Thatcher's account of her father can be understood as the 'family romance', with all its promise of success, achievement and public recognition. Her recollections of her mother are much more ambivalent and recall the constrained love of the aspirant daughter for her trapped mother found in the 'weepie' maternal melodrama *Stella Dallas* (Vidor, 1937) that enthralled Thatcher as a girl (Thatcher, 1995:14).

Responsibility and sound finance

> Choice in a free society implies responsibility. There is no hard-and-fast line between economic and other forms of personal responsibility to self, family, firm, community, nation, God.
>
> (Thatcher, 1977:55)

> [Politicians'] place is mid-way between the counting house and the pulpit.
> (Gilmour, 1977:170)

In this story, Thatcher's father signifies the route out of domestic insularity. This escape route is open as long as emotional and improper excess are replaced by a temperate masculine endeavour – and the taking on of the father's dictates of sober industry and fiscal rigour. Thatcher states: 'Responsibility was my father's watchword; sound finance was his passion. I was so much his daughter' (1995a:1). The construction of her early and formative years offers another story between the lines. The pleasures of femininity are overshadowed with an emotional poverty. Yet the pleasures of masculinity have to be continually earned and guarded. When recalling her father's influence upon the formation of her character one phrase sprang to Thatcher's lips: 'That which thy father bequeathed thee, earn it anew, if thou wouldst possess it' (Harris 1989:60).

Within this masculine economy, the insistence on a proper return for investment involves the maintenance of established hierarchies, an obsession with clear classification and fixed meanings and the closure of a systematic exchange of goods, ideas, power and property. This bounded and ordered framework armours the idealised masculine identity. In Thatcher's memoir her legacy from her father is an adherence to duty, responsibility for self and the ability to lead. This is linked to the form, control and regulation of her Methodist background and then mapped onto her economic and political beliefs. She offers 'a moral world in which there are precepts which must be repeated with dogmatic precision and rules to be honoured and obeyed' (Samuel, 1983:10). In Thatcher's speeches the imagery of Babylon, of the Egyptian exile, of wilderness and the tablets of stone, of Heaven and the battle with Satan, were frequently used. She often cast herself as the solitary pilgrim. Translated from Thatcher's Grantham childhood experience and Methodist upbringing, her promise of redemption resided in the fantasy of a society without concessions, where moral and political deliberations were pared down to the simplicity of stark contrast. Raphael Samuel noted of Thatcher's moral individualism that she emphasised 'sin rather than grace, law rather than charity' (Samuel, 1983:10).[13] In 1978, Thatcher spoke at St Lawrence Jewry, and bemoaned a contemporary religion 'stripped by certain sophisticated theologians of its supernatural elements'. She added that, 'the majority of English parents' wanted their children brought up 'in the same religious heritage' that was handed to her: 'To most ordinary people, heaven and hell, right and wrong, good and bad, matter' (Thatcher, 1978:64).

Hugo Young (1989:123) suggested that Thatcher's rhetoric grew in fundamental severity around early 1977 once her accession to party leadership was secure. In the Iain Macleod Memorial Lecture in July 1977, Thatcher claimed that 'economic choices have a moral dimension. A man is enabled to choose between earning his living and depending on the bounty of the State' (Thatcher, 1977:55). She located the origins of Conservatism in the Old Testament: 'our spiritual roots go back to the early days of civilisation and man's search for God' (p55-6). To the General Assembly of the Church of Scotland, a decade later, she crystallised her interpretation of Christian faith as the 'fundamental right to choose between good and evil ... and to use all our *own* power of thought and judgement in exercising that choice' (Thatcher, 1988a:251). Omitting ethical complexity or Methodism's radical political potential, Thatcher summarised the scriptural injunctions she had learned as a child as: 'a view of the universe', 'a proper attitude to work' and 'principles to shape economic and social life' (Thatcher: 251). This is closely linked to Conservatism's religiously informed tenet that man is a fallen creature: 'The imperfection of human nature meant that the tendency to evil rather than good could not be ignored' (Ball, 1995:30). From this perspective, social policy and collective state action fail to allow for the fundamental flaws of human nature. Thatcher's discourse, then, was in keeping with a longer tradition of thought in which religion underpinned political service.[14] But she offended some political peers by ignoring the social obligations of the caring Christian, supplanting evangelical fervour for 'balanced and prudent' inspiration and perverting politics into a secular religion (Gilmour, 1977:102; Heffer, 1983:12-13; Samuel, 1983:8-10; Winter, 1988).

Thatcher's political discourse was aggressively demotic and, as such, had the potent appeal of simple clarity: clear boundaries between good and evil, right and wrong. She outlined her political leadership as an extension of her religious values and presented herself as lay preacher:

> You've got to take everyone along with you ... You can only get other people in tune with you by being a little evangelical about it ... I'm not a consensus politician or a pragmatic politician: I'm a conviction politician. And I believe in the politics of persuasion: it's my job to put forward what I believe and try to get people to agree with me.
>
> (Thatcher in Harris, 1988:109)

Speaking at the St Lawrence Jewry in March 1978, Thatcher attacked socialist theory and practice as 'bad theology', because it assumed that if social institutions were equitable in the provision of education, health and social welfare then 'we shall have exorcised the Devil' (Thatcher, 1978:67). She claimed that the 'vast efforts and huge amounts of money' expended in her lifetime to improve the human condition had failed. She warned that 'The Devil' was 'still with us'; his presence could be read 'in the crime figures and in all other maladies of this society, in spite of its relative material comfort' (Thatcher: 68). In contrast she advocated a free enterprise economic system embedded within a moral and regulatory framework: 'man is inherently sinful and in order to sustain a civilised and harmonious society we need laws backed by effective sanctions' (p69). Man's destiny and salvation, exhorted Thatcher, lay in his ability to face 'moral dilemmas' and to meet these with 'self-discipline' (p70). To do so enabled society to pursue material interests and wealth: 'Christ did not condemn riches as such, only the way in which they were used and those who put trust in them. It is one of the Church's tasks to guide us about our use of this world's wealth' (p67). Thatcher's concept of evil was opposed to a 'fiscal morality' or 'spiritual capital' that renewed the 'spiritual assets' of the nation. Consequently the sanctified and moral spaces were either the institutional seats of finance or the family home. In March 1981 Thatcher returned to the St Lawrence Jewry in the City of London. In her speech she set out the foreboding spectre of a nation in which 'crimes of violence are increasing' and 'murder can be justified on the grounds that it is political' (Thatcher, 1981:127). In contrast 'ethics and national economics' were located in the regulated borders of the City's square mile: 'outside this City we can no longer assume that a man's word is always his bond' (Thatcher: 127).

Thatcher's memoir then continues this emphasis on wealth and parsimony. Her politics are presented as enabling material envy and acquisitive desire harnessed by proper emotional and behavioural constraint. 'Mastery', 'control', 'curb', 'calculate', 'order', 'discipline' are the watchwords throughout her memoir and are values intimately related to 'capitalism', her 'creed for the common man' (Thatcher, 1995:156). Interviewed by Pete Murray on *The Late Show* in March 1982, she told the radio audience that her childhood was 'rich in the right values' which overrode material scarcity: 'There were no silver spoons in my childhood' (NSA: LP 40788). Like most provincial towns in the 1930s Grantham was a town without the benefits of modern domestic appliances; her family did not possess a vacuum cleaner, refrigerator, or bath but were 'scrupulously clean'. She added that in these circumstances 'work was a part of our lives'. In *The Path to Power*, Thatcher prides in her family's thrift and reveals that their social status was built upon the work of maintaining a respectable façade in straitened circumstances. She claims: 'There was hardly time to draw breath. Nothing in our house was wasted, and we always lived within our means. The worst you could say about another family was that "they lived up to the hilt"' (Thatcher, 1995:12). Her comments reveal the central ascetic values of Methodism latched onto a lower-middle-class policing of self and an instrumental adaptation of economic circumstance to sober social identity. Involved here is a sense of superiority and even mastery over others who are seen as spendthrift, lazy, or pleasure seeking.[15]

Alison Light (1991:150) has captured the 'emotional and linguistic constipation' of this form of well-policed respectability in which 'laxity' often implies either 'moral or social "looseness" and usually both'. The inter-war years and the construction of a particular form of defensive and protective English middle class sensibility form the backdrop to 'the anxious production of endless discriminations between people who were constantly assessing each other's standing'

(Light: 13). Light suggests: 'The grocer's wife in Grantham, the female bank clerk in the metropolis, the retired memsahib in Surrey, were far more likely to be aware of their differences than their mutual attitudes' (p13). The creation of the 'cut-glass accent' in the 1920s and 1930s is one illustration of the way the body, the voice and their demeanour were used to assert superiority. Containment of feeling and of gesture, and avoidance of the vulgar accompanied this assertion. Control was the measure of one's social standing (p50). In 1975, soon after becoming leader of the Conservative Party, Thatcher was asked about her television persona as 'a cool, collected, very controlled type of person, and therefore lacking in feeling, in compassion, rather a cold person' (Harris, 1988:61). She replied that her parents had taught her the maintenance of control:

> I was brought up to believe that you *never* lost your temper, at least not in public. That you didn't complain. You counted your blessings. You never spoke of your failures – of course you had failures and disappointments, but you didn't talk about them; you just got on with the job.
>
> (Thatcher in Harris: 61)

In her autobiography Thatcher recalls the triumphant moment when she won the Finchley constituency through a salute to Tory decorum. The 'controlled' Tory cheers are contrasted with the unbridled response of 'Liberal or Socialist lips' (Thatcher, 1995:101). Throughout her memoir, the utterances of the political opposition are constructed as immoderate: 'shameless', 'immoral', 'a stream of crude invective' (Thatcher: 401, 363). Her precarious self-mastery suggests that any kind of generosity or immoderation 'is bound to be suspiciously extravagant or even suggest incontinence' (Light, 1991:50). Waste is wrong, 'but even worse, it's vulgar' (Light: 50). Furthermore, verbal excess and social chaos 'are only words apart'; 'Any exposure of feeling is a kind of squandering and is demeaning: the most verbose are likely "to give themselves away" and only the most costive of communications is deemed proper' (p50).

For Thatcher, Conservatism is about a 'middle-class' will to responsibility that aims to develop 'heroes from all backgrounds' (Thatcher: 47). Following her recent third general election victory in 1987, she informed *Sunday Telegraph* readers that a misplaced conscience had fuelled the 'British guilt-complex' and a misplaced egalitarianism through which the middle class had been made to feel guilty about well-earned success. In contrast, at the core of Wesley's Methodism, and by implication Thatcherism, was 'the Parable of the Talents' with its ethic of work and duty (Thatcher in Young, 1989:420-1). For Thatcher, this ethic is related to a 'proper' masculinity played out in virile, muscular and 'hard-headed' political activity. In her populist political rhetoric she articulated a range of civilised and 'new[ly] oppressed' masculinities – the tax payer, the parent, the home owner, the share-holder, the entrepreneur – who were released by the self-regulation of the free market.[16] The figure of the soldier-hero and the police officer were cast as necessary defenders of the civilised man and his family. By extension the 'Iron Lady' was frequently set as an embodiment of that symbolic law 'at its most self-inflated and rigid' (Rose 1993a: 245). As Jacqueline Rose has indicated this was a construction of self and social mastery that could not acknowledge 'its own sense of aporia' and instead remained entrenched 'in a vision of its own self-fulfilment' (Rose: 245).

The Path to Power replicates earlier media interview and biographical representations of Thatcher throughout the 1970s and 1980s: forms of femininity are presented and then denied in favour of the most phallic of images. There is no failure in this constructed identity, no gap is allowed between word and deed. The blurb for the autobiography presents Thatcher as a figure of 'magnificent coherence' and announces that 'in our uncertain and increasingly rudderless world, here is a woman who knows what she thinks and why she thinks it' (1995: cover blurb). *The Path to Power* sets up Thatcher as the bulwark, or place of maximum intransigence, the point between responsibility and irresponsibility, the frivolous and the thrifty, control and excess, mastery or defeat. Riviere suggests that such a fantasy of the self and its rich and varied stagings was 'the mainspring' of the masquerading woman's 'whole life and character': 'she came within a narrow margin of carrying it through to perfection. But its weak point was the megalomanic character, under all the disguises, of the necessity for supremacy' (1929:42). As a new Conservative Party leader, Thatcher told the *Financial Times*: 'I do take some small consolation that there is only one small vowel sound between ruin and run. The small vowel sound is "I"' (Thatcher in McFadyean and Renn, 1984:9).

References

1. I shall explore the publication of *The Downing Street Years* (1993) more fully in the concluding chapter.
2. For a detailed linguistic analysis of Thatcher's voice and speech pattern see

Max Atkinson's *Our Master's Voices: the language and body language of politics* (1984).

3. The immediate context of Riviere's work is that of the work of other analysts writing in the 1920s on sexual difference and who attempt to engage with female sexuality and gender difference. Riviere refers to Ernest Jones's 'The early development of female sexuality' published in *The International Journal of Psychoanalysis* in 1927. She also refers to Melanie Klein's 'Early Stages of the Oedipus Conflict' published in the same journal in 1928. For a full account of Riviere and her personal and intellectual relationship with Freud, Jones and Klein, see Lisa Appignannesi and John Forester, *Freud's Women* (1992:Ch 12).

4. For masquerade as resistance see Mary Anne Doane, 'Film and the Masquerade: Theorising the Female Spectator' (1982) and 'Masquerade Reconsidered: Further Thoughts on the Female Spectator' (1988-9) reprinted in Doane (1991). See also Stephen Heath (1986) and Judith Butler (1990) and Pamela Robertson (1996).

5. Her speeches were made in the context of the forthcoming Helsinki conference on human rights and East-West *détente*.

6. For an analysis of the 'paranoid style' of politics see Richard Hofstadter (1967).

7. Here I am indebted to Martin Shingler's discussion of masquerade in Bette Davis's star persona (1995:181-5).

8. For mocking humour and the masquerading woman see Shingler (1995).

9. In the same period as these photographs, Virginia Woolf analysed the masculine structures of Britain's Inns of Court, Army and University and the parades, rituals and costumes they adopted. She declared of the medal laden, robed and beribboned men of rank: 'Your clothes in the first place make us gape with astonishment ... every button, rosette or stripe seems to have symbolical meaning' (Woolf, (1938) in Heath, 1986:56).

10. The exception is Leo Abse's *Margaret: Daughter of Beatrice* (1989).

11. The effects of the cinema upon provincial life in the 1920s and 1930s have been well recorded. Robert Roberts's *The Classic Slum* (1973), an autobiography of life in Salford in the early part of the century, places cinema as crucial to the broadening of the cultural imagination beyond the parochial (Roberts in O'Shea, 1996:25). Sally Alexander charts how cinema in this period was used by young women as an escape from hard work and the restrictions of family and respectable femininity (Alexander, 1989).

12. Riviere located the masquerading woman's desire to placate the imaginary mother in this appearance of supremely competent housewifery. Underlying this is a fear of the mother's anger and an accompanying

narcissistic belief in supremacy over the mother and other women (Riviere, 1929:41).

13. Religion holds a prominent place in the armoury of Conservative thinking. Ian Gilmour (1977) cited the religious fundament of Conservative thinkers such as Burke, Coleridge, Lord Hugh Cecil and Disraeli. In recent years Churchill's self-proclaimed first principle of liberty was, amongst other things, upheld by a temperate religion that opposed dogma or extremism (Gilbert, 1981:18, 110). Quintin Hogg contended that no new Conservatism existed without a bedrock of religious faith as the basis of civil obligation and political principle (1959: 19-22).

14. In a recent survey undertaken by *New Statesman* the Bible ranked in the list of top ten books or authors claimed by Conservative MPs to have an influence on their political beliefs (*New Statesman*, 7 October 1994:19).

15. See Weber's *The Protestant Ethic and the Spirit of Capitalism* (1904-5).

16. See Maureen McNeil's reference to the 'new oppressed' of the Thatcher decade (1991).

CHAPTER FOUR:

Let Our Children Grow Tall

The Start Rite child

> Let our children grow tall and some grow taller than others, if they
> have it in them to do so.
>
> (Thatcher, 1975a:16)

I once met Margaret Thatcher in person. The year was 1971 and the
venue was a draughty hall somewhere in Peterborough. The event, I'm
afraid to say, was not particularly significant in the grand scheme of
political things. It was the 'Golden Egg' competition. I was an eleven-
year-old contestant and Margaret Thatcher, then into her second year
as Secretary of State for Education, the only woman in Edward
Heath's Conservative Cabinet, was the competition's judge. At the
time this meeting made quite an impression on me. I knew she was
important from the deferential attitude of my normally strict teachers
and, ushered to speak to her, I recall quite clearly being struck by her
rather 'posh' voice. She had very formal clothes on; she seemed regal
and quite aloof. Unlike my teachers' sensible shoes, when she walked
alongside them her shoes tapped distinctly on the hall floor. Local
dignitaries surrounded her and, when she spoke to us children, they
seemed to crowd in around her and the result was overwhelming.
Unfortunately, the questions she asked me are all of a blur, I recall
only being anxious not to sound too stupid, not to show myself up.
The only other emotion I associate with Margaret Thatcher at that
meeting was disappointment because she did not select my 'adventur-
ous' egg and sage pie as the winning recipe. By 1971 Margaret
Thatcher had already achieved a certain notoriety which was fanned
by sections of the media who were later to celebrate her. Little did I
know that the woman judging me had recently been publicly derided
as 'Thatcher the Milk Snatcher'.

At this point in Thatcher's political career, a broader cross-party commitment to welfarism inevitably informed her political actions. Both the Labour and Conservative Party were in at least partial accord that the Welfare State was necessary for the protection of the most vulnerable of British citizens. The analogy of state as a caring parent nurturing its citizen-offspring was an obvious way imaginatively to shape this relationship. When Thatcher entered the Cabinet in a period of disorganisation and restructuring, she adopted some of these parental metaphors as she promoted and pushed through areas of educational policy. As Heath's Education Minister, from 1970 to 1974, she personally promoted a number of policies that fitted within the welfarist ethos which had been sustained by Conservative and Labour progressives since 1945.[1] Fighting against the wishes of the recently deceased Iain Macleod, Heath's first Chancellor of the Exchequer, (who had died within a few days of the 1970 election), Thatcher fought to preserve the Open University which expanded higher educational opportunities to the part-time student. She has since claimed that she endorsed it as an inexpensive means to widen access and 'above all because I thought it gave people a second chance in life' (Thatcher, 1995:179). She vociferously defended the demolition of Victorian school buildings and their replacement with new primary schools in poor areas (Young, 1989:69). In December 1972, she introduced the Education white paper *Framework for Expansion* in which her plans to expand nursery school provision were outlined. Thatcher presented her plans as the state's opportunity to 'help redress the balance of those born unlucky' (Young: 70; Abbott and Wallace, 1992:27).[2]

However, these aspects of her educational tenure were largely eclipsed in the public imagination by a decision which catapulted her into the media spotlight and made her, for the first time, a notorious national politician. In December 1970, free milk for 8 to 12 year-old schoolchildren was abolished. In her account of this moment, Thatcher claimed the decision was naïve. At the time she thought that the resulting welfare cut of £9 million would be popularly understood as a necessary sacrifice for a better funded education service (Thatcher, 1995:182). However, throughout 1971 the assault on her by the political opposition and the media escalated. The *Guardian* described the cut as 'a vindictive measure which should never have been laid before Parliament', the *Daily Mail* told her to 'think again', the *Sun* asked 'Is Mrs Thatcher Human?' (Thatcher, 1995:181). This criticism drew on connotations of class as well as gender as Thatcher's self-image as a woman who cared for underprivileged children was turned against her. She was represented as the upper-middle-class Tory woman in a hat, remote from the problems of the poor for whom she had claimed to speak. The decision triggered abuse and the first batch of nick-names: 'Milk Snatcher, Ice Maiden, Cave Woman, Open Refrigerator, Salome, and so on' (Wapshott and Brock, 1983:97). The incident enhanced an incipient reputation for unforgiving coldness. 'Something happens to her eyes,' a journalist had written the previous year, liken-ing the effect to 'a cold wind passing over a Norfolk beach' (Wapshott and Brock: 97). Newspaper stories sometimes descended into farce with, for example, accounts of a Labour council considering buying a herd of cows to provide milk for its children. Thatcher's gender fuelled a deeper unease which reached a culmination in the *Sun*'s declaration that she was 'The Most Unpopular Woman in Britain' (Harris, 1983:80). The accompanying article alleged: 'At a time when Mr Heath's Government is desperately seeking an image of compas-sion and concern Mrs Thatcher is fast emerging as a liability' (Harris: 80). The connotations behind such criticism were clear: for a woman to deprive children of milk implied an aberrant femininity, and Thatcher was represented as a woman divorced from the caring instincts of motherhood.

To understand Thatcher's particular mobilisation of the child and the horizon of expectations that she was seen to attack in her milk-snatching incident, it is important to remember how, in the early 1970s, the child was still shaped imaginatively and physically by the Welfare State. In 1971, the provisions of the Welfare State that Thatcher was to challenge vigorously a few years later had influenced my childhood. Like many others, I was brought up on the free extras that the state provided for the growing child: rose-hip syrup, orange juice, Marmite and, at primary school, free milk. The significant year of the Golden Egg competition was my first at a former grammar school which had just turned comprehensive, a practice which Wilson's Labour government had promoted as a levelling of the educational field. In conversations about my childhood I have some-times tried to encapsulate the welfarist ethos that fed into my early years with the nostalgic statement that: 'I was a *Start Rite* child'. Clark's sensible children's *Start Rite* shoes with cross bar, flat low heel and wide leather uppers – with room for growth – were what I was made to wear until about the age of ten when I put my foot down and demanded something more fashionable. The shoes were advertised as giving children's feet a good start in life. The *Start Rite* advertising poster for the shoes was a line drawing of young children, seen from behind, gaily walking away from the viewer down a long road towards a glorious horizon. The advert suggested an infinity of care and the child as symbol of a golden future. Here the child can be interpreted as symbol of a certain form of investment: the advert an address to the adult's desire, hope and demand for a better life which fixes onto the child. As Dorfmann and Mattelart suggest:

> adults create for themselves a childhood embodying their own angelic aspirations which offer consolation, hope and a guarantee of a 'better' but unchanging future ... Adult values are projected onto the child, as if childhood was a special domain where these values could be protected uncritically.
>
> (Dorfman and Mattelart, 1972:30-1)

In the *Start Rite* advert, the image of childhood as the adult's future health and potential was harnessed to consumerism. However, this commercial image also borrowed from more powerful understandings of the role of the child in modern culture. In the late nineteenth and early twentieth centuries the child became the contested site of a range of political discourses and actions that sometimes challenged, sometimes justified, the developments and social conditions of a modern industrial capitalist nation. Central to a range of conservative, philanthropic and reformist debates was a general consensus about the role of the child. Modern children were supposed to be segregated from the harsh, dangerous and disciplined world of urban industrial life. The modern construction of childhood arises out of these assumptions and, belonging as it does to the feminine sphere of family and private life, it reveals the broader hierarchical gendering of the relations between public and private, workplace and family, production and consumption, need and desire. Set up as a 'privileged domain of spontaneity, play, freedom and emotion', childhood provides the contrast and ground for the ideologies of public life with their emphasis on 'discipline, work, constraint and rationality' (Stephens, 1995:6). Central to this modern construction of the child then was the ideal that they should be protected from the laborious tasks and mechanised relationships of the urban and industrial world. Carolyn Steedman describes the 'sacralisation' of the child that occurred in the late nineteenth to early twentieth centuries (Steedman, 1990:63). As children were withdrawn from the work force and economic activity they became 'emotionally priceless', as symbols of social hope, objects of reformist study and subjects of legislative attention (Steedman: 62-4). Just as turn-of-the-century socialist reform was informed by 'a widespread use of an evolutionary theory in which children provided the key point of development', so post-war welfarism conceived of a people who had to be 'acted *for*', supported and helped on the road to independence (p171-2).

In its interpretation of the child as golden future, the advertising image of the *Start Rite* child could be seen as analogous to the welfarist dream, a dream pragmatically supported by both Left and Right of the political spectrum for over twenty years.[3] 'From the cradle to the grave' was the phrase used by the Labour Party after the Second World War to encapsulate the all-encompassing care that the Welfare State would bestow upon its citizens. In the late 1970s and 1980s Thatcher promoted a shift of perception in which the market usurped the place of the state in providing for the child. In January 1979, just months before she won the general election, she was interviewed on Jimmy Young's Radio Two chat show (NSA: LP385 18). She summoned up an image of the vulnerable members of society: 'the elderly, the sick, the children'. These, she claimed, were the victims of trade union strikes and disputes held over the previous winter. She contended that the previous need for legislation to protect the 'working chap' had been overtaken by an unlawful scramble, 'not a free-for-all', but a 'free-for-some to hold the country to ransom'. She claimed that she was the barrier that would hold back such unlawful demands and maintain the 'essential liberties of the country'. The welfarist claim to protect its citizens from the cradle to the grave was swiftly undercut by Thatcher's suggestion that the old, the sick and children were now in need of her protection from the state that had failed them. Thatcher, as a new Prime Minister, stressed that the state's provision of lifetime care had come to an end. At a memorial lecture in early 1980 she maintained: 'We should not expect the State to appear in the guise of an extravagant good fairy at every christening, a loquacious companion at every stage of life's journey, the unknown mourner at every funeral' (CPA: TS 174/80).

When recalling her path to power Thatcher stressed the importance of her mentor Sir Keith Joseph (Thatcher, 1995:262). The week after Edward Heath's election defeat in mid-October 1974, Joseph argued, in a speech at Edgbaston, Birmingham which was published in full in *The Times*, that Conservative focus on economics during the election had been instrumental in their loss. Joseph crucially signalled the importance of a Conservative realignment of moral and economic discourses. Joseph's speech is most widely known for controversial remarks on working-class single mothers and the comments on the resultant degeneration of 'our human stock' which lost him his chance of leadership and paved the way for Thatcher. He argued that the cause of many social and moral problems was explicitly linked to welfare spending which, through its encouragement of dependency upon the state, generated poor parenting and the dereliction of familial responsibility:

> Parents are being divested of their duty to provide for their family economically, of their responsibility for education, health, upbringing, morality, advice and guidance, of saving for old age, for housing. When you take away responsibility from people you make them irresponsible.
> (Joseph in Abbott and Wallace, 1992:47)

He went on to propose that the major 'problem' was poor single parent families in which unmarried mothers produced a delinquent future generation:

> They are unlikely to be able to give children the stable emotional background, the consistent combinations of love and firmness which are more important than riches. They are producing problem children, the future unmarried mothers, delinquents, denizens of our borstals.
> (Joseph in Abbott and Wallace: 47)

Here Joseph laid bare the harshest connotations of the evolutionary template that also informed Thatcher's model of the developing consumer-child. He expounded an individualist model of self-sufficiency for the well-being of future generations. This model was in direct opposition to welfarist arguments that financial deprivation led to the physical, emotional and educational detriment of the child and therefore society's responsibility was to remedy this lack. Furthermore, for Joseph self-sufficiency was a role assigned primarily to the idealised patriarchal family in which the father worked and provided for the mother who maintained the family and the home.

In 1975, Thatcher appointed Joseph to chair an advisory committee to consider the family. The resulting 'Notes towards a Definition of a Policy' argued that a range of government policy had undermined the family and induced broader cultural factors: urban redevelopment, the increasing dependency on two incomes, too much television, easily available divorce and thereby increasing numbers of single-parent families. The report replicated Joseph's speech in the location of the irresponsible family and particularly the single mother as the source of social decay: hooliganism, truancy, child abuse, alcoholism and criminality (Abbott and Wallace: 48). The withdrawal of Welfare State-induced dependency and the restoration of the 'traditional' patriarchal family were seen as the fundamental route to a revival of self-dependency and morality in private and ultimately national life.

Such thinking chimed with and extended one aspect of Conservative philosophy in which the bond between parent and child and the natural dependence of child upon adult are used as a legitimating model for the natural hierarchies of society. Implicitly, the fundamental relationship between parent and child is patriarchal: knowledge, property and power being passed from father to son. A byword of Conservative thinking is inheritance: the transmission of property and privilege unites generations. As Roger Scruton put it in *The Meaning of Conservatism*: 'The parent at rest with *his* child has a dominant desire, which is this: what I am and what I value, I here pass on' (Scruton, 1980:145, my emphasis; see also Levitas, 1986:94-5).

In her recollection of Joseph's speech Thatcher suggested that the 'powerful messages' were lost in the outcry about his more controversial remarks. Side-stepping his slippage into genetics and natural selection, she signalled key areas of his speech about 'the decline of family, the subversion of moral values and the dangers of the permissive society' and connected these 'with socialism and egalitarianism' (Thatcher, 1995:262). She identified with Joseph's proposed 'remoralization of Britain' and added that his message was a much-needed 'backbone' for Conservative social policy. Thatcher's own formation as Conservative leader was recalled through the image of a radical moral agenda misunderstood, a message refashioned as 'mortal sin in the eyes of mediocrities' and turned into a violent and intrusive attack upon the politician and his family (Thatcher: 262). To emphasise her empathy with Joseph, Thatcher compared his savaging by Conservative and Labour opponents and the media to her traumatic first encounter with the national press as the 'milk snatcher' in the early 1970s. She described the press's 'fierce attack' on Joseph's speech: 'The press camped outside his house and refused to leave him or his family alone. He had probably never experienced anything quite like it. Having been vilified as the "milk snatcher", I felt his hurt as if it were my own' (p262). Thatcher suggested that her decision to stand against Heath was fuelled by a desire to represent their mutual political viewpoint when Joseph stood down from the leadership campaign.

THATCHER, POLITICS AND FANTASY

In the face of 'malicious' rumours spread about her in the press and 'an ugly streak of contempt' from 'some of the Tory hierarchy', Joseph became the measure of a political destruction she would not contemplate: 'I was bitterly upset ... Sometimes I was near to tears. Sometimes I was shaking with anger. But as I told ... a friend: "I saw how they destroyed Keith. Well, they're not going to destroy me"' (p268-9).

Children are at the centre of this memory of personal and political empathy with Joseph and his moral plan. For, underpinning Thatcher's narrative of public onslaught, radical vision, political morality and personal vulnerability, there are two moments of political engagement with the child. Joseph's lamentation about the high and rising number of children being born to young working-class mothers and Thatcher's proposal to remove free school milk from primary school children are interconnected as catalytic messages that triggered ill-deserved abuse (Thatcher: 262). Here then the child underpins a story of misunderstood moral radicalism. In Thatcher's account children are both the crux of the Conservative political agenda and also the politician's stumbling block. Joseph's plea to the party to seize the popular appeal of a moral agenda erupted in his face around the rights, or not, of certain mothers to have children. Thatcher claimed that her similar experience entailed a toughening of her persona and political will.

The Joseph débâcle and the 'milk snatching' incident were symbolically central to Thatcher's self-reflection on the tempering of her political persona and subsequent route to power. The controversy around the removal of free milk was the point, she claimed, when she learnt a very public lesson about how political attack could be inflected through her gender, a lesson that perhaps informed her later hardened persona of 'Iron Lady': 'In one respect at least, the Department of Education was an excellent preparation for the premiership. I came under savage and unremitting attack that was only distantly related to my crimes' (Thatcher, 1995:178). She recalled that for her withdrawal of school milk she 'had incurred the maximum of political odium for the minimum of political benefit', that she had been 'caught up in battles with local authorities for months' and had suffered 'constant sniping from the press' (p182). Memories of her 'hurt and upset' at the attacks provoked the insight that: 'It is probably true that a woman – even a woman who has lived a professional life in a man's world – is more emotionally vulnerable to personal abuse than most men' (p182). She described the images of her 'callously attacking the welfare of young children' as 'deeply wounding' for 'someone who was never happier than in children's company' (p182). This was a fleeting acknowledgement of a female vulnerability that provided critics with a weapon that could cause her both political and emotional damage. She described this experience as a lesson and a formative political moment in which she upped the stakes for any political move on her part: 'I resolved not to make the same mistake again. In future if I were to be hanged, it would be for a sheep, not a lamb, still less a cow' (p182). In this passage, she moved from her gendered vulnerability to a description of the event in more neutral terms. It became a moment of blooding, a kind of selective initiation rite, that all aspiring politicians must go through: 'Some are broken by it, others strengthened' (p182). The story acquires an epic political status, as 1971 becomes the crucible in which Heath's government faltered under strain to buckle into 'various elements of the U-turn' in early 1972. In contrast, Thatcher suggested that 'although under greater strain than any time before or since', in this moment her own self-confidence 'held' (p188). Significantly she described her success- ful political survival as a hardening of the spirit, a closing down of emotion and a distinct wariness about how her gender might influence other politicians' or the media's interpretations of her. In 1976, one year into her leadership, Thatcher had seized the sobriquet 'Iron Lady', but it was, she claimed, the earlier milk-snatching incident of 1971 when 'Iron entered my soul' (Wapshott and Brock, 1983: 105; Young, 1989:74).

Consumption: a heaven on earth

> More than coal, more even than nuclear power, children are our great- est resource, *The Authorised Childcare Handbook*, HMSO.
> (McEwan, 1987:205)

In September 1975, on her first intensive tour of the United States, Thatcher drew upon the symbol of the child to animate her vision of a future in which healthy competition and the success of the fittest meant that some children would 'grow taller than others'. She told her New York audience that her legacy to future generations would be freedom from dependency on the state and moral and economic vitality (Thatcher, 1975a:3,16). The speech, 'Let Our Children Grow Tall', introduced what would become a long-term strategy in which she contrasted 'ordinary people' to 'pressure groups outside Parliament and the democratic framework'. She claimed that such groups were 'assisted' in orchestrating their demands for 'redress and justice' by the expanding opportunities for 'publicity and press which the media have nurtured' (Thatcher, 1975a:13). She maintained that past political attempts to redress genuine 'injustice and inequality' in society had been replaced in contemporary Britain by groups with fabricated social injustices: 'You know how it goes. It is "my rights at all costs regardless of who has to pay", or "society has a duty to me", not "I have a duty to society"' (Thatcher: 12-13). Thatcher implied that the child was hindered by this iniquitous system and she would return the child to its rightful owners, ordinary parents, and, through the promotion of individual economic rights, would redress the imbalance of power wrought by the state. In December 1976 she informed the Social Services Conference that the parents' desire for their child was crucial to the establishment of a stable and moral society. She stated: 'We believe the family is the foundation of society and the desire of parents to give their children a better start in life is honoured as one of the most powerful influences for good' (Thatcher in Thomas, 1992:64ff).

In July 1977 Thatcher delivered a lecture called 'The Dimensions of Conservatism' to commemorate the life and works of Iain Macleod. Macleod was her personal friend. He was also one of the post-war progressives of the party who had determined to use the agencies of the Welfare State to assist society and industry. Thatcher likened her Conservative Party to the post-war party in the sense that both of them had been impelled to define themselves anew to meet the demands of the time, both were 'continuous and evolutionary' (Thatcher, 1977:48). In keeping with long-held Conservative beliefs, she suggested that natural hierarchies and obligations between social groups linked society into an organic whole: 'man is a social creature, born into family, clan, community, nation, brought up in mutual dependence' (Thatcher: 53).[4] She then swiftly disconnected this dependency from any association with the obligations of the Welfare State. She suggested that belief in the state's unique capacity to recognise and provide for the socially and economically deprived was deficient. Her tale of sociality and dependence contradicted the post-war emphasis on welfarism and reworked the conventional Conservative emphasis on kinship as exemplar of social stability through inheritance of property and wealth. She latched the child's evolution as a social being onto the impulses informing consumerism:

> Self-regard is the root of regard for one's fellows. The child learns to understand others through its own feelings: at first its immediate family;

> in course of time the circle grows ... Because we want warmth, shelter, food, security, respect and other goods for ourselves, we can understand that others want them too ... People must be free to choose what they consume in goods and services (p54-5).

Here the child illustrated the movement from self-regard to consumption. Thatcher suggested that the child's 'self-regard' and subordination to the natural hierarchy of the family provided a model for the 'drives' of a free consumerist society. In this process desire for material goods, consumer services and prestige developed into a recognition of one's moral obligations and responsibilities: 'Choice [of goods and services] in a free society implies responsibility. There is no hard-and-fast-line between economic and other forms of personal responsibility to self, family, firm, community, nation, God' (Thatcher: 55). The child symbolised both the stable, natural foundation of social life and also a social anticipation that he or she would fulfil their civil duty in the transmission of 'traditional' moral values. Furthermore, the child naturalised the market as the impetus to self-improvement and exchange.[5]

Thatcher declared at the beginning of her leadership that: 'What is right for the family is right for Britain' (*Sunday Express,* 29 June 1975:17). By 1979, her speeches revealed how the family had become for her the 'driving force' of society, with the desire of 'millions' for 'a better life' for their children being the motor of that drive (Thatcher in McFadyean, 1984:15). Thatcher's agenda was to return responsibility and independence to the private sphere and to recover the family as the basic 'building block' of society where the right values were instilled in children as tomorrow's citizens. Throughout her premiership she reiterated that: 'children come first because children are our most sacred trust' (Thatcher in John, 1995:122). Throughout the 1980s, the idealised scene of family life was a commonplace reference in her speeches and interviews, with the home pictured as shelter replete with material goods in which the child and its mother were the anchor-point. This harmonious private sphere was set up as essential counterpoint to the autonomous, enterprising responsibility of the adult realm of consumerist capitalism. This adult (often implicitly masculine) world of enterprising consumption, in its turn, was invested with sincerity and worthiness by its contrast with the alleged 'dependency culture' of the Welfare State. The self-reliant consumer was contrasted with the unworthy recipient of state benefits who, as a figure of infantile and immoderate greed, rose up to claim his or her 'rights' with an all-consuming appetite.

In a speech to the 1986 Conservative Women's Conference, Thatcher pictured her audience out canvassing and asked them to remember the words of Mrs Yelena Bonner, wife of the Soviet dissident, Andrei Sakharov. Yelena Bonner had contrasted her own life in Soviet Russia with that of her children and grandchildren in the United States, and Thatcher reiterated Bonner's dream: 'My dream, my own house, is unattainable for my husband and myself, as unattainable as Heaven on Earth' (Thatcher, 1986:212). Thatcher proposed that this fantasy of 'Heaven on Earth' was 'an everyday, attainable reality in Britain' (p212). She conjured up the typical little Heaven that the female Conservative canvasser would happen upon: a comfortable home in which security was evident in a plethora of consumer and financial goods: videos, deep freezes, telephones, the possession of privatised company shares. In the midst of this scene Thatcher pictured the figure upon whom the women canvasser's eyes would finally rest: a child, in the warmth of the sitting room, using a home computer, moreover using it more 'expertly', 'far better ... than mother or father' (p212). This description of material prosperity assumed consumer knowledge on the part of the Conservative women, but more importantly it offered a vision of a better present and future in which consumer capitalism relieved everyday hardships and ensured self-fulfilment. In her use of Yelena Bonner, a woman apparently excluded in her own land from realising the pleasures and desires of consumer capitalism, Thatcher countered the imagined objections of the hardiest ascetic 'Socialist' with an endorsement of consumerism as the purpose of production:

> some commentators think that it is crudely materialistic to describe the everyday things that families want in the way I am doing. And then they go on to contradict themselves by complaining that not everyone enjoys them! Well *our* aim is to spread these good things, and others, more widely – by leaving people with enough of their money to afford them. Remarks about our society being debilitated by 'consumerism', so-called, is simply Socialist sour grapes ... There's no earthly point in making goods unless someone's going to buy them.
>
> (Thatcher, 1986:212)

The fantasy of the comfortable home has been a central component of Western capitalism. It has provided ideological justification for the

public world of work where, particularly men's labour, has been legitimated as 'for the good of the family', its needs and desires. Women
and children have peopled and secured the harmony of the private
family refuge away from the masculine sphere of politics, culture and
production. Through the figure of Yelena Bonner and the child
tapping at his computer, Thatcher acknowledged a desire for, and a
pleasure gained from, material comfort. Here I am reminded of
Carolyn Steedman's suggestion that her mother's working-class
Conservatism gave her 'a public language' that allowed her mother 'to
want, and to express her resentment at being on the outside, without
the material possessions enjoyed by those inside the gate' (Steedman,
1989:121). Expressing anger at accusations of greedy materialism,
Thatcher asked the readers of *Woman* magazine: 'What's wrong with
wanting to have enough to enable [your children] to have private
music lessons, to take them abroad, to see that they have better clothes
and better food?' *(Woman,* 4 June 1988:30). Furthermore, the child of
her imaginary domestic scene was a signifier of the 'euphoric values'
of consumerism – a life of possibilities, a life without restraints.[6] But
this child was also carefully contained to avoid the disruptive potential of a purely libidinous existence of, for example, the child
entranced by the computer screen. Thatcher suggested he was motivated, more skilled than his parents and, importantly, represented
childhood off the streets and satisfying the technological needs of the
future.

Thatcher frequently presented an economical view of salvation that
melded money to morality and consumer responsibility. In this
scenario, the child was central to securing the family's stability for the
child's presence indicated that the pursuit of wealth was not materialistic and self-centred but for the protection and betterment of the
family. In Thatcher's interviews throughout 1987 and 1988 accounts
appeared of the good son who worked diligently and used the wages
from this industry to re-carpet his mother's flat one Christmas. This
thrifty devoted son was used to endorse her broader claim that there
was nothing wrong with the pursuit of wealth *(Woman's Own,* 31
October 1987:10; *Woman,* 4 June 1988:30). At the 1988 Conservative
Women's Conference Thatcher revealed that 'the British miracle' in
which 'the spirit of enterprise had returned to Britain' was illustrated
by the widespread prosperity of the 'moderate majority':

the latest figures show that the living standards of the poorest families
have been rising faster than those on average incomes. 98 per cent of

households now have a television. 83 per cent have a telephone. 82 per cent have a washing machine, and over 70 per cent central heating.

(CPA: 229/88:6-7)

In the language of calculation and gratification the 'repaying of debts' was represented as 'lifting the burden off the shoulders of our children' (p7). The purchase of one's own home or previously rented council house was presented as 'a substantial legacy' that 'most families' could 'pass on to their children' (p12). Thatcher reinterpreted care and support as restriction and oppression; the overwhelming sense gained from her speeches was of the Welfare State as a suffocating formation that stunted the subject's path to adult individuation. Consumer 'choice' was equated with self-control. Financial self-sufficiency enabled charitable giving and independent provision for one's family. It signified a breaking away from the suffocating anonymity of collectivity and a semi-dependent, infantile existence where everything was mapped, selected, categorised and ordered for you.

What can be seen here is a displacement of the welfarist possibilities of universal responsibility for all adults and all children into the atomised and individual achievements of the individual family and its (implicitly male) breadwinner. In both sets of discourses the child operates as a symbol of hope and as an investment in the future. In welfarist discourse the child was primarily a focus for the combined efforts of the community. However in Thatcherite discourse the child became a focus of the limited and private competitive unit. This was a unit buying its way into Yelena Bonner's 'dream' of 'a little bit of Heaven on Earth':

It's too easy to lay off your conscience with more and more public spending. But compassion can't be nationalised. It's individuals that count. A responsible society is one in which people do not leave it to the person next door to do the job. It is one in which people help each other, where parents put their children first and friends look out for their neighbours, and families for their elderly members. That is the starting point for care and support – the unsung efforts of millions of individuals.

(Thatcher, 1986:218)

Such fantasy scenes combining narcissism and reparation are difficult to maintain. The fantasy of warm, soft-carpeted, private homes only partially conceals the instability and unfulfilled lack that also infuses family life: the petty squabbles, private rivalries and the conflict born of intimacy that are also present in the lived reality of any 'family' home. Speaking of the volatility of the fantasy *mise en scène*, its mutability and instability, Laplanche and Pontalis suggest it is a 'favoured spot for the most primitive defensive reactions, such as turning against oneself, or into an opposite, projection, negation' (1968:26-7). In Thatcher's speeches, the external political world outside the home continually boiled with subversion and discontent; the imagery of social instability and volatile public battles deflected from and partly consolidated the unreal harmony of the private sphere. While conflict and dispute on the part of unions, nuclear protestors and social movements were continuous throughout the Thatcher years, they were frequently presented in her discourse as irrational, disharmonious and often dangerous infractions of an otherwise prosperous and secure national and private life.

Thatcher's secure family home then was 'ground' won through the Government's 'many battles' from the Falklands to the recent Miners' Strike and the current print workers' union protest at Wapping, East London (Thatcher, 1986:220). She warned her female audience that the Conservative's 'first duty' was 'to defend and hold that ground against all-comers' (p219):

> You are the best guardians of our liberties. Continue with the Conservative Party to build on the great open site of human freedom: the homes, the families, the values, the enterprises – in a word, the good society. For it's that which can bring, as Yelena Bonner herself has testified, a little bit of Heaven on Earth (p221).

Furthermore, there was no space here for those excluded from the pleasures of consumption or those exhausted by the effort needed to live up to the dream of material abundance. The family on a low income, the unemployed and the child without material benefits became harder to imagine throughout the 1980s amidst the plethora of public images of the prosperous family. In this respect Thatcherite discourse resembled the advertising industry in its repetitive display of a 'good society' in which the purchase of goods, insurance policies or mortgages for the family was equated with benevolence and protective responsibility. In contrast to the rich detail afforded the consuming family was the virtual invisibility of the poor family in the public domain. Patricia Holland illustrated this contrast in her analysis of the new Family Income Supplement leaflet issued in 1978-9 to publicise the revised form of welfare credit for poor families on low incomes (Holland, 1992:50).[7] In particular, she highlighted the anonymous cut-out of the nuclear family that appeared on the leaflet's front cover. Bereft of features, the stark outlines of two adults and two children were clustered into the recognisable family grouping but reduced to the anonymity of the institutional signs that mark out roads or public toilets. This could be interpreted as the DHSS's attempt to appeal to all families. However, Holland reads the empty shapes as indication of a family virtually simplified out of existence, unacknowledged by the dominant representations of the market (Holland: 50). The disjuncture between consumer plenitude and welfare austerity can be read in the contrast between the stark anonymity of this silhouette and the rich detail that accompanied the political and commercial images of the smiling, purchasing, charity-giving family (p50).

For Thatcher the system of social benefits inherited by the Conservatives encouraged young people to be idle and to see benefit as an acceptable substitute for work (CPA: 229/88). In mid-1982, her concern that the young should not be deprived of personal responsibility led to the formation of the Family Policy Group with the assistance of New Right thinker Ferdinand Mount.[8] The Group proposed the shifting of responsibility for public and welfare services away from the state and onto the family. Thatcher has suggested that a combined 'commitment' to economics and the 'traditional values' of self-responsibility was behind their ambitious programme of tax reforms, education vouchers, widened council house sales and curbs on welfare and education professions (Thatcher, 1993:279). State reliance was increasingly seen as undignified, a 'burden' and infantile. The Family Policy Group 'sought to transmit free market values to the young via the family', and the proposals included the suggestion that children be taught to 'manage their pocket money' (Edgar, 1986:75). The family and home, then, was the site in which children would be introduced to their potential role as responsible and discriminating consumers.

Infantile pleasures and consumption

To think about the Thatcherite family then is to think of an enclosure, the space where commerce comes home. It is the hub of the network of consumer goods, commodities, places of production, sites of financial exchange and commerce that sustain it. The illusion given is of a self-sustaining intimacy that is nonetheless linked to hybrid networks of communication and convergence that characterised the equally self-sustaining New Right vision of the free market. Here is Ferdinand Mount on consumer capitalism as the 'redistribution of privacy':

> The material triumph of the masses – the access they have finally gained to a decent standard of living – is not to be used for making society more public and collective. On the contrary, it is to be used for dispersing the delights of privacy to all ... The other domain, the domain of home and family, here asserts its primacy over the public domain and its tired old quarrels of class and race (Mount, 1982:175).

Mount, an adviser to Margaret Thatcher in the early 1980s, produced an extended thesis that characterised the nuclear family as 'timeless' and at present under attack from 'the State'.[9] *The Subversive Family* (1982) was a trenchant engagement with Marxist and socialist feminist critiques of the family which had emphasised its relation to gendered and class structures of power. Mount characterised these theorists as false 'subversives': 'feminists, anarchists, hippies, utopians and radicals' all attacking the 'customs and obligations of the family' (Mount, 1982:2). He claimed to speak for 'the ordinary man' who was elided with 'the ordinary family' to become 'the ultimate and only consistently subversive organisation' (p162) which continued across time to be 'an enduring enemy of all hierarchies, churches and ideologies' (p1). He suggested that the family was 'in permanent revolution against the State' and celebrated the working class as 'the only true revolutionary class' (p162).

Mount's thesis illustrates how the language of 'rights' and 'freedom' could be disengaged from the radical political discourses of the 1960s and rearticulated as a Conservative defence of property, consumerism and individual responsibility over state interference. He knowingly parodied the style of libertarian Marxist critiques of the family as a repressive extension of the capitalist state. But he reversed the terms so that the family became a 'subversive' class on its own countering the repressive structures of the Welfare State. Mount, like Thatcher, refused to condemn consumerism. He denied that the purchase of and the desire for consumer goods by 'ordinary people' was materialistic and saw it rather as a recognition, on their part, that these goods were 'of potential social and spiritual value and capable of altruistic use' (p164).

Mount's reworking of politically left-oriented celebrations of working-class culture shared some of their tendencies to romanticisation and the same rendering invisible of working-class women. His 'ordinary family' members were almost child-like in their spontaneity. The organic community they inhabited was male: their 'pub talk' was free of ideology and intellectual 'claptrap' (p163). Their loyalties were uncomplicated, bound as they were by family blood and bone. Their acceptance of boring work was not passive or pragmatic but an assertion of a man's elemental sacrifice, 'in order to *provide a better life for his family*' (p163: his emphasis). He evoked a working class community that was sceptical of politics but 'markedly free of *serious* utopian sentiments' (p163: his emphasis). Their utopias were 'playful and sensual – Big Rock Candy Mountain, Lubberland, Cockaigne, places of leisure and plenty' (p163). Furthermore, he added, their satisfaction with consumer goods was not purely materialistic, rather it was a valuation of the ease it brought to their lives:

> working men do not tamely register contentment with their car, their washing-machine, their extra weeks of holiday and their warm, dry houses ... these are, simply, good things because they make life easier *for one another*: wives are not worn out at the age of thirty-five, children are educated, husbands pay more attention to their wives, go out to pubs together (p164, his emphasis).

Mount's thesis was written partly as an attack on the work of social historians such as Philippe Ariès and Edward Shorter who had, in the previous decade, foregrounded the cultural specificity of the family and the man, woman and child's place within it (Ariès, 1960; Shorter, 1975). It was also a riposte to socialist writers, such as Jeremy Seabrook, whose chronicle of the loss of the working-class organic community berated 'consumer capitalism' for eroding working-class identity.[10] In response Mount not only emptied working-class identities and spaces of history, but also singled out one imaginary form of 'family' as a privileged site of authentic community.[11] This simple consuming unit was refused any psychological complexity and the material conditions of working class lives and how these may be experienced – boredom, dissatisfaction, pain, poverty, anxiety, desire, greed – were washed over with a veneer of uncomplicated, earthy emotional simplicity. He exhibited nostalgia for an imaginary pure, uncomplicated and implicitly white community in which women stayed home and received consumer gifts while men brought home the wages and children were loved but not heard. He projected lofty hubris onto socialist politicians and left-wing intellectuals, while his own perspective was grounded inside the family:

Seen from outside and above, from some Olympian spectators' stand, these goods may seem to be greedily devoured by materialist families; seen from ground level and *from inside the family,* the goods are seen as gifts and transfers between one member and another, charitable gifts which express affection and repay filial, parental and marital debts, thus blessing both the giver and receiver (p164).

Images of childhood and childish pleasures uncomplicated by the taint of capitalist and materialist greed abound. Envy, hunger, survival and need are erased as consumption becomes an almost prelapsarian act of selfless generosity. The figure selected to represent the intrusiveness and authoritarianism of the Welfare State revealed how intimately the realm of childhood and the childish were connected to Mount's family. He claimed that the state was the family's 'most dangerous enemy' (p174). He encapsulated the collective statutory and administrative powers of 'education officers, children's officers, housing officers, architects, planners, welfare workers' in the malign figure of the 'District Health Visitor' (p174). The 'Visitor' was split into good and bad *alter ego.* On the one hand she was the mother's intimate friend: 'sweet and sensitive and genuinely useful' (p174). On the other hand, she was a 'Stalinist' super-ego, who inculcated in the mother a sense of surveillance through her continuous awareness that the 'Visitor' was 'there as an inspector as well as an adviser' (p174). In his narrative the child became a symbol of the family's vulnerability. The child was object of the Visitor's 'roaming eye' as she roamed the room and its body 'for evidence of dirt, neglect, even brutality' (p174). The child who was not read as 'clean and proper' became the catalyst for the Visitor's 'disposal' of 'a Stalinist array of powers': to remove the child from its mother, to condemn the home as unfit for human habitation, to 'clap the mother and father in jail' (p174). Mount's dystopian scenario excluded the possibility that intervention by the welfare worker may be needed and did not address the state's categorisation and intervention in the (primarily working class) 'problem' home. Such complexities were reduced to his representation of 'an unde-clared war between two domains': a professional 'overclass, bossy, acquisitive of power and security' and a resentful 'gulled and harried' 'underclass' whose children may be snatched and privacy intruded upon (p174-5).

Mount was one of Thatcher's favoured political speechwriters and policy thinkers. They shared a desire to valorise the family unit and, in their similar ways, to render consumerism as entirely benevolent ngaged from the difficult questions of poverty, survival in and exclusion from the market place. Importantly, they both indicated a shared recognition of the 'demands of home and family, the pulls of psychic as well as social structures', and in that concern reveal that these were areas that Conservatism and New Right discourse took seriously politically (Light, 1991:14). Furthermore, they both acknowledged people's everyday fear of intrusion from outside authority and the fear that one's child would not be clean enough or fit enough to meet the Welfare State's criteria of adequate parenthood. Thatcher elevated the self-governed, consuming family to the status of characteristic national identity. However an anxiety attended this celebration, for the libidinous connotations of consumerism stood in contrast to the stability and morality that Thatcher associated with the family space. One means to address this anxiety was to locate the child as the motivating force behind a responsible consumerism, and here public and political debates about education and discipline were central.

Discipline, the child and the parent-consumer

> Upbringing and environment not only offer benefits in the way of love, but also employ other kinds of incentive, namely rewards and punishments.
>
> (Freud, 1915:71)

Thatcher considered that Mount's formative thinking on areas of social policy was central to her long-term plans for Britain. In 1982, her respect for him increased when he succeeded John Hoskyns as Head of her Policy Unit (Kavanagh, 1987:255). In the wake of the 1981 urban riots in London, Liverpool and Manchester, Thatcher claimed that her interest turned to Mount's areas of concern: 'social policy – education, criminal justice, housing, the family' (Thatcher, 1993:278). In late May 1981, he presented a paper to her which foregrounded 'many of the themes and ideas which would dominate [her] third term of office' including the Conservative reform of the education system and the restoration of 'parent power' (p278).[12] Thatcher quoted his paper to illustrate the valued authority and obedience that she wished to instil in the British people. Here the disciplined child and authoritative parent were the template for the respectful democratic society:

> in the early stages of life it is the experience of authority, when exerted fairly and consistently by adults, which teaches young people how to

exercise responsibility themselves. We have to learn to take orders before we learn how to give them. The two-way relationship between obedience and responsibility is what makes a free, self-governing society. And in the breakdown of that relationship we can trace the origins of so much that has gone wrong with Britain.

(Mount in Thatcher, 1993:278)

Thatcher tapped into broader fears of the child as unconfined or unregulated. These were, as illustrated below, translated at their most abject into imagery of a hideous gestation and reproduction of ideology or poisonous addiction coursing through the education system. The fear of the contaminated or indoctrinated child acting out its terrible chaotic potential was an integral part of Thatcherite attacks on education and progressive teaching throughout the 1980s. Anxieties concerning the transmission of proper knowledge and culture to children were condensed into an attack on left-wing local authorities, teachers, cultural workers and politicians. The Thatcherite address to a range of constituencies – the responsible or worried parent, the good teacher, the caring mother, the family, the taxpayer – extended the perspectives from which concern about the child could be authoritatively registered.

A good ten years before Thatcher came to power, debates about education and discipline and concerns about open or student-centred teaching practices and acceptable knowledge were the subject of intense cross-party political and cultural concern.[13] Thatcher therefore latched onto a series of highly charged fears about the child and its protection, education and control, mobilising a populist register on educational decline that had been in gestation throughout the years of Wilson, Heath and Callaghan's governments. Crucially, however, she reworked the terms of the debate to emphasise the market as the appropriate mechanism to gauge and inform the role and performance of educational institutions. In Thatcherite terms education was not a social responsibility or civic duty but primarily a commodity in which the parent was the consumer (Donald, 1992:124-5). Within the new consumerist paradigm the purported ideal was for education to respond to a different calculus of interests and values. These included: cost effectiveness, response to consumer needs, preservation or reintroduction of the pedagogic values of rote learning, training the future employee and the prioritisation of a limited notion of the family, morality and culture.

Importantly, Thatcher had to divide off any sense of self-gratification or selfish pleasure from her notion of responsible consumerism. Long-held anxieties about the individual's participation in the market have been intimately tied to commerce and the libidinous connotations of consumerism: untrammelled desire, narcissism and the dissolution of responsibility. Treating one's self, letting go, unwinding and pure enjoyment are the trademarks of many commercial appeals to buy a product for more than its material value. Self-indulgence, personal gratification without guilt, and the freedom of play have all been common associations of childhood. Consumer goods have often been sold as a route back to the imagined liberty of childhood. Discourses that appeal to a responsible family-driven consumerism attempt to stave off the charge of solipsism and abdication of responsibility that such pleasure implies. Most telling is Thatcher's location of the 1981 urban riots as the backdrop to the initial moves towards a re-disciplined and consumer-driven education market. It reveals a complex set of displacements in which fears of the child, of desire and appetite are woven into complex racially inflected images. The riots were drawn on as evidence of the collapse of adult responsibility, discipline and violation of consumerism.

Press reports of the 1981 riots emphasised, with voyeuristic fascination, the image of the unruly crowd. The tabloid papers in particular laid bare the mix of horror and fear that has informed public narratives about youthful spontaneity and lack of discipline since at least the 1950s. The fears expressed were racial and also generational: readers were presented with nightmare images of 'black youth' rejecting social control and acting out their dreadful potential. The urban and commercial setting was significant. 'Black youth' on the streets, or silhouetted against huge bonfires as they looted smashed shop windows, became stock images whether of Brixton, Wood Green or Toxteth (Waddington, 1992:165). The eruption of protest onto the streets and shopping centres of Britain revealed how those excluded from the dominant fantasies of urban civilisation can become, nonetheless, symbolically central. The *Sunday Mirror* (12 July 1981) stressed the Brixton protesters' 'delight in injury and destruction'. It located children as the prime focus of fear: 'Much as you understand the tremendous pressures they are under, the sight and sound of children of 14 and 16 crowing and bragging about inflicting pain brings you to the depths of despair' (Holland, 1992:117). The *Daily Mail* (8 July 1981) similarly evoked the fantasy of the corrupted child. Under a front page photograph of silhouetted figures ransacking a Liverpool supermarket, the article stated: 'At midnight, by the red light of fires they have lit, the young of Liverpool look truly scary, like stunted demons emerging from the shadows with throwing arms raised' (Holland: 117).

As with the images of the out-of-control children of the 'underclass' that appeared in the 1991 disturbances in Oxford, Cardiff and Tyneside, crime, community and out-of-control youths on the streets became conflated in highly charged popular symbols of a brutal intrusion upon civilised urban space. Beatrix Campbell has suggested that 'historically, riots express a crisis – the impossibility of politics and protest'. She argues that they are 'a moment when challenge becomes chaos, when disorder becomes danger' (Campbell, 1993:93). These riots were the incendiary response of young people excluded from the central subject positions of Thatcher's Britain: seen and seeing themselves as 'neither legitimate citizens nor consumers' (Campbell: 95). There were consequential social changes that provoked the street disturbances. In variant ways, unemployment, policing methods, changes in community, schooling and family life, ideas about masculinity and about independence and self-assertion through force, fed into the destruction of property and aggressive behaviour. The newspapers rightly registered social anxiety, despair and fear at mainly young male anomie and the violence that ensued. But they did so in imagery that excluded them not merely from acceptable versions of the child but often from humanity itself.

Adult rationality, its discipline and ordered self-restraint, have been counterpointed to the irrationality, chaos and lack of control that are associated with childhood. In the construction of the modern (Western) subject, both race and gender have added texture to this childish other, wedding blackness and masculinity to the nuances of uncontrolled libido and uncivilised threat. Crucially the image of the young, in particular the young black male, pillaging supermarkets or stores or, in the early 1990s, poor white boys 'nicking' and joy-riding cars, pointed up the centrality of consumer goods to the conceptualisation of 'civilisation'. Depicted as dangerous and euphoric, and outside the legitimate channels of exchange and distribution, these 'children' embodied a greed that was tapped into but contained in dominant images of the purchasing family. They also indicated how central consumerism has become to a sense of citizenship from which they were, or felt themselves to be, excluded.

In the House of Commons (14 April 1981) Thatcher was asked whether high unemployment, social deprivation and inadequate housing had contributed to the history of tensions between police and community in the areas where the riots took place. She flatly refused any such interpretation: 'nothing that has happened with regard to unemployment would justify these riots' (Thatcher in Young, 1989:233-4). The problem was one of lack of discipline, 'motivated by nothing more complicated than human wickedness' (Young: 234). As such the response she advocated was the reinvigoration of moral discipline, backed up by the regulative forces of the law. In consequence, the Home Secretary William Whitelaw saw through substantial expenditure on the police force to enhance crowd-control technologies and equipment, including weaponry and vehicles, communications devices and protective body-armour (Smith, 1994:176-7). These resources were subsequently to be crucial to the defeat of the National Union of Mineworkers in the strikes of 1984-5 (Smith: 177).

The immediate response to the riots of several New Right spokesmen was well publicised in the press. These were part of a network of journalists, lobbyists, academics and politicians committed to attacking post-war social democracy and to building a populist consensus for the Conservative Party. This loose grouping of graduates from Peterhouse College (Cambridge University) advocated that Thatcher adopt an invigorated social authoritarian Conservatism and emphasised Conservative allegiance to authority, discipline and social restraint.[14] In the *Sunday Telegraph* Peregrine Worsthorne's immediate response to the riots warned: 'More violence there is certain to be. If not in the inner cities, then it will be on the picket lines' (12 July 1981). He mused that: 'those who voted Mrs Thatcher into office did so in the belief that a Tory Government' would control such 'violent convulsions' (Edgar, 1986:72). George Gale, in the *Express* (7 July 1981), blamed the unrest on a 'revulsion from authority and discipline' wrought in 'the permissive revolution' of the 1960s (Edgar: 72). At the same time Colin Welch, a regular contributor to the *Spectator* (17 December 1983), blamed a society in which 'all fidelity, restraint, thrift, sobriety, taste and discipline, all the virtues associated with work, with the painful acquisition of knowledge, skill and qualifications' had been impaired (Edgar: 72). An image of young people corrupted by the liberal politics of the 1960s informed Welch's theory of national and educational corruption. Thatcher's commencement of leadership of the Conservative Party seemed implicitly linked to the resurrection of 'reason' over the dark forces of 'adult barbarism' that he charted for *Spectator* (20 October 1983) readers:

> The decade of the 1960s (or perhaps more precisely of '65-'75) is often remembered ... as a horrendous episode which ended in tears, after

which reason resumed her sway and wiser counsels prevailed. This is
but a comforting illusion. The poisons then injected into our system,
though doubtless diluted, course still through our veins ... The revolting students of the 1960s are the revolting teachers of today,
reproducing themselves by teaching as received wisdom what they furi-
ously asserted against the wisdom received from their own teachers.

(Edgar: 73)

In February 1982, political attention on the previous year's riots was
revitalised following the release of police figures which claimed to
expose the level of involvement of black youths in violent street crime.
In the resultant debate about hooliganism, crime and family breakdown, junior education minister Rhodes Boyson informed
Loughborough Conservatives that the fault lay in the 'permissive'
1960s which had 'created a pathless desert for many of our young
people' (Boyson in Edgar: 55). He conjured up the depraved exhibi-
tionism of modern urban life where 'many of our city streets and
entertainments flaunt debased morals and false values' and the
'cement' of society had been replaced by 'a destructive, naïve arro-
gance' (p55). The dissolution of 'stable families' was a plague 'with a
malignant effect on many of our children'. The authority of parents
and teachers had been undermined resulting in more children in care.
He concluded that: 'society has reaped dragon's teeth in the form of
juvenile revolt' (p55). One month later, Thatcher pinpointed liberal
educational theories as part of the broader disintegration of social
discipline. Contemporary educational practice was one of the 'disqui-
eting features' of everyday 'family matters' that were threatened. She
drew a correspondence between the work of child-centred education-
alists and 'the permissive society' in which the child symbolised a
conflict between freedom and control:

Children have been encouraged to grow up faster and see themselves as
independent of parents. Parents have been told by self-appointed
experts that their duties to each other and to their children should be
balanced by more emphasis on self-fulfilment. In other words we have
seen the birth of the permissive society.

(Thatcher in McFadyean and Renn, 1984:118)

Here, the feared reversal of child and adult roles was clear: children no
longer represented dependency and limitation, while adults were
becoming childish through the 'permissive' mandate to seek personal

gratification. Thatcher suggested that re-disciplining the child and adult entailed latching education onto the market and re-infusing both with the structures and values of family life. In debates leading up to the 1987 general election and on into the 1988 Education Reform Act (commonly known as the Baker Act) the child featured as a counter to be wrested from the hands of progressive educational 'producers' and into the rightful control of 'consumers'.[15] In early 1986, Kenneth Baker took over from Keith Joseph as Secretary for Education. He characterised his role at the Department of Education and Science as an attempt to break the hold on education of local authorities, teachers, left-wing bureaucrats and trade unionists in order 'to empower' 'the consumers of education' whom he defined as 'businessmen and groups of parents' (Baker, 1993:210-11, 161).

Shirley Letwin, a Director of the Centre for Policy Studies, New Right philosopher and publicist, has written an extensive justification of Thatcher's 'vigorous virtues'.[16] In *The Anatomy of Thatcherism* (1992) she revealed the social and psychic effort that accompanied attempts to secure the drive and initiative of children as future responsible consumers. She attacked progressive education for its replacement of 'old-fashioned "passive reception"' with a form of learning based on the child's 'active participation' (Letwin, 1992:231). Letwin clearly demarcated duty and responsibility from pleasure and desire: 'Far from learning to put duty before pleasure, pupils were encouraged to pursue instant gratification of desires and to resent any discipline that interfered with "spontaneity" or "self expression"' (p231). This included the replacement of 'literary classics' with 'unknown writers who did not use idiomatic English or meet literary criteria' and the abandonment of conventional grammar and spelling standards as 'children were "stimulated" to naturally "express themselves" (p231). She described the 'progressive' reshaping of English schooling as a dismantling of borders and boundaries in which: 'rules, assemblies, rituals, set subjects, timetables, games – were repudiated. In the new open-plan schools, classes were not held in separate rooms and children were not required to remain seated, keep quiet, learn tables or memorise dates' (p230-31).

In such discourse the child featured as a point of tension between public and private worlds, order and chaos, discipline and loss of control. The pupil was described as potentially deviant; in receipt of forms of knowledge constructed as perverse, a practice which was associated with the breaking down of pedagogic and cultural boundaries. Letwin's list of problems included the erosion of standard

English through racial equality initiatives, the encouragement of children to examine class and social structures and 'old subjects ... crowded out' with discussions of 'peace studies ... racism, feminism, community problems, and homosexuality as well as other unconventional sexual practices' (p231). In *Family Portraits* (1986), a collection by the New Right Social Affairs Unit, Valerie Riches similarly argued that school education on 'one-parent families, cohabitation, homosexual relationships and deliberate child-free marriages' eroded family values. Along with advice on contraception and abortion it attacked 'the consciences of children by encouraging the pursuit of personal pleasure' (Riches in Anderson and Dawson, 1986:101). Here, anxieties about the containment and regulation of the child's body were inextricable from fears about the collapse of social order enshrined in the nuclear family and, underlying that, the dissolution of the ordered and controlled subject. Riches suggested that the proliferation of options afforded to the child be closed down and replaced by an ethos of self-control. The child should be encouraged to understand that: 'the life-long struggle of human beings is the need for self-mastery in which the intellect and will wisely control the sensual appetites' (p101). Important questions about the child's access to legitimate knowledge and how that should be defined were collapsed into generalisations about the internal fragmentation of 'our' national culture and ordered social identity.

Letwin defined herself as a libertarian freeing parent-consumers and their children from the dictates and political indoctrination of progressive teachers. Yet her message endorsed restraint of the child through reinforced cultural, gender and sexual boundaries. Similarly, Thatcher's notion of 'parent power' and fiscal reward for good teaching involved invigorated government control of educational practice and an emphasis on firm authority over the child. At the 1987 Conservative Party Conference, Thatcher spoke of her worry about the 'plight of individual boys and girls' 'in the inner cities' as she introduced forthcoming educational reform. She drew directly from the right-wing Hillgate Group's tract *Whose Schools? A Radical Manifesto* (1986) as she described children victimised by 'hard Left education authorities and extremist teachers' (Thatcher, 1987:226; Wagg, 1996:17). She warned:

> Children who need to be able to count and multiply are learning anti-racist mathematics ... who need to be able to express themselves in clear English are being taught political slogans. Children who need to be

taught to respect traditional values are being taught that they have an inalienable right to be gay.

(Thatcher, 1987:226)[17]

I suggest that, through the demonisation of politically-driven teachers and their juxtaposition with the caring responsible parent, consumerism could be disengaged from popular connotations of euphoria, desire and excess and located as central to 'the pursuit of excellence in education' (Thatcher, 1987:219). Kenneth Baker claimed that his role as Education Secretary in the 'sweeping reform of education' was fuelled by 'two watchwords: standards and choice' (Baker, 1993:164). In Thatcher's government of the late 1980s it was held that these values would be expressed through the establishment of a national curriculum with testing, city technology schools and grant-maintained schools which would meld the aims of the parent-consumer and the 'businessmen' who would oversee these new structures (Baker: 164). Against the image of parent-consumer responsibility was set the abuse of ideologically motivated state schoolteachers and the disruption of teachers' strikes over pay held during 1986-7. As Thatcher informed her party, the option for schools to leave local authority control, the establishment of a national curriculum and the maximisation of parent-governor control (all aspects of the then forthcoming 1988 reforms) would break this 'extremist' hold on the child (Thatcher, 1987:226). The market entered as the regulating principle that would guarantee uniformity of quality, meet parental aspiration and represent the future for the child. Furthermore, educational purchasing, whether of books, educational toys, private schooling, or computers, represented an acceptable, responsible form of consumerism for the productive, entirely focused and disciplined learning child.

Thatcher rehearsed a familiar pedagogic fantasy in which the well-turned phrase and the disciplined linguistic structure closed down the hybridity of language, identity and culture, in which education is both forcing house and guardian of a pure national culture and a regulated child. Furthermore, along with like-minded New Right thinkers, she revealed how adults stave off fears about the instability of language and identity through the concept of the well-educated child. The breakdown of cultural, linguistic and generational hierarchies was associated with the breakdown of order within the school. Letwin painted a dystopian image of 1970s schools: 'the effects on the behaviour of children were dramatic. In the year 1971-2, more than two thousand violent incidents and nearly a thousand threats of violence were reported' (Letwin: 232). Thatcher went further, and in successive speeches throughout 1987-8 directly linked bad teaching to crime. She highlighted countless parents' fears, giving political credence to their everyday worries about, for example, truancy and vandalism. The force of her imagery lay partly in the diagnosis of the child's incipient aggression or transgression: a condition awaiting the trigger of progressive education or left-wing political indoctrination. It lay also in the fantasised solution of a regulated and disciplined privatised child, constrained by a successfully internalised moral consumerism. The fantasy of this disciplined and productive child was plagued by and dependent upon its criminal violent other who signified the child's 'deadly' potential.

The (un)safe family and the endangered child

> In the marrow-bones of the grown man I can, it is true, trace the outline of the child's bone, but it itself has disappeared ... The fact remains that only in the mind is such a preservation of all the earlier stages alongside of the final form possible.
>
> (Freud, 1930:259)

Childhood, as Freud indicated, exists largely in the minds of adults. He foregrounded the impossibility of the adult's pure recall of a child-hood event. Childhood is constantly reinvented in the adult mind; images of the child are fashioned from a mix of memory, fantasy, desire and anxiety and are recharged with the colour of contemporary events. Furthermore, adult memories of simple childhood pleasures or uncomplicated gestures are a weave of condensation and displacement that often flee from and conceal attributes that are perceived as monstrous or unacceptable in the adult self: greed, for example, or sexual urges or aggression.

Public images of childhood – in advertising, films, newspapers, government department information leaflets, for example – are crucial to the maintenance and negotiation of the difficult distinction between adult and child. It is difficult to disentangle commentary on the lived experience of 'real-life' children from these powerful representations. Fears and anxieties about the status of childhood, and behind these anxieties about 'the uncertainty of adult status', are both projected onto real children and reworked in changing public images of the child (Holland, 1992; Holland, 1997). Public images of the child set up patterns of interpretation, expectation and desire which sediment into the common-sense cultural assumptions of childhood. But contrary to the sense of childhood as a fixed, unchanging, innocent space of pleasure and play, in the late twentieth century contradictory images of childhood proliferate in the accelerated and image-saturated world of commerce, politics and social exchange. The Thatcher years saw a growing public consciousness and concern about the perceived assault (in various forms) on the space of childhood and on wider representation of damaged or abused children on British television screens, advertising hoardings and in the daily newspapers (Stephens, 1995a; Scott, 1996).[18] The dominant theme was of children 'as innocent and vulnerable victims of adult mistreatment, greed and neglect'. But running alongside this was the theme of 'lost childhood' and the erosion of a space and time of innocence and safety (Stephens: 9). Here the media itself was the target of a set of debates about dangerous effects upon children leading to a series of video and broadcasting regulations. Crucially, Thatcherite discourses on the child within the family negotiated and often amplified a set of cultural and political representations of the endangered child who was the repository of experiences beyond its years.[19]

Throughout the 1980s, the phrase 'children at risk' was attached to a range of social and political concerns including education, family breakdown and media effects. The phrase's force was no doubt strengthened by the blaze of publicity that surrounded a number of tragic child abuse cases that instigated a public critique of the welfarist approach to childcare. The post-war practice of state social work with children and families was imbued with the broader welfarist premise that intervention and support for deprived or needy children within their family structure would compensate for socially caused deprivations.[20] In the mid-1980s sensationalist media coverage introduced the public to the physical and sexual abuse of children within the family. The focus on the public inquiries into the deaths of three young girls – Jasmine Beckford, Tyra Henry and Kimberley Carlile – provoked public and professional debate and increasing criticism of state policy and practice in child care and the competencies of social workers (Parton, 1996:47).

The prevalence of such disturbing cases in the media was central to changing conceptualisations of the child in Thatcher's Britain. Firstly, the private lives of children moved beyond the institutional confines of police and judiciary, hospital and social service department and entered the wider field of cultural representations. Secondly, there was a (reluctant) recognition of the pathology at the heart of the family and the domestic space, reluctant because Thatcherite discourse thrived on representations of external threat to the social order. Furthermore, Thatcher frequently extolled paternity as an emblem of wider social responsibility. Yet regularly within the press the public was confronted with examples of violence within the home and the perpetrator was frequently the father or stepfather. In national news-papers the photographs of these dead children, often pulled from family albums, catalogued the repeated and ultimately fatal injuries they suffered within the family space.

In 1987-8, as the Thatcher government campaigned and won its third term in office with an electoral emphasis on the restoration of parental rights and family responsibilities, the 'Cleveland crisis' received massive media visibility. The family space, revered in populist Conservative discourse, became infused with tension. The revelations in the media of the large number of children diagnosed by two paedi-atricians, Dr Marietta Higgs and Dr Geoffrey Wyatt, as sexually abused within the family introduced complex uncertainty into the idealised image of the home, replete with consumer goods and with the protected child at its core.[21] In the confusion that ensued, the media tried to locate clear-cut heroes and villains from the cast of doctors, lawyers, childcare experts, social workers and parents whose differing interpretations they quoted at length. The focus was increas-ingly on varied institutions involved as potential sites of exploitation and violation of the child; the hospital, the police station, the doctor's surgery, the courtroom and the social services department all came under scrutiny. The increasing attempt to analyse and locate blame away from the homes of the seized children revealed a fundamental disquiet about the family space as potentially dangerous. For Cleveland suggested that family relations could also be transgressive.

Speaking of the Cleveland crisis and its media coverage, Beatrix Campbell suggested that 'child torture came to haunt Thatcherism during the 1980s' (Campbell, 1988:118). The public unveiling of pathological fathers who destroyed their own children unsettled the sanctified political image of responsible family life central to remoralised Britain. Certainly, Thatcher's own responses to child abuse reveal a process of displacement and simplification. In the late 1980s, in a number of woman's magazines, Thatcher addressed the female audience she placed as the stable influence on family life. Here she touched on and swiftly veered away from the issue of 'child cruelty'.[22] Her use of 'cruelty' was significant on its own for it avoided any clear reference to physical or sexual 'abuse'. She also avoided placing such events in any social or gendered context that would acknowledge hierarchical power relations within the family. She reflected on child abuse as a 'sin' or a sign of the 'problem of human nature' (*Woman's Own*, 31 October 1987: 10). It signified the timelessness of 'evil' that no amount of social welfarism could ever effectively counter. At the height of moral panic about Cleveland, just four months after her re-election to a third term, Thatcher addressed child abuse in a somewhat veiled and unsure manner in the now infamous interview with *Woman's Own* where she said that 'there is no such thing as society'. She suggested that 'child cruelty' was rooted in the flawed human subject: 'We now realise that the great problems in life are not those of housing, food, and the standard of living. When you've got all these you're still left with the problem of human nature' (*Woman's Own*, 31 October 1987: 10). To *Woman* magazine Thatcher spoke, foremost as a mother and former Secretary of Education, on the role of the family and of good parenting on the moral fibre of the nation (4 June 1988:32). She proposed that schools were a sanctuary for children who had been 'neglected' or had 'suffered at the hands of their parents' (p32). She added the aside: '(and I might say it is difficult to teach the scriptures, 'God is a Father', when your own father is violent)' (p32).

Significantly, these references occurred in Thatcher's interviews for mass weekly women's magazines: *Woman, Woman's Own, Woman's Realm, Chat.* In the 1980s, these magazines shared a pragmatic form of feminist address which tackled women's problems at work, in relationships and with child care mainly through an individualistic approach in which self-help, self-transformation and individual resourcefulness were the key to overcoming trauma or difficulty (Winship, 1987:66-98). In a sense then this format was in accord with Thatcher's broader political stance and her own persona, both of which avoided any feminist stand but which afforded women a pragmatism that was able to identify and prevent a whole host of social problems within the family. As she told Conservative women at their 1988 national conference:

> The family is the building block of society. It is a nursery, a school, a hospital, a leisure centre, a place of refuge and a place of rest. It encompasses the whole of society. It fashions our beliefs. It is the preparation for the rest of our life. And women run it.
>
> (CPA: 229/88:4)

In an interview for *Woman's Own* entitled 'Granny's Guide', Thatcher's 'record-breaking' achievement of ten years in office was combined with 'another first – [Thatcher's] first grandchild' (17 April 1989:8). As a grandmother her maternal credentials were extended a generation to fuel Thatcher's political vision for the next twenty or so years.[23] Politics was transformed into a 'granny's guide' to the nation's ills and hopes for the millennium and the world in which her grandchild would grow up. Focusing on the moral and spiritual welfare of the child, Thatcher emphasised the need for women's vigilance so that 'a gradual deterioration in the importance of home-life' did not occur (*Woman's Own*, April: 10). Careful to acknowledge that the modern woman may want to work, she more strongly stressed the need for a proper mother for today's children and voiced concern for the 'gradual increase in children born to single parent families' and the 'latch-key children' of career women. Discipline, rules and talk across generations were presented as 'fundamental' and common sense attributes of good parenting which, along with the nuclear family unit, gave 'children the strength and capacity to say no' (p10). Once again, Thatcher suggested that violent crime, drugs and alcoholism were always 'fundamental problems of human nature' which would never be alleviated by welfarist intervention, the building of hospitals or education and training of people. Predictably, paternalism returned as a benevolent assessor and keeper of moral well-being: 'I don't think a government can change human nature. My father always said to me, "There's good and bad in every single person. And the whole of family life is to try to bring out the good and put down the bad"' (p10).

Thatcher's response to the abuse or assault of children, then, was twofold. On one hand, the family was rehabilitated. Here, in part, she drew upon religious discourse, which opposed the sins of the flesh to the (potential) purity of the soul. Representing the future, children were seen as primarily 'creatures of the flesh', only potentially good or evil adults. Echoing the overt theme of Thatcherite discourse on education, children were seen to inhabit bodies as yet unregulated by spiritual or moral awareness, they required adults to give them the 'capacity to say no' (*Woman's Own*, 17 April 1989:10). In addition, responsibility for the protection of children narrowed to the imaginary scene of the nuclear family and narrowed further to the 'interior reaches' of the inner individual and their conscience.[24] On the other hand, the connotations of abuse were removed from the home. The child became part of sullied nature, scarred by rubbish, dirt, vandalism, crime and ultimately the practices of socialism itself.[25]

Thatcher's uncharacteristically muted response to an area of major public concern and confusion revealed her broader reluctance to engage with any issue to do with sexuality. Yet sexuality and the body were central to this event. The Cleveland case concerned married men who were alleged to be sexually abusing their young daughters and sons. The crisis, though was also about the eradication of the fantasy of the innocent child, and the psychic crisis that is experienced by the child as object of adult longings, desires and fantasies is thrown very publicly into relief. At the centre of media confusion over victims and perpetrators, there were underlying cultural and institutional difficulties in acknowledging a child's testimony and its relationship to truth and 'adult' sexual knowledge (Campbell, 1988; Nava, 1988; Gittins, 1998:183). After Cleveland, a shift occurred in emphasis, in political and much media representation, away from the trauma of children at risk and towards the alleged incompetence of social workers and professionals in their medical diagnosis of abuse. The attacks invoked long-held fears of strangers stealing into the home and kidnapping 'our children', and the accusations of abuse were condensed and displaced onto the social workers themselves. In the process more complex discussions of power within the family or state intervention into domestic lives was largely left unexplored (Nava: 157).[26]

The conflicting discourses that responded to the Cleveland trauma highlighted attempts to relocate and strengthen eroded cultural boundaries of acceptable behaviour towards the child. These attempts were also present in much more benign but still deeply troubling and ambivalent forms in the Thatcherite claims for consumerism and the debates about education. Debates about the protection of the child and the accompanying imagery of lost or disappearing childhood were not only signs of a growing awareness of children in danger or at risk, but also an indication of adult fear that children were a contemporary source of danger or risk. The Conservative and New Right anxieties about the parameters of children's knowledge and their potential to make claims upon adult space, authority and even physical safety were one particular set of political responses which tapped into and amplified a broader set of cultural articulations of anxiety about the contemporary child. As the 1980s progressed the dominant imagery of innocent childhood became irreconcilable, not only with the representation of abused children but, increasingly, with political and media images of aberrant or monstrous children. Throughout the decade, calls for the protection of the child were often fuelled by fears of the monstrous overtaking the child. Towards the decade's end, with the

LET OUR CHILDREN GROW TALL

Cleveland crisis fresh in the public's mind, the image of the vulnerable and abused child expanded into a general vocabulary of abuse. The object of the ensuing protective measures and the focus of moral panic included the culture industries, professional social workers, single parents and teachers. In the early 1990s, political and popular discussion of fears about children 'surfing' the Internet for unsuitable material reinvigorated the previous decade's fears about 'video nasties' or sex education.[27] These discussions shared an anxiety that the contemporary child had slipped the net of childhood and the adult's regulation of his or her knowledge and pleasure. For Thatcherism, the figure of the precocious or transgressive child was deeply unsettling for it not only undermined the much hailed stability of the family but also unsettled the fantasy of the responsible consumer-driven home as successful lynchpin of social order.

References

1. Thatcher was appointed opposition spokesperson on Education on 21 October 1969 in succession to Edward Boyle. She became Secretary of State for Education and Science on 18 June 1970 when Edward Heath became Prime Minister.
2. Hugo Young has called this white paper 'the last great expansionist package to issue from the DES before the oil shock [of 1973]' (1989:71).
3. The analogy between the *Start Rite* advert and the Welfare State was developed from art historian David Mellor's discussion of the artist John Stezaker's uncanny images of the family in his 1990 series 'Care' (Williams, 1994:26).
4. In his legitimisation of the family, the right-wing theorist Ferdinand Mount cited Edmund Burke: 'To be attached to the subdivision, to love the little platoon we belong to in society, is the first principle, the germ as it were of public affections, it is the first link in the series by which we proceed towards a love to our country and to mankind ... We begin our public affections in our families. No cold relation is a zealous citizen' (Mount, 1982:172).
5. Here the influence of New Right economic thinking on Thatcher is evident, especially the New Right emphasis on the free market propounded by Friedrich Hayek and Milton Friedman (Gamble, 1988:56-9). Also the influence of the ideas of early liberal economists like Adam Smith can be traced in the emphasis on exchange to the mutual benefit of all concerned, the consumer as sovereign and the emphasis on the market as non-coercive exchange between free individuals (Heywood, 1992:17, 36-8).
6. Roland Barthes in 'Rhetoric of the Image' referred to the 'euphoric values'

of certain advertising images (Barthes, 1977:35). I am drawing here on Patricia Holland's analysis of 'the child' in advertising imagery (Holland, 1992: 18).

7. Family Income Supplement leaflet (FIS 1/Nov 78) issued by the Department of Health and Social Security (DHSS).

8. Thatcher placed the initial meeting of the Family Policy Group as early June 1982 and the first official meeting was in July (Thatcher, 1993:279). The Conservative ministers involved were Keith Joseph, Willie Whitelaw, Geoffrey Howe, Norman Tebbit, Michael Heseltine, Norman Fowler and Neil MacFarlane. Janet Young was invited to join in October 1982.

9. Mount, chief architect of the Family Policy Group, advised Thatcher in the early 1980s through his post in the Central Policy Review Staff Policy Unit.

10. Mount drew from Jeremy Seabrook's *What Went Wrong: Working People and the Ideals of the Labour Movement* (1978) (Mount: 167-9).

11. In this sense Mount could be seen to be replicating many of the nostalgic traits of Seabrook. For a critique of Seabrook see Carolyn Steedman's autobiography, *Landscape for a Good Woman* (1986).

12. The slogan 'parent power' was used during the run-up to the 1987 election and appeared in political and media response to the 1988 'tightening' of the curriculum. Critics within Thatcher's party of 'parent power' and the emphasis on 'parental choice' in the discussions surrounding the education reforms of 1988 included the former Prime Minister Edward Heath and Sir Ian Gilmour, who had been a member of Thatcher's first Cabinet (Gilmour, 1992:161-174; Wagg, 1996:19).

13. See for example the controversy over the 'Black Papers'; a collection of articles (appearing from 1968) authored by Brian Cox, Professor of English at Manchester University, Tony Dyson, a teacher of literature and Rhodes Boyson, Head of Highbury School. These were written in response to the inauguration of comprehensive schooling during the late 1960s. The authors argued for the restoration of 'discipline' and 'standards' to schooling (Wagg, 1996:12). See also the controversy over the 1976 'William Tynedale affair' in which the staff of a London borough primary school came into conflict with parents over progressive educational practices (Holland, 1992:76-81; Letwin, 1992: 232; Wagg, 1996:16)

14. Maurice Cowling, a fellow of Peterhouse, Cambridge University edited a collection of *Conservative Essays* (1978) that included Peterhouse graduates George Gale, Roger Scruton and Peregrine Worsthorne. Other prominent Peterhouse social authoritarians included novelist Kingsley Amis, Thatcher's biographer Patrick Cosgrave, John Vincent (regular writer for *The Times*) and Colin Welch (contributor to the *Spectator* and

the *Telegraph* group). Scruton produced a sustained argument for social authoritarianism in *The Meaning of Conservatism* (1980) (Edgar, 1986).

15. The central provisions of the Act were the introduction of a national curriculum of ten compulsory subjects, arranged around the core subjects of maths, science and English; the entitlement for state schools to 'opt out' of local authority control and become government grant maintained; regular tests for children with results made public; the opportunity for schools to enrol as many children as they thought appropriate (Wagg, 1996:18).

16. Letwin also had strong links with the Institute of Economic Affairs and was a member of the Tory Philosophy Group.

17. Anne Marie Smith provides a detailed account of the campaign for and implementation of Section 28 of the Local Government Act 1987-8 during 1986-7 that prohibited the teaching of the acceptability of homosexuality as a 'pretended family relationship'. She argues that this campaign prepared the way for homophobic elements in the subsequent 1987 Conservative Party election campaign (Smith, 1994:Ch.5).

18. One example of this contemporary concern over endangered, lost, stolen or disappearing childhoods can be signalled by a few examples of recently published book titles: *The Rise and Fall of Childhood* (Somerville, 1982), *The Disappearance of Childhood* (Postman, 1982), *Children without Childhood* (Winn, 1984), *Innocent Victims* (Gilmour, 1988), *Broken Promise: The World of Endangered Children* (Allesbrook and Swift, 1989), *Stolen Childhood* (Vittachi, 1989). These texts are all cited by Sharon Stephens in her introduction to the published collection of papers from the 1992 international conference 'Children at Risk' (Stephens, 1995a:9).

19. Market forces and the development of new media forms were important, for example, in the deregulation of the charity sector under Margaret Thatcher at the same time as the development of the glossy, advertisement filled Sunday supplements in the 1980s. Consequently, alongside the new extended magazine-format discussion of current issues such as domestic child abuse or child starvation in the Third World in the Sunday supplements one could see disturbing representations of the homeless, starving or abused child in adverts for charities (Holland, 1992:166ff; Scott, 1996:109ff).

20. Critics have argued that the welfare system of social policy and practice was itself imbued with class and gender-inflected assumptions about appropriate domestic circumstances and child-rearing practices which informed the state's willingness to intervene in and regulate primarily working-class 'problem' families (Muncie and Wetherall: 1995).

21. Between the spring and early summer of 1987 these two paediatricians diagnosed 121 cases of sexual abuse of children aged, on average, between

6-9 years. After months of legal contestation, 26 of these children from 12 families were declared by the judges to have been wrongly diagnosed. In contrast, the account that continues to be repeated in the media is that most cases were cleared (Campbell, 1988; Nava, 1988). Stuart Bell, the local Labour MP for Middlesborough, who supported a number of families in their campaign against the decision to remove their children into local authority care provides an alternative account in *When Salem Came to the Boro* (1988).

22. *Woman's Own*, 31 October 1987:10; *Woman*, 4 June 1988:32; *Chat*, 18 March 1989:3; *Woman's Own*, 17 April 1989:8.

23. Grandson Michael was born to Mark and Diane Thatcher on 28 February 1989.

24. Marilyn Ivy (1995) has noted a similar narrowing of responsibility in America during the Reagan-Bush presidencies. She draws interesting parallels between the moral panics arising over drug and child abuse in the United States and the conservative emphasis on the breakdown of the nuclear family as the source of the so-called outbreaks of abuse. She makes links between this political discourse and medical and psychoanalytical discourse on recovery from addiction (from shopping to drugs) which focus on the location and healing of the 'lost inner child'. She suggests that both the political and the medical or psychoanalytic avenues narrow the responsibility of abuse and addiction to the 'dysfunctional' family and ultimately the dysfunctional subject within it.

25. In 1989, Thatcher brought this emphasis on the child as part of a polluted environment to the fore. Once again her status as a grandmother was stressed as she tapped into the 'great burst of public interest' in green politics (Thatcher, 1995:638). Her concerns as a grandmother were stressed in reports on her speech to the 44th United Nations General Assembly (November 1989). The *Express* (9 November 1989) reported that she 'sounded a dramatic Doomsday warning' on overpopulation and pollution. In an interview in *Chat* (18 March 1989:3), Thatcher moved from describing the graffiti and litter-strewn Britain to her 'crusade' against such vandalism, graffiti and violent crime. Part of the polluted environment was, Thatcher warned, 'terrible crimes on children' (p3).

26. A number of Conservative women were unsympathetic of their critique. This perhaps indicated the long legacy within the Conservative Party of female support for law and order fuelled by an identification with the belief that women were the bulwark against feared versions of rampant male sexuality (Campbell, 1988:158; Nava, 1988:154-5).

27. In late 1991, these themes returned at the time of the implementation of the Children Act, whose purview included the codification of the rights of

children and of the family, alongside the need to restrain and limit social work intervention. The press coverage of the 'zealous ideology' and 'hysteria' of social workers returned in response to the removal of children from families in Nottingham, Rochdale and the Orkneys, following allegations of ritual or satanic abuse (Winter and Connolly, 1996).

CHAPTER FIVE:

The Nation Rampant

In that second election, at least, there can be no doubt that one of the things which Thatcher stood for was the desirability of war.

(Rose, 1988:48)

In this chapter, I move outwards from the previous discussion of the family as the microcosm of the Thatcherite nation to its national boundaries and imagined international enemies. The previous chapter was concerned with fantasies of restoration of harmony, self-suffi-ciency and ambition on the very local level of family life. This chapter is concerned with grander claims for national strength, the restoration of the national image in the eyes of international allies and enemies and, critically, the primary role of militarism in achieving these aspira-tions. The smallest and the largest components of national life are interlinked. Thatcher disavowed dependency, powerlessness and passivity in both the private and the public sphere and promised, instead, autonomy, control and activity in both spheres. The private space of the family was not only the model for public behaviour but also the utopia to be striven for and the 'Heaven' to be protected against the hostility and destruction that characterised her vision of the public political world.

The 1983 general election is central here because Thatcher's success in the election enabled her to consolidate her leadership and resolute persona. Importantly, the campaign foregrounded law and order and defence, issues which were central to both her construction as a notable political leader and to the popular appeal of Thatcherism.

In this chapter I consider the public articulation of core elements of Thatcherism: the promotion of a law-abiding but combative nation, the celebration of the military man as idealised public figure and the endorsement of nuclear armament as prerequisite of national survival. The election campaign illustrated a broader political strategy in which both anticipation and recollection of war provided powerful imagery of violence, disorder and fear that was displaced onto imaginary scenes of civil strife within the nation. Popular Cold War imagery of Stalinist dictatorship, of totalitarian oppression, spies and subversive agents plotting for democracy's downfall, all fed Thatcher's attack upon the allegedly 'militant' Labour Party. Such imagery was deployed in order to associate Labour and peace campaigners with communism, to portray them as subversive enemies within the nation's borders.

The accumulation of these images and the way that they were bound together in this moment constituted a posture that I designate the 'nation rampant': the nation poised to do battle, a nation convinced of 'the desirability of war' (Rose, 1988:48). Thatcher's investment in a bellicose nationalism and her fascination with the fighting man was acutely revealed in the emblem she selected to hand down through the Thatcher generations as an icon of her era. In 1994, three years after her removal from power, Thatcher's heraldic coat of arms was unveiled as she was given the title of Baroness of Kesteven. The coat of arms, which had taken two years to draft, featured two men holding a shield. On the right was the figure of a bewigged Sir Isaac Newton, carrying a set of scales, representing Thatcher's interest in science. Unsurprisingly, on the left was a military man, an officer of the Royal Navy, representing the Task Force that had sailed to and fought in the 1982 Falklands war. The motto underneath declared: 'Cherish Freedom' (Malone and Cohen, 1994:9). One year on, amidst a series of publicised celebrations of her seventieth birthday, Thatcher gave an exclusive interview for the *Mail* with her journalist daughter, Carol Thatcher. She acknowledged poet Rudyard Kipling's influence upon her, in particular his poems about heroic imperial masculinity. She confessed to her own private act of commemoration to the heroic imperial masculinity of the 'Unknown Soldier':

> Wherever I've been abroad I've visited war graves – those who gave their lives for us, buried halfway across the Empire. As you go along the rows of graves you come across a beautiful stone at the head of an Unknown Soldier and engraved upon it is 'Known to God'. And I thought – what a wonderful way to put it … [Kipling] chose it as the inscription for gravestones above unidentified bodies when he was literary adviser for the Imperial War Commission.
>
> (Thatcher, C., 1995:9)

Such identification with the soldier-hero was frequently made throughout the 1980s and hence is unsurprising in an article which attempted to shore up Thatcher's image as principled and passionate premier who made 'colossal changes' (Thatcher, C.: 9). She frequently invoked the glory of war: war transmuted destruction into heroism and reaffirmed the strength and international significance of the nation. She continually posed 'war' as an always-potential state for Britain and 'peace' as a temporary and volatile interlude between wars. This notion of war found its support in a range of civil and international conflicts which Thatcher used to summon up her own righteous battle and aggressive national defence.

1983 General Election campaign

> NOW IS THE HOUR – MAGGIE IS THE MAN
>
> *(Daily Express*, 9 June 1983:1)

> Who do we want, who do we need?
> It is a leader who is bound to succeed:
> Maggie Thatcher – just Maggie for me.
> These British Isles have found a fighter
> With the coolest of styles,
> No other politician comes within miles,
> Two, three, four, Thatcher, Thatcher, Thatcher,
> Not a man around to match her.
>
> (Thatcher's 1983 election campaign song, Cockerell, 1983:2)

There are certain moments of intense public scrutiny in the life of political parties: the replacement of a leader, a political scandal in the ranks, a grand national or international trauma – war, natural disaster, deep economic or socio-political instability – or, in democratic nations, the periodic electoral contest for government. An election campaign is an opportunity for national reassessment of the governing party and its leader. In such moments of public scrutiny political parties overtly flag nationalism. Politicians attempt to quicken patriotic fervour and link nationalistic sentiments to their party by conjuring up images of social disintegration should the 'other side' win. The nationalistic address is a powerful one that builds upon a range of familiar symbols, myths and narratives of community and of exclusion. Benedict Anderson famously suggested that the members of a nation 'will never know most of their fellow members, meet them, or hear of them, yet in the mind of each lives the image of their communion' (1983:15). A process of routine practices and unobtrusive representations largely maintains this communion: media images of the homeland, sporting events, political discourse on borders and migration or devolution (Anderson, 1983; Billig, 1995:42-3). National identification becomes emotionally and politically charged when the security of the nation appears troubled or threatened or when national celebrations or large-scale spectacular events punctuate everyday life. In such situations 'regressive' forms of identification can occur as individuals invest libidinal energy in collective-insularity and they succumb to the lure of strong authoritative leadership (Strachey, 1957 and 1960; Giddens, 1987:218). It was crucial to a successful re-election that Thatcher's image as authoritative Conservative Party leader was consolidated. Her general election victory on 9 June 1983 after one month's vigorous campaigning prepared the way for her continued clearing out of the 'wets' from her Cabinet and its refashioning in the Thatcherite mould. It also signalled a clear move away from the earlier domesticated media images of her, and while there were later fleeting attempts to soften her uncaring image, the establishment of Thatcher as heroic and authoritarian national leader held sway from this moment onwards.[1]

It is important to remember that from mid-1981, the Conservative government was deeply unpopular and consistently came third in opinion polls, while Thatcher received the lowest popularity ratings for any Prime Minister since the Second World War. The bleak backdrop to this public disaffection was high unemployment, rising inflation and disturbing scenes of civil unrest as frustration and racial tensions erupted in urban violence on the streets of Manchester, London and Liverpool, all of which continued into 1982.[2] When the Argentineans invaded the Falklands Islands in April 1982 they initiated a conflict which may have been fairly small-scale in military terms but which symbolically was of great significance to the ailing popularity of Thatcher and her government. Prior to the Falklands, Thatcher was still 'the most unpopular Prime Minister since polls began'.[3] After the cessation of conflict in June 1982, Thatcher's popularity rating had soared from a lowly 28 per cent to 51 per cent and the Conservative's ratings had also risen from 28 per cent support to 47 per cent support (*Guardian*, 14 April 1982:5; Negrine, 1989:157). The Falklands war was a leitmotif during the build-up to the 1983 general election. It provided the backdrop to the October 1982 Conservative Party Conference slogan, 'The Resolute Approach'. Militarism was crudely symbolised in the delegates' main platform, which resembled a grey battleship. The widow of 'war hero' Colonel 'H' Jones of the Second Battalion was present on the platform when Defence Secretary John Nott paid tribute to the 'guts' of the armed forces during the Falklands campaign. This was followed by an endorsement of Thatcher as 'a great national leader' (*Guardian*, 6 October 1982:24). The Falklands theme continued in a televised account of Thatcher's five-day visit to the Islands in January 1983 and in speeches leading up to the campaign (Barnett, 1982; Cockerell, 1988; Auchlich, 1992). Journalists cited the Falklands war as evidence of Thatcher's patriotism and intransigence and it became the key signifier in a series of counter-productive attacks on her by members of the Labour Party. The conflation of Thatcher and military supremacy extended the earlier widely-circulated descriptions of her leadership style as combative and conviction-led. The Falklands war gave concrete historical expression to this image and the accompanying Thatcherite moral discourse of individual struggle and national destiny.

The general election contest commenced on 9 May 1983 and finished one month later. Despite Thatcher's recollection that the Conservative campaign avoided the 'gladiatorial sport' of the 'media circus', in fact the sound bite and focus on political personality held sway (Thatcher, 1995:287). Contemporary public cynicism about political parties plus a Labour Party wrought with internal conflict enabled this personalisation of politics, and the Conservative Party exploited the phenomenon of 'leadership stretch' and represented Thatcher as outside government bureaucracy and in tune with 'the people's perspective (Foley, 1993:263-66). Cecil Parkinson, former Conservative Party Chairman, recalled Thatcher as the Conservatives' 'key weapon': the country was scoured months in advance for suitably photogenic locations, and tours concentrated on firmly Tory seats to avoid images of confrontation or voter dissatisfaction (Cockerell, 1988:279). The symbolic marking of the nation's territory as one's own is central to the campaigning process. Beginning in the West Country, Thatcher held a series of photo opportunities as she visited farms, factories, bakeries and chip shops. She posed in Harry Ramsden's famous fish and chip shop in Leeds, a police convalescent home, the Aston University Science Park and on Padstow harbour front where she brandished a 2lb lobster at a crowd of supporters. On 27 May, virtually every paper carried a photo of her eating fish and chips as the *Sun* gleefully commented on her inability to finish her 'man-sized meal' (p2). On 7 June, three days before the election result, she was shown in the *Sun* in frilly cap and overall at a marzipan factory under the headline 'Sweet Life for Maggie' (p2). Thatcher's image was of a leader engaged with everyday life surrounded by her supporters. But the quotidian was overlaid with her exceptional standing as a woman who had brought her nation to triumph in the recent Falklands war. Roland Barthes has explained the combination of complicity and idealisation offered in such promotional imagery:

> What we are asked to read is the familiar, the known; it offers to the voter his own likeness, but clarified, exalted, superbly elevated into a type ... the voter is at once expressed and heroized, he is invited to elect himself, to weigh the mandate which he is about to give with a veritable physical transference: he is delegating his 'race'.
>
> (Barthes, 1973:91-2)

The election campaign drew on popular images of the Empire and two World Wars, and heroic masculinity and military supremacy were erected to cover up the inadequacies and failures of the Thatcher government. Throughout the campaign Labour were represented as 'the pessimistic party' and the Conservatives as enterprising, brave modernisers open to change and opportunity. Thatcher was surrounded with adoring supporters and kept aloof from the potentially volatile unselected crowd as she travelled by plane, helicopter or well-equipped 'Robust Bus'. Worries about security and about disruptive hecklers led to all-ticket audiences for the six speeches at major rallies. At the Wembley Youth Rally in early June, Thatcher's audience was billed as 'Britain's Youth Strong and Free'. The three thousand young supporters were dressed in 'I love Maggie' T-shirts, hats and badges. In this stage-managed display of mass adulation an array of show business and sports celebrities – Jimmy Tarbuck, Steve Davis, Bob Monkhouse, Cilla Black and Kenny Everett – endorsed Thatcher amidst streamers, balloons and loud music. The words of speechwriter Ronald Millar's song 'Maggie for me' were distributed on cassette to the crowd and played on loudspeakers (CPA: GE 364/83). It was the first time that a British political party had produced a specially written campaign song and revealed the broader innovative approach to electioneering in which the Director of Marketing, Christopher Lawson, drew upon American presidential techniques.[4] Thatcher addressed the Wembley audience as the 'Party of today and tomorrow' who joined her in keeping 'Britain's future ... strong and free', for 'the age of the microchip has dawned in Britain and we're determined to see that the sun rises here too' (CPA: GE 554/83:1-3). Labour's manifesto was described as 'a grim catalogue' promising the youth standing before her 'a future wholly controlled by the operations of the Socialist state. To each, his own pigeon hole. From each, total conformity' (p6). Thatcher claimed that her party opposed dictators and invoked the Falklands: 'we think freedom is worth defending – even though it be challenged eight thousand miles away'. Drawing on Pericles of Athens, she added that: '"Freedom is the sweet possession of those alone who have the courage to defend it"'. This courage marked 'the great divide' between Conservatives and their opponents' (CPA: GE 554/83:10).

The themes that had prevailed throughout the campaign of leadership, patriotism and advanced technology were skilfully linked in this penultimate rally speech and extended in the final photo opportunity. Conservative Central Office provided four helicopters to fly her and the press to the Isle of Wight. In front of the British Hovercraft Corporation's hanger doors, which featured the biggest Union flag in the country, she was captured on film with arms outstretched. She then made an amphibious landing on another section of the island and was photographed posing like a figurehead on the prow of a military hovercraft (Cockerell, 1988:284). Although other Conservative ministers rarely capitalised upon the Falklands in this outspoken way in campaign speeches, it formed the implicit foundation to their portrayal of the party and Thatcher as strong and resolute. Such imagery was an attempt to wed Thatcher to a concept of British identity in which militarism, technology and the fulfilment of the nation's destiny were combined.

Defence

Thatcherism was strongly committed to an uncompromising and tough defence policy that was fuelled from the onset of Thatcher's leadership by vehement anti-Soviet rhetoric. Her first four years in office had seen an aggressive assertion of Britain's defence interests in both monetary and ideological terms. In the lead up to the 1979 general election, Thatcher combined an appeal to 'one nation' with an aggressive call to Britain to 'reassert itself as a force of freedom'. She claimed that her party continued with vigour the 'war on poverty and squalor' waged by her predecessors, but equally emphasised the aggressive defence of Britain as a 'fortress of freedoms' (CPA: GE 601/79:6). The Labour Party was maligned as the route to 'social disintegration and decay, the path to the pitiless society in which ruthless might rules, and the weak go to the wall' (p7). With direct reference to her 'Iron Lady' persona she located herself as 'the barrier of steel' between 'millions of people who are deeply frightened and anxious' and a menacing array of Communists, benefit 'scroungers', 'muggers' and Labour extremists (CPA: GE 601/79:7; *Guardian* 20 April 1979:4).

The vigilance counselled in her speeches was matched by an injection of government funds into defence. This involved an increase in public spending on defence which meant that in 1982-3 defence expenditure was 16.7 per cent higher in real terms than the last Labour government of 1978-9 (Riddell, 1983: 220-33). As she informed the Young Conservative Conference in February 1983: 'Peace is not bought cheaply. It cannot be won without cost. The cost of Britain's defence is the price we pay to prevent war. The money for our armed services is truly our "peace tax"' (CPA: 73/83:1). Furthermore, the Conservative Party was committed to nuclear weaponry allied to a strong identification with American foreign policy. This entailed the support of American troops siting Cruise missiles at Greenham Common and, some three years later in 1986, allowing British bases to be used for American air attacks upon Libya.

In the 1983 election, the three main parties disagreed fundamentally on the issue of Britain's nuclear deterrent.[5] The *Sun* captured the centrality of defence and of the nuclear debate in its gung-ho announcement of the electoral contest: 'Maggie Presses The Button' (10 May 1983:1). The election campaign was bracketed by Thatcher's emphasis on defence. At Prime Minister's Question Time at the beginning of her campaign she stressed: 'I am only too delighted to discuss defence. There will be no more important subject for the next four and a half weeks' (*The Times*, 11 May 1983:1). At the end of her campaign she told supporters at her Flyde Coast Rally: 'Never have I known defence play such a large part in a General Election campaign' (CPA: GE 583/83:4). The electorate was confronted with a set of choices on defence. The Labour Party was the first major political party in electoral history to offer a manifesto commitment to complete unilateral disarmament.[6] They endorsed a non-nuclear defence policy which included the removal of American bases and nuclear weapons from British soil, the abandonment of plans for Trident and Cruise missiles and planned to phase out Britain's existing nuclear arsenal within one term of office (Curtice, 1989:144). The SDP-Liberal Alliance was also locked into the nuclear debate. They supported the deployment of Cruise missiles at Greenham Common and NATO's 'dual-track' policy,[7] although unlike the Conservatives they agreed to the inclusion of Britain's existing Polaris nuclear weaponry in the Geneva negotiations between America and the USSR. They agreed with Labour that the proposed modernisation of Britain's weaponry through the Trident system should be abandoned. The Conservative Party were firmly committed to the planned deployment of Cruise missiles at Greenham Common in the immediate future, they supported NATO's dual-track policy and were strongly opposed to the inclusion of Britain's nuclear weapons in present negotiations on arms control (Butler and Kavanagh, 1984:256, 282).

More broadly, defence was a central issue. In campaign addresses, 98 per cent of Conservative and 92 per cent of Labour candidates, 88 per cent of Social Democrats and 87 per cent of Liberals dealt with the issues of defence, nuclear weapons and occasionally the risk of nuclear war (Butler and Kavanagh, 1984:255). In the crucial middle two weeks of the campaign, just under a third of the fifty-one Conservative ministerial speeches or addresses by letter to party workers prioritised defence.[8] On 17 May, the Defence Secretary Michael Heseltine sent a letter to Conservative candidates warning of the subversive threat of Campaign for Nuclear Disarmament (CND) agitators in marginal constituencies (CPA: GE 357/83).[9] The same day he gave a speech to the Watford constituency about the dangers of Labour's anti-nuclear defence policy (GE 367/83). The next day Douglas Hurd spoke to the Royal United Services Institute about the political implications of 'Arms Control' (CPA: GE 363/83). Hurd informed Littleborough and Saddleworth party workers that Labour's policy of unilateral disarmament was 'the real threat to peace', and former Conservative premier Edward Heath focused on defence in his address to party workers at Saltash (CPA: GE 393/83; GE 404/83). This prioritisation of defence and of nuclear weapons as campaign issues was echoed amongst the electorate (Marsh and Fraser, 1989:14). In surveys of the electorate, defence was consistently the second or third most important issue facing the country.[10] Correspondingly, the theme of defence was the most prominent in the lead stories on the election in the daily newspapers.[11]

Freedom from fear
In the 1983 election campaign, nuclear weaponry and military strength were tokens of virile national security and progression. Thatcher expressed an outspoken admiration of 'fighting men'; war and battle became the means to endow her own political identity with the

strength she admired in them. As indicated in Chapter Three, analogies can be drawn between the protective façade of female 'masquerade' and the camouflage of male 'display'. The attributes of the war leader or soldier-hero – the macho language, displays of physical zeal, rituals of collective control and obedience, pride in technical and military hardware – mask the vulnerability of the fighting man and attempt to conceal a collective lack of mastery. Thatcher's identification with fighting men and military leaders was well known and it was bound up with a bellicose stance which concealed, or attempted to conceal, her femininity and also the inevitably flawed, impossibly hyper-phallic masculinity that she adopted as her own.

This aspect of her persona was replayed in numerous journalistic sketches of her as the incarnation of wartime Conservative premier Winston Churchill. As early as 1978, a portrait of Thatcher in the *Sunday Times* was illustrated by a front-page photograph in which she stood, in blue patterned dress and pearls, completely dwarfed by a towering stone sculpture of Churchill (Peters, 1978). The caption read: 'A Portrait of Margaret Thatcher'. There is something vaguely uncanny about this photograph, and something acutely prescient for, in retrospect, it seems to foreshadow the immovable and colossal claim to power that Thatcher promoted as her self-image in her own years as premier. But also, this image revealed the debt that Thatcher held to the phallic father figure and the forms of embattled authority that she attempted to accrue as her own. In the accompanying article the photographer Eve Arnold captured Thatcher in a 'picture essay' on 'women in pursuit of power' (Peters, 1978:8-9). In the first photograph, Thatcher again stood dwarfed before a huge sculpture of Churchill by Oscar Lemon, who was then working on a portrayal of her as well. In the second photograph, the stone bust of Thatcher supplanted Churchill; in contrast with her regal bearing Churchill appeared almost humbled or bowed, the stone Churchill placed so its gaze rested on the flesh and blood Thatcher who dominated the frame.

Throughout the early 1980s Thatcher frequently referred to Churchill and drew directly from his speeches; for example in the Falklands conflict she compared her residence at Chequers with Churchill's respite from the stress of war there during World War Two (Keay, 1982). She also laid claim to the spirit of Conservative colleague and war hero Airey Neave who was a famous escapee from the Nazi prison camp Colditz and who had spoken and written extensively on his ordeal. Furthermore, he was a central figure in the promotion of Thatcher against Heath in 1975. At the First Airey Neave Memorial

Lecture in 1980, Thatcher recalled his spiritual strength to escape from Colditz. She stressed that the implements of escape, shovels and maps, for example, were never enough without the necessary spirit: 'a philosophy of freedom was an integral part of his character in peace, and in war' (CPA: TS 174/80:2). She added that the philosophy that guided Neave, in his wartime escape and in his life's work, was 'close' to her own (p4). Similarly, Thatcher regularly stressed her empathy with Napoleon and Wellington and attempted to bestow upon her own political reasoning their embattled imperialist protectionism (Barnett, 1982:Ch.3).

As a woman campaigning for a return to government office during 1982-3, she thus refused the limitations that were conventionally assigned to her gender in national discourses of battle and of war. Under conditions of 'total war' women have been conscripted to stand in for men on the 'home front', yet this mobilisation of fighting women has been hedged with provisos and anxieties about the erosion of femininity and of gendered and familial roles. In the imaginary total war that Thatcher invoked, the role of mobilised women was left for her female electorate as she adopted the masculinised role of authoritative, experienced war leader. The severance of Thatcher from 'ordinary' women, who watched and waited, had been achieved during the Falklands war and amplified in the media's reportage of that limited military engagement. The relatives of those serving the Task Force had a key function in the representation of the British home front. The 'wives, mothers and sweethearts' of the Task Force were used in numerous television and press accounts of the conflict to score the division between feminised relatives at home and masculinised fighting personnel.[12] Emotive images of waiting women were the media's surrogate for human and personal emotional involvement in a battle thousands of miles away (Glasgow University Media Group, 1985:Ch.6).[13]

To the Conservative Women's Conference held in the midst of the Falkland conflict, Thatcher spoke of 'the reality of war' and the shared knowledge that her audience held about 'the hazards', 'dangers' and 'formidable task' that faced 'our fighting men' (CPA: 405/82:2). Her speech set up a division between a female rationality that propelled Britain to war over an island that was 'family' and male tactical analysis from in the thick of the fighting, 8000 miles away. Immediately following the conflict, Thatcher frequently explained her engagement in combat in domestic and matriarchal terms. She informed George Gale of the *Express* that the conflict and its outcome obsessed her. Her comment was characteristically grandiloquent: 'I had the winter at the back of my mind. The winter. What will the winter do? The wind, the cold. Down in South Georgia the ice, what will it do? It beat Napoleon at Moscow' (Barnett, 1982:91). This self-comparison with a warring Emperor was immediately domesticated as Thatcher located her decision-making skills in the experience of being one of an army of housewives who managed and organised and planned and 'were on the job 24 hours a day' (Barnett: 91). Interviewed by Douglas Keay in *Woman's Own* in August 1982, Thatcher spoke with emotion of the Task Force invasion back in May. She placed herself as anxious woman in contact with, but absent from, the dangers of the frontline:

> I assumed the landing was taking place, but when there's something big going on you never want to worry about your communication line back from the front. You must let the men get on with it. Don't fuss them. Their main job is to do the task efficiently. We who are waiting must wait.
>
> (Keay, 1982:33)

At the 1982 Conservative Women's Conference the pressure of reconciling gender roles was crystallised. Here, Thatcher spoke as a woman but primarily as party and war leader bound to the fighting men she led and to whom she occasionally deferred. There was a perceptible strain in Thatcher's speech between first and second person pronouns that registered her attempted manoeuvre across the gender divide. 'You' was used to signal Thatcher's separation from the Conservative women who were engaged in 'debating fighting policy' while 'our' 'fighting men' were 'engaged in one of the most remarkable military operations in modern times' (CPA: 405/82:1). Thatcher revealed her own intimate knowledge of soldierly activity, fighting skill and resolution in the face of 'formidable problems in difficult terrain with a hostile climate' (p2). 'We' was both the nation and often Thatcher and her government who had the power to despatch 'more than a 100 ships, and 27,000 sailors, marines and soldiers' across the South Atlantic (p1). Thatcher distanced herself from the women who had heard second hand of military attacks upon the Task Force, and she joined them in trepidation as women who did not yet know the number of casualties. She frequently switched identification between 'the British' or 'the people' and sometimes the Conservative women whose 'hearts go out to all those who had men' in the damaged *Atlantic Conveyor* or sunken *HMS Coventry* (p1). Foremost, she situated herself as the military commander who bore the strategically powerful political and territorial gaze. She witnessed failed international peace negotiations, knew the positioning of the 'amphibious landing at San Carlos Bay' where the men waited to 'retake the islands', had 'studied seven sets of [diplomatic] proposals' and moved with the military 'to recover by force what was taken by force' (pp2-4).

In the much quoted Cheltenham Address, made in the immediate aftermath of the Falklands war, Thatcher placed her idealised resolute and victorious nation in a masculine lineage of 'fathers and grandfathers' who had met 'the demands of war'. The 'Falklands Factor' was bandied as evidence of national affiliation under the threat of aggression and the Task Force was 'an object lesson' that revealed the ability of each man and woman to fulfil their allocated task competently and with speed for the greater good (Barnett, 1982:149-53).[14] At the Flyde Coast Rally, during the 1983 campaign, she extended this message under the heading 'In Tune With The People', in which she presented her premiership as a reaching out to 'real people' and the 'real world'. The common-sense restoration of political and national order was expressed as the logical outcome of this reforged link with a self-managing, self-defining people. She positioned herself on the side of 'families' not 'political theorists and sociologists', 'trade unionists' not 'their leaders', 'parents' not 'educational experts' and, in doing so, articulated a distinction between civil society and a Labour Party that exploited people's 'natural fear':

> The British people want to see their country properly defended ... This country has stood alone so often in the defence of liberty. People do not want us to be the first to crumble in the test of resolve. The Labour Party, I think, hoped to exploit the natural fear and dislike of nuclear weapons ... Labour's defence policy would create a new and frightening instability in Europe. It would put peace at risk. It would make war more likely. And the British people know it.
>
> (CPA: GE 583/83:4)

At the subsequent Wembley Youth Rally, Thatcher condemned Labour's ability to defend and fight for the nation. Its nuclear policy was 'one-sided abandonment of our deterrent'; it would break the 'balance' of strength between East and West. She claimed that Britain would be 'wide open' to Russian 'blackmail' and domination (CPA: GE 554/83:11). Here as in other campaign speeches she reduced the abstract nature of nuclear warfare to the armed conflict of more conventional military engagements. She associated her electoral promises of freedom within the law to 'the swift and sure response of young men' in the Falklands war and her own militaristic precision in dealing with aggressors.

In May 1984 Thatcher reflected on the key principle that had informed her campaign. In 'What Unites Us As A Nation' she informed her all-female audience that she believed 'freedom from fear' was the crucial defining element of national affiliation: 'I believe that people want freedom from fear: fear of violence; fear of intimidation; freedom to go about their daily duties and interests unhindered and freedom to express their views however controversial those views might be' (CPA: 376/84:7). This was a familiar form of Conservative address to female party members which summoned fantasies of their potential vulnerability. It is on this 'terrain of fear' that feminism and Conservatism meets and divides (Campbell, 1987:148). Contemporary feminism has engaged with the broader social structures that render women vulnerable. In contrast, Conservatism has conventionally operated within a more individualised preoccupation with political mobilisation of good against bad, right versus wrong in which women have been addressed as moral guardians, their role condensed into a doctrine 'of eternal vigilance – a kind of permanent war economy' (Campbell: 148).

Thatcher's abstract 'fear' was, in keeping with other speeches, grafted to a number of political enemies or contemporary moments of political dissent. At this moment the miners' strike was in the forefront of political and media debate. Thatcher located 'fear' in the 'ugly scenes of violence which have disfigured our television screens night after night' in which striking miners allegedly intimidated those who wished to work and support their families (CPA 376/84:7). She appealed to the Conservative women as physically vulnerable but also as the moral fibre of the party, in need of protection but also able, like her, to galvanize their personal discipline against the random forces of rogue masculine assault. Furthermore, she defined theirs and the nation's freedom negatively, for it was, first and foremost, a freedom *from* fear, as if this was the existent condition of the nation-state.

Gender was thus central to Thatcher's political mobilisation of the nation and its defence. Its significance was underlined by Thatcher's outspoken claims to aggressive, war-like national leadership, because the modern Western European nation and its strength and protection rest upon the 'naturalised equation of masculinity, military prowess and the nation' (Dawson, 1994:17). Primarily it is men who have been, and still are, expected to answer the state's call to arms and the deeds of battle are expressed through images of heroic masculinity. Metaphors of battle operate through gendered notions of separate spheres in which men are called upon to act for love of country and women are called upon to sacrifice their loved ones to the greater good. The complexity of men and women's participation in the nation is reduced to compelling narratives of triumph and duty. Thatcher's speeches to the Conservative women on 'fear' reproduced this divide which she implied that she alone could span.

From the outset, the imagined community of Britain (or frequently England) has been yoked to aggressive fantasies of atavism and civilisation, of territory to plunder and of the vulnerable British islands. These fantasies were generated and given shape through the antagonisms of expansionist trade and war. The cohesion of British national identity, its 'sense of mission and providential destiny' and the protection of its borders, were secured through successive acts of violence (Colley, 1992:18, 53). Thatcher's Churchillian rhetoric at the Flyde Coast Rally (cited above), made blatant the political investment in the fantasy of war in times of peace: '"It is in the years of peace that wars are prevented ... peace will not be possible without the virtues that make victory possible in war"' (CPA: GE 583/83:10).

In this emphasis Thatcher was not alone. In the modern Western nation-state definitions of 'peace' as, for example, quiet or tranquillity are usurped by an emphasis on peace as a precarious condition. Peace is considered an interlude for the nation or a buffer between bouts of war or civil strife and Thatcher accentuated the nation's constant spectre of violence. In 'The Modern Janus' (1977:348), Tom Nairn insisted on the intrinsically two-faced nature of nationalism: 'through nationalism, societies try to propel themselves forward to certain kinds of goals (industrialisation, prosperity, equality with other peoples etc.)'. They do so *by a certain sort of regression* (Nairn: 348, his emphasis). He stressed that nationalism, whatever its 'constructive, democratic impulse' contained a 'dark, rapacious chauvinistic side'. All nationalistic mobilisation stirred up 'the powers of the Id': 'prejudice, sentimentality, collective egotism, aggression' (Nairn: 348). Thatcher's prolific use of military rhetoric, her discourse of punitive law and order and emphasis on aggressive defence re-presented the violent possibilities of the nation-state as the people's constitutional and legal entitlement to peace, order and safety. The Thatcherite inflection of nationalism brought 'chauvinism', 'prejudice' and 'collective egotism' to the fore (Nairn: 348). Sarah Benton proposed that Thatcher's gender compounded a familiar Conservative nationalist address. She suggested that 'Conservative leaders on the whole are like women inciting men to take up arms and behave like true men': 'That's who we were under Thatcher – independent pirates and warriors ... Perhaps that is part of the thrill of being a Conservative Home Counties lady representative; without shifting her bottom from the conference seat, she can fly off in her head to lay waste to Marxists, miners, muggers, whoever is the enemy of the hour' (Benton, 1996:27).

Fear of nuclear attack and national enemies

> Whatever the uncertainties surrounding it, the idea of nationality remains deeply embedded in the political unconscious, and the sleeping images which spring to life in times of crisis – the fear, for instance, of being 'swamped' by foreign invasion – testify to its continuing force. Fantasies of national rebirth remain a stock-in-trade of political rhetoric ...
>
> (Samuel, 1989:xxxii)

The 1983 general election represented the consolidation of Thatcher's ideological movement away from 'one nation' Conservatism and its replacement with an adversarial and divisive form of national address. Thatcher, through her invigorated emphasis on aggressive national interest, revealed the unconscious undercurrents of aggression, which inform all nationalistic demarcations of territory, people and place. Freud, in *Civilisation and its Discontents* (1930), clarified the ambivalent identifications that hold together a national community and, importantly, emphasised discord as a core element of the address to, and construction of, the national subject. Rather than the physical boundaries of a nation, Freud focused on the structure of feeling and affect that protects and unifies a nation's inhabitants. The modern nation, he implied, was inherently fragile and also unstable. Thatcher's consistent deployment of extreme right wing discourses of national identity and authority overtly demonstrated the projected aggression and the attendant fear of its return that inform fantasies of national strength. Paradoxically, the emotional ties that bind together the disparate people of a nation are maintained through the very instability that Thatcher exacerbated and laid bare: aggression and fear. Freud used the analogy of constant feuding or ridiculing between people of adjoining territories – the Spanish and Portuguese, Northern and Southern Germans, the English and Scots – to illustrate the ambivalent identifications of love and hate that bind a community together. The nationalistic address, then, is partly about the binding together 'of a considerable number of people' so long as there are others 'left over to receive the manifestations of their aggressiveness' (Freud, 1930:305). In addition, the nation is always split between an external border with other nations outside and constantly changing internal imaginary borders, which locate and contain dissenting spaces and subjects.

Thatcher pushed at the extremes of nationalism, proclaiming aggression in international debate and nuclear armament as the best defences of the beleaguered nation. In the 1983 general election the fantasies of annihilation and exclusion that underpinned this nationalistic message overwhelmed and supplanted her emphasis on the freedom of the economic market. She summoned up a vision of legitimate extreme force and of potential war to match the might and danger of calculating national enemies. Freud's rumination on war described the ambivalence of national identification worked to a pitch. In war, the fears of one's mortality and annihilation and the consolatory fantasy of an afterlife (at the very least in other's memories) spill into the tortuous identification with and horror of the uncannily powerful and indestructible enemy who may be hiding very near (Freud, 1915). The ambivalent identifications of love and hate occupy the same psychic space and in war they are writ large. 'The paranoid projections "outwards" return to haunt us and split the place from which they are made' (Bhabha, 1994:149). In Thatcher's campaign speeches, love of nation was inextricable from hate of enemies without and within the nation's borders. She brought into focus the rampant aggression that subtends national identification. Throughout the 1983 campaign Thatcher argued that a safe nation was dependent on nuclear weapons for 'peace' to be maintained and claimed that a powerful nation was defined by its possession of nuclear weaponry and their ability to annihilate the enemy. This argument was accompanied by a concerted vilification of the British anti-nuclear lobby.

The decision by NATO in December 1979 to deploy American Cruise missiles in Western Europe meant that Britain was faced with the prospect of a large nuclear arsenal being placed on its soil from the latter part of 1983. This met with widespread public disapproval, not necessarily of nuclear weapons *per se* but sometimes of American colonisation and the possible launch of Cruise missiles from British soil.[15] Under President Reagan's leadership, the White House altered its nuclear strategy from a thirty-year-old concept of mutually assured destruction (MAD) to the notion that a nuclear war was winnable. In

March 1983, President Reagan made his 'star wars' speech allocating 25 billion dollars to the Strategic Defence Initiative: a defence umbrella to protect America (Kennedy Martin, 1990). Simultaneously, the Conservative government's decision to replace Britain's own independent nuclear system Polaris with the new Trident missile was met with deep ambivalence on the part of the public. The replacement of Polaris with multi-strike warheads signalled a more aggressive nuclear stance. Opinion polls indicated that while many of the public were for retaining some form of independent nuclear force, a large number were strongly opposed to Trident (Butler and Kavanagh, 1984:282; Rootes, 1989:99; Taylor, 1986:211). In the early 1980s membership of CND, the anti-nuclear pressure group, soared as nuclear weapons became a major public concern. In January 1980, a Gallup poll revealed that 57 per cent of respondents believed there was 'much danger' of world war compared with only 15 per cent of respondents in 1975 (Rootes, 1989:99). Fear of nuclear attack, of extinction, formed an imaginary reservoir that was drawn on by 'pro' and 'anti-nuclear' campaigners and, in the light of growing popular support, the anti-nuclear lobby was styled as a palpable enemy within the nation for the Conservative Party.

In a tense alliance, CND and the women protesters at Greenham Common (who had become the subject of intensified media criticism since late 1982) brought nuclear weaponry into the public domain. They attempted to present the public with an alternative image to challenge the imposing official discourses that conventionally and imposingly presented nuclear weaponry in scientific, technological and militaristic jargon. They humanised the dangers of nuclear warfare and frequently expressed the very physical and emotional consequences of threat from nuclear escalation and the arms race. The Greenham women in particular drew upon deeply feminine imagery of birth, nature, parenting and artistic creativity to counter the scientific and technologically informed discourses of rationality in which the nuclear arms race was politically framed. The women wove photographs of loved ones, children's toys, paintings and handicraft into the barbed wire perimeter of the military base in an attempt to conjure up the horrible potential human loss contained in each missile. During the 1983 election, CND recognised the prominence of nuclear defence as a campaigning issue and used professional advertising people for the first time (Taylor, 1986:209). The main CND advert published in the press captured their message of human vulnerability and potential eradication of the future with a prominent image of three children anchored by the caption: 'In the nuclear election vote for them. You *can* influence the nuclear arms question on June 9th … it's your choice' (*Sun*, 6 June:2).

CND General Secretary Monsignor Bruce Kent, E.P. Thompson (a founder of the peace movement) and Labour leader Michael Foot (also one of the original founders of CND in 1957-8) countered Conservative claims that nuclear weaponry had maintained the peace since 1945. They argued that the increasing complexity of the weapons made them vulnerable to human and mechanical failure and the constant rearmament process was, in fact, an endless struggle for power that could only end in mass extermination. The CND protest was pitched as civil society against a potentially violent state. They focused on political protest which took the nuclear issue onto the streets via petitions, 'die-ins', the promotion of nuclear free zones, marches and so on. Their arguments were often linked to protest over welfare distribution and a waste of resources.[16] The initial impetus for people joining CND during the early 1980s was expressed by members as fear of a world out of control; in response CND adopted a political message that emphasised physical security in hard economic times (Rootes, 1989:97-9). It could be argued that CND's emphasis on individual vulnerability and their increased focus on American occupation of British bases was a differently inflected response to the same fear of social disorder, of a world out of control, that fuelled voters allegiance to Thatcher's authoritarian response.

Minister of Defence Michael Heseltine developed and co-ordinated political propaganda in reaction to the growing success of the anti-nuclear movement. Conservative production of pro-nuclear speeches, publicity and information literature was covertly handled following Labour opposition to their plans to commence a £1 million campaign against CND. Most was produced through the newly established Ministry of Defence special propaganda unit Defence Secretariat 19 which was disbanded in the September after the 1983 election due to Conservative confidence that they had reclaimed the nuclear argument (Young, 1990:129-33).[17]

Late March 1983 also witnessed Conservative opposition to disarmament on the part of Tory women. Achieving much more favourable coverage in the press than the Greenham campaigners, Lady Olga Maitland, (Conservative *Sunday Express* columnist) and Conservative MP Angela Rumbold formed the counter-pressure group 'Families for Defence' to challenge the peace movement on its own terms. Originally named 'Women for Defence', it was swiftly decided that men should not be excluded from the group or its title. Lady Maitland acknowledged the womanly virtues that she saw in the Greenham protest as inspiration for this Conservative counter attack: 'it was a brilliant idea to have women only, who are home and hearth by nature, doing a great demonstration which involved great hardship' (Campbell, 1987:135).[18]

Families for Defence had strong links to the Conservative government (The Ministry of Defence and the Foreign Office both published leaflets and pamphlets for them). They also had links with the recently formed Conservative umbrella organisation Committee for Peace with Freedom headed by the MP Winston Churchill who had been appointed by Thatcher to mobilise a campaign against anti-nuclear protesters in the run-up to the general election (*Economist*, 5 February 1986:36; Young, 1990:129). They achieved positive coverage particularly in the *Times*, *Sunday Times*, *Express* and the *Mail* in which their 'true' family values and 'womanliness' were emphasised often as a means to authenticate their desire for peace and, by contrast, to condemn the Greenham women (*Times*, 2 May 1983:18; Young, 1990:132-3).[19] Headlines such as 'Greenham invaders bring babies' and 'Baby on front line at air base' in the middle market newspapers signalled the protestors' contrasting dereliction of maternal care (*Mail*, 2 May: 6; *Mail* 12 May: 17). While the Greenham women aroused a degree of hostility that far exceeded the bother caused by their pickets and their encampment outside the Cruise missile base, the Families for Defence received far less opposition and most from within the higher reaches of their party. This contrast resulted not only from their different political ends, one group for and one group against nuclear armament. Rather they represented different, powerfully symbolic inflections of a feminised concern for the nation. Families for Defence drew upon the conventional Conservative emphasis on women as essentially passive, as nurturing, as mothers and wives who bore responsibility for the protection of the private sphere. While the Greenham protestors also drew on maternal and passive imagery, they embodied social marginalisation and they explicitly linked warfare to institutionalised patriarchy. They lived 'on the wire', 'on the perimeter' of a closed, monumental, military complex (Stallybrass and White, 1986:24). Furthermore, unlike the Conservative women, they lived only with other women, their peace movement included only women and they occupied common land in tents and plastic sheeting. As such they triggered powerful associations seeming to transgress 'gender, territorial boundaries, sexual preference, family and group norms'

(Stallybrass and White: 24).

Authority and disorder

> Civilisation, therefore, obtains mastery over the individual's dangerous desire for aggression by weakening and disarming it and by setting up an agency within him to watch over it, like a garrison in a conquered city.
>
> (Freud, 1921:316)

> Given the choice, the nation will infinitely prefer the vision of Maggie in a Union Jack to the Beast in a Red Flag.
>
> (*Sun*, 3 June 1983:6)

So far I have outlined the Conservative commitment to strong defence and the corresponding emphasis on the possession of nuclear weaponry to secure that image of strength in the face of feared international threat. There was a fixated and compensatory aspect to the fantasy of encroached borders and subversion within the nation's boundaries that could be found in Conservative campaign speeches. Attempts to conjure up the fortified nation also inevitably summoned scenes of the social bond's dissolution. The nuclear bomb as a symbol both of utter destruction and of unquestionable salvation locked the party into vacillation between two extreme positions. Nuclear weaponry was praised as the only power omnipotent enough to match the potential for annihilation threatened by other nations' possession of equal nuclear arms. In this sense the nuclear bomb was endowed with almost magical powers of survival: its possession alone, rather than its use, would instil fear and respect in adversaries and would fortify borders.

Guilt, greed and aggression underpin collective identification as much as, perhaps more, than generosity, innocence and love. In Freudian theory, the founding of civilised identification rests upon the precarious repression of aggressive drives and illicit desires. Fantasies of abandon, and of an armoured and controlling self, struggle within each subject. Conservatism, with its emphasis on the preservation of stability and its attendant fascination with social chaos, may be understood as a political form attuned to and invigorated by this struggle. Thatcherism amplified and exulted in fantasies of this dynamic: violent transgression and absolute control were continually replayed. The 1983 campaign illustrated how Thatcher held together these oppositions and placed herself at the centre of extreme violence and

154

extreme social control. That positioning, and its force, leads to an interpretation of her persona as the punitive super-ego.

In *Civilisation and its Discontents* (1930) Freud described the super-ego as a perverse, cruel underside and bolster to the social law. The subject's inclination to aggression is at odds with the ordering imperatives of civilisation. Crucially, Freud illustrated that the subject's aggression is introjected, 'sent back to where it came from' (Freud, 1930:315). It forms that portion of the ego that splits off and, as super-ego, draws on the violence it controls in the tortuous scenes of guilt it inspires. The harsh strictures of the super-ego are formed out of redirected transgressive drives as the subject's aggression is mobilised against him or her as social or moral injunctions. Thus a fear of authority results in renunciation of violence, greed, lust – the dark and dangerous pleasures – alongside a masochistic desire for punishment (Freud, 1930:315-323).

Lacanian readings of this relationship between the law of the symbolic order and its underside stress the dependency and the slippage between the two. The super-ego is the point at which obligation to obey is reversed into 'an enslavement of the subject to the imperative of enjoyment' (Silvestre in Salecl, 1994:100). It is the point at which duty and desire bound to the law are always marked by the 'stain' of surplus enjoyment and potential transgression (Salecl, 100-104; see also Copjec, 1989; Žižek, 1991:32-4 and 257-259; Rose, 1993:154-5). As Freud illustrated, the more one renounces enjoyment in the name of desire within bounds, the more one is obliged to renounce it: 'Every renunciation of instinct becomes a dynamic source of conscience and every fresh renunciation increases the latter's severity and intolerance' (Freud, 1930:321). In a society in which external authority is reinforced with vigour, the self-regulating interdictions proliferate (Freud: 320). In Chapter Three, I discussed Thatcher's endorsement of the self-regulation of guilt, conscience and moral discipline. While she sanctioned the strictures of the law, she suggested that in the final instance 'individuals are ultimately accountable for their actions', they must draw on their moral reserves to counter and redirect 'the timeless and bottomless resources of old-fashioned human wickedness' (Thatcher, 1995:626). In speeches, interviews and biography she presented herself as the exemplary model of self-discipline and self-direction, her moral values allegedly informing her political beliefs. But I would argue that she operated as a harsh and ferocious super-ego for the nation. As such, the force of her persona derived from its dependency on the 'timeless and bottomless resources of old-fashioned wickedness' that she continually raised as her enemy without and within. Thatcher exerted a vengeful authority, an Old Testament 'eye for an eye' unyielding discipline, that drew upon all the images of irrational, chaotic or violent energies that she claimed to tame. In her speeches she staged imaginary scenes of endless punishment and endless transgression. This is why she was often presented by Conservative colleagues as heroic but terrifyingly intransigent.

The 'horror' of nuclear warfare

Thermonuclear weaponry can be seen as the latest high-technological extension of the industrialisation of warfare that coexisted with the consolidation of the modern state. Nuclear warfare, by necessity, relies upon the horrible anticipation of its effect. The balance of power between nations is maintained through the imagination of likely violence and the fantasy of total obliteration. Unlike the two modern world wars, here there would be no messy carnage, no surviving witnesses, and no bloody engagement of bodies on the battlefield. Thatcher's advocating of nuclear warfare revealed the modern nation-state's symbolic use of military violence. She presented herself as the modern utilitarian hero: she met the military challenge of nuclear opponents through the calculating use of modern scientific knowledge and technology. She constructed herself as the warrior at the outpost of modern scientific warfare and used the imagery of nuclear escalation and the adversity of the arms race to cast her role as national leader who sheltered and protected. At her Harrogate campaign speech, she contrasted 'peace' attained by the possession of a '[nuclear] deterrent' with the terrible carnage that had occurred beyond the boundaries of 'the West': 'Outside Europe, where there is no deterrent, peace has been hard to come by. 158 wars since 1945 – ten million people killed – millions more maimed. There are vast numbers who cannot take peace for granted. Theirs is a terrible warning' (CPA: GE 438/83:17). She told her audience that 'everyone wants peace. We know the horror and sacrifice and waste of war'. But, she admonished, 'peace doesn't come by accident. It is a rarity in the world today' (CPA: GE 438/83:17). Thatcher warned that 'outside Europe' there were hundreds of wars, millions killed or maimed, whereas the nuclear deterrent had 'kept the peace in Europe for thirty-seven years' (CPA: 73/83:5).

This equation of nuclear weaponry with political authority exposed the masking operations of 'phallic' power. At the National Young Conservative Conference, just before the election campaign, Thatcher focused on defence and disarmament. In her speech force, or rather the threat of force, was an integral element of national self-definition and that force was the only means to survival. She declared: 'What a cruel irony it is that the word "peace" has been hijacked by those who seek one-sided disarmament. Ironic because if only one side disarms the other is far more tempted to aggression' (CPA: 73/83:1). She claimed that the logic of the unilateralists was faulty, they relied on a misplaced 'trust' that the Soviet enemy would not abuse a disarmed Britain. 'Sadly', she mused, 'there are many in CND who minimise the danger from the Soviet Union and refuse to acknowledge its tyranny in order to promote their scheme of one-sided disarmament' (p2). 'The sheer horror of modern warfare', reflected Thatcher, could 'drive people to unreason. For as Edmund Burke said, "No passion so effectually robs the mind of all its powers of acting and reasoning as fear"' (p2). In contrast her own authority, armoured by 'sensible' thought processes and the 'coolest' of heads, guaranteed that she could be trusted to defend the nation from a position of aggressive nuclear strength.

Nuclear weaponry was, in such speeches, the insignia of Thatcher's authority, the fetish that concealed the decreasing influence of Britain's power in world events. It was a 'compromise' reached to partially mask over the 'weight of the unwelcome perception' of Britain's loss of international influence (Freud, 1927:353). Alongside the fantasy of control, the fetish always carries an underlying horror: 'the horror of castration' (Freud: 353). Seen in this light, nuclear weaponry was an illusory and ultimately disturbing 'token of triumph' (p354).[20] The always-present sense of imminent castration that the weapon signified was partly displaced onto Labour's ineffectual leadership. As Thatcher told her audience at the Perth rally: 'Britain's defences were undermined and our police demoralised under the last Labour government … We had to rebuild the nation's ability to defend itself in an increasingly dangerous world' (CPA: GE 347/83:1-2). Thatcher claimed that nuclear defence was part of a broader backing of police and army 'to the hilt in enforcing the law'. 'Friend and foe' had to be sure 'that those who looked to us for their defence would find once again that our word is our bond' (p2). Thatcher's defensive nationalism relied on a certain trust; if the nation were challenged she claimed she could be trusted to respond with full force. The Sun (10 May: 1) trumpeted on day one of the campaign that 'Maggie' alone was prepared to push the nuclear button. In contrast to Labour, Thatcher claimed that she was prepared to undertake the ultimate and most destructive of war strategies to destroy the enemy. Unlike Labour, there was no gap between her promise and the deed, her word was her bond: 'There are no escape clauses: no small print in our policies. We say what we mean, and we mean what we say' (CPA: GE 539/83:21).

The authority of 'phallic' power lies in the promise that its force and knowledge can be fully deployed. However, the strength lies in the *potential* of this power, for if put to the test too often or too far, the limitations of the phallus will be unveiled. Thatcher maintained that the nation's power lay in keeping the threat of a nuclear reserve: the intention was not to deploy this ultimate weapon but to wield its horrific potential. The Lacanian idea of 'plus-One' *(Je plus-Un)* can be drawn on to explain this economy:

> Every signifying set contains an element which is 'empty', whose value is accepted on trust, yet which precisely as such guarantees the 'full' validity of all other elements. Strictly speaking it comes in excess, yet the moment we take it away, the very consistency of the other elements disintegrates.
>
> (Žižek, 1991:250)

The idea of a 'reserve' was (and is) a potent force in sustaining the power of 'advanced' Western nations. 'Reserves' of money were allowed to lie in vaults to maintain 'monetary balance'; food was allowed to rot in silos to maintain our food 'reserve'; 'weapons not meant to be used have been accumulated to guarantee the "balance of fear"' (Žižek, 1991:251). Thatcher argued that unilateral disarmament – the taking away of our nuclear 'reserve' – would result in the disintegration of our image as a powerful nation. The government propaganda unit DS19 together with pro-Thatcher journalists encouraged the replacement of the term 'unilateral disarmament' with 'one-sided disarmament'.[21] Her speeches underlined the 'horror' of nuclear weaponry while simultaneously stressing its status as bargaining chip; she presented them as terrible but usable products of progressive scientific rationality. She almost compulsively repeated the word 'horror' throughout an extensive justification of nuclear defence to the pre-election Young Conservative Conference. Horror, terror, devastation and tyranny were the central themes. A longer quotation demonstrates the relentless repetition involved here:

The horror of the nuclear bomb needs no underlining from me. None of us can ignore the devastation which would result from a war waged with nuclear weapons. It is no wonder that many people – particularly young people – are so concerned and fearful.

Indeed, it is precisely because the Government has faced up to the horror of war that we have gone to such lengths to prevent it ...

Those who support unilateralism believe that the nuclear weapon is so horrific that we should have nothing to do with it. Some of them would counsel the West to give up its deterrent. That would leave the Soviet Union with a virtual monopoly of nuclear arms: that tyrannical regime, which cares not one jot for human rights, uniquely able to blackmail mankind ...

The trouble is that the sheer horror of modern warfare can drive people to unreason ... Yet it is precisely when the dangers are greatest that our heads must be coolest. It cannot be sensible for the West to disarm and abandon this most terrible weapon ...

Nuclear war is a terrible threat; conventional war a terrible reality. Yet we have saved these horrors of war in Europe for almost the longest time for 200 years ... The so-called balance of terror keeps the peace.

(CPA: 73/83:1-5)[22]

Thatcher's speech underlined her apparent relentless commitment to instrumental reason, to the ideals of rationality: measurement, calibration, balance of power, mutual disarmament, equally-weighted armament and the counterbalance of power. But the speech remained caught within a contradictory dependence on the opposite traits: abandon, tyranny, unreason, imbalance of power and an uneven monopoly of weapons. She yoked together signs of 'supreme logic and consistency' with terror, horror, irrationality and the immeasurable and paradoxically revealed these as elements of 'attraction' at the same time as they were being denied (Rose, 1988:62-64). The horror of nuclear devastation became a kind of sublime fixation, a dreaded terror that wove through Thatcher's speeches and was projected onto the 'folly' and 'unreason' of the unilateral argument of Labour, CND and the recent Church of England report *The Church and the Bomb* (1982). In a strange conjunction nuclear armament was 'sensible' and unilateral disarmament reduced to 'unreason' induced by fear (CPA: 73/83:3, 7).

The fantasy of contemporary technological warfare sometimes

involved the suspension of 'raw physical violence'; the brute reality of bloody battle and death was often translated into 'abstract data': 'location of the target', statistics on arms accrual, strategic weapon count, potential bombing score (Žižek, 1994:73).[23] This fantasy of nuclear warfare as clean, direct and scientifically contained was a politicised mechanism for disavowing the anxiety of 'the real': the eruption of violence and the rupture of the physical body on the battlefield. The 'real' is within the symbolic order but, in a sense, is outside it. It represents 'the impossible': it is that which resists symbolisation, it cannot be attained or integrated because, in a way, it marks the death of our social world. It is this which lends the 'real' its traumatic status (Lacan, 1964:167; Evans, 1996:159-60). Thatcher acknowledged the horror of being a powerless 'witness' to the possibility of nuclear devastation, an event 'whose comprehension exceeds our capacity of representation' (Žižek, 1994:74). Her subsequent response, though, was to reassert her role as bearer of historical truth and as the unflinching gaze that had lived through and 'faced up to the horror of war' (CPA: 73/83:1). Thatcher informed the Young Conservatives, too young themselves to have witnessed mass bombing or nuclear devastation, that 'the destruction of Dresden rivalled that of Nagasaki'. She reminded them that the people of Lyons that same week were 'reliving the horrors of the Nazi occupation: the torture, the death and the concentration camps' and that it was 'exactly fifty years since Hitler became Chancellor of the German Reich' (CPA: 73/83:1-2). She claimed that her memory of past atrocity enabled her and her government to bear the terrible possession of nuclear arms with good conscience:

> Nagasaki and Hiroshima were not attacked because Japan *had* nuclear bases and missile sites on her soil ... Would the nuclear bomb have been dropped if Japan could have retaliated? I doubt it. Nagasaki and Hiroshima show just how vulnerable a nuclear free zone really is ... The bully sets upon the weak and not the strong.
>
> (CPA: 73/83:4)

In many of her campaign speeches she translated nuclear warfare into the imaginable reality of conventional military battle. Nuclear battle was frequently characterised as the most modern culmination of a long line of military engagements in the history of civilised nations. Here support of President Reagan's Strategic Defence Initiative became part of a venerable legacy of defensive weaponry: 'Every weapon in history has called forth a corresponding defence: the shield against the sword, armour against the lance, in modern times, guns and missiles against aircraft' (CPA: 310/85:12). Hence, Reagan's Strategic Defence Initiative was yet another 'defence against that most lethal and destructive of all weapons, the ballistic nuclear missile'. Reagan's aim was 'a system which destroys those terrible weapons before they destroy people' (p12).

Predictably it was the Second World War and the Falklands war which featured regularly in the campaign speeches. Although fresh in modern memory, it is probable that both wars were only familiar to a large portion of the electorate through the 'fictions' of the mass media. Throughout the election period the newspapers were packed with references to the Falklands. Stories ranged from the horrific to the banal. *The Times* (9 May 1983: 6) on the first day of the election campaign reported the growing concern in Washington that Argentina were pressing ahead with plans to explode a nuclear device as a political warning to Britain over the Falklands. The *Sun* (3 May 1983:7) included breezy updates on the lingerie-clad female singers July and Diana off to entertain the Falklands troops. The *Mail* (16 May 1983:9) crudely linked a 'tribute' to the Falklands task force to the Conservative Party by photographing a Conservative bride-to-be holding the new rose 'Invincible' with her future husband, Neil Hamilton, the Tory candidate for Tatton where the rose was grown.[24] The *Mirror* (17 May 1983:9) included a full-page advertisement by the Royal Air Force Museum for an authentic scale pewter replica of the 'Harrier' aircraft which had 'earned a place in history through its brilliant combat performance in the Falklands'. These frequent media references provided an imaginative landscape and a means to express the wickedness, prowess and honour of war and to latch these attributes onto either Labour or the Conservative Party.

It was the fictionalised and romantic elements of these modern wars that enabled Thatcher to embed technological warfare in understandable narratives of violence and glory, helping to marginalise the actual experiences of suffering, discomfort and defeat of modern soldiering. Furthermore, she drew on public anxiety about the visible increase in range and power of new and improved nuclear weapons. Their capability eroded the imagined border between the battlefront and the safer hinterland. Recent government 'civil defence' circulars sent to the public had exacerbated this anxiety. They had 'emphasised the need for the state to control the sick, starving and dying survivors of a nuclear attack through commissioners with dictatorial powers, armed police, special courts and internment camps' (Keane, 1996:55-56).

The horrific images of Nazi violence – torture, death and concentration camps – translated the unknowable consequences of nuclear warfare into an understandable landscape of militaristic systematic oppression. At Harrogate, Labour's disregard for the Russian offensive in Afghanistan was distinguished from the collective British memory of World War Two:

> Labour overlooked the invasion of Afghanistan and the Russian tanks in Hungary and Czechoslovakia, and the events in Poland. But the British people haven't forgotten. They remember even further back. They remember how our weakness once encouraged a Nazi dictator.
>
> (CPA: GE 438/83:18)

And the Young Conservatives were reminded that 'moral gestures' of 'one-sided disarmament' ignored the supremacy of Britain's strategic position: 'Just look at a map. Our position is so important we could not be immune if war were to come between the two super-powers'. The audience was bid to recall 'the experience of two World Wars' where 'neutrality' was 'no bar to invasion' (CPA: 73/83:4).[25]

Thatcher projected onto the Labour Party a chaos and destruction which formed the fascinating underside of her own political discourse. She postured as the ideal father, the military leader, advocate of law and order, supporter of the police and the force of the law. However her real force lay as punitive super-ego, for a key part of the horror and appeal of her iconic image was its dependence on the imaginary breakdown of the social order: 'at one and the same time, the law and its destruction' (Lacan, 1953-4:102). She presented herself as just, reasonable and consistent. She told the Young Conservatives that the Conservative political message was 'idealist', 'realistic', 'practical' and 'proven' (CPA: 73/83:7). But these attributes were defined against an imaginary backdrop of 'tyranny'. Conservatives, claimed Thatcher, sought peace but also aimed to release those who longed to escape tyrannical oppression. Conservatives had a clear rational 'measure of those who threaten our way of life' (p7). Simultaneous with this claim to rationality and reason, Thatcher drew upon horrific images of imminent nuclear attack. She conjured up the monstrosity of totalitarian government and the 'anarchy' that loomed at the edge of the law to undercut the dream of national and individual self-control. In asserting the power of the law over personal responsibility, Thatcher played with and revealed society's failure to secure and regulate the subject's inclination to aggression: 'freedom cannot survive without personal responsibility. Without the framework of a just law impartially administered, it becomes anarchy. Without order it degenerates into the tyranny of the strong' (CPA: GE 554/83:9). Thatcher's vision of the nation-state then produced its own symptom. The violence that defined the difference between the free and the dictatorial state was transformed into a split within the nation between two political approaches to nuclear enforcement. Her image as forceful national leader benefited from this frequent juxtaposition with tyranny. At her opening Perth speech she stressed the electoral contest as a 'battle':

> For the choice facing the nation is between two totally different ways of life. And what a prize we have to fight for: no less than the chance to banish from our land the dark divisive clouds of Marxist socialism.
>
> (CPA: 347/83:12)

In Freud's narrative of civilisation, the dictatorial and excessive primal beast is slain and, in his place, civilised standards and communal inhibition and regulation are installed. In Thatcher's speeches, the process of national deliverance involved the abolition of a 'dark divisive' enemy and the election of the Conservative Party. To restore 'freedom' she demanded 'courage' to do battle and to lead the exemplary life, but her speeches frequently returned to scenes of social breakdown or dictatorial excess. According to Freud, the super-ego's interdictions constantly suggest the possibility of transgression. The super-ego's injunctions work most effectively when they carry about them the hint of forbidden pleasures. 'In forbidding excess enjoyment', the injunctions appear to be the 'only obstacle; the subject ... is thus free to dream of their removal and of the bounty of pleasure which will some day be his' (Copjec, 1995:292). The totalitarianism to which Thatcher frequently returned is a specifically modern form of rule and represents the extreme and horrific possibility of the modern state (Giddens, 1985:294-310). Thatcher charged the Labour Party with excessive surveillance, the license of mob violence, extreme bureaucracy and with political reason pushed into irrational propaganda. In doing so she invoked those authoritarian practices which the democratic nation contains as its terrible underside and must necessarily suppress.

Concluding comments: 'freedom not licence'
I suggest that part of the unconscious appeal of Thatcher's punitive right-wing discourse derived from the fantasy of the public law failing

and thus the spectacle of illegal enjoyment. She endorsed total order, the disciplined operation of the law, the 'responsible' possession of nuclear weapons, and the moral desire to work for consumer items and the good life. This endorsement (over) compensated for her status as a woman as she laid claim to the role of war leader. But in her speeches she frequently set out images of the law's infraction and of violent social insurrection. It has been argued that regular transgressions or temporary suspensions of the public law are an integral part of maintaining social order (Stallybrass and White, 1986). The distinctively bourgeois, pure, closed, ordered sense of self that emerged alongside the rise of the modern European nation-state was accompanied by the protracted withdrawal of this subjectivity from the impure, disordered, violent and chaotic aspects of social and collective identity. These last elements re-emerge in displaced and distorted form as phobic or fetishised objects and repressed desires which function as a primary constituent of fantasy life: 'the result is a mobile, conflictual fusion of power, fear and desire in the construction of subjectivity' (Stallybrass & White, 1986:5). While there is no simple fit between these fantasies of transgressive enjoyment and our collective political and social organisation, this chapter indicates how the two are intimately connected.

When the narcissistic image of the nation is humiliated, demeaned or edged with threat of degradation, one result is a depression creeping into subject or group practices and representations (Kristeva, 1993:52). The alternative extreme to counteract this collective cynicism and apathy is an appeal to 'the narcissistic excitement of rediscovering strengthened, super-egotic, hyperbolic "ideals"' (Kristeva: 52). Here, the dangers of aggressive excess are clear. Kristeva states: 'Between suicide and barbarity, there is not much leeway' (p52). Accompanying her presentation of 'a dangerous and uncertain world' Thatcher offered herself as 'strength and security' dependent on sacrifice: 'I did not promise you an easy road in 1979. I do not promise you one now. But I promise you that we shall stay true to our principles and our country' (CPA: GE 583/83:10). Against the image of abject chaos, national depression and the spectre of emasculated leadership Thatcher's persona was of national leadership as strong, resolute, punitive: she offered 'freedom not licence' (CPA: GE 554/83:6). The self-defined role of Thatcher as super-ego is clear: she was the prolongation of social authority, the return of conscience, the knowing site of national control. In 1983, she recalled her newly-elected 1979 government as a stronghold beseiged on all sides by 'the thickets of bureaucracy', battling off profligate collectivism (CPA: 347/83:2). Appositely, Freud likened the super-ego to 'a garrison in a conquered city', an agency set up by 'civilization' whose force is drawn from the dangerous and illicit desires it purports to weaken and disarm (Freud, 1930:316). Kristeva pointed out the dangerous lure of self-inflated political leadership. She warned against the political leader who took shelter in a defensive nationalism and argued that the promise of a strongly secure national identity could backslide, too easily, into persecution of those who do not fit the 'impregnable "aloofness" of the uncompromising nation' (1993:3). She signalled the ready appeal of such a grandiose public persona:

> such a thirst for the absolute is appalling but on a deeper level it satis-
> fies our narcissistic passions for 'all or nothing', our desire for an
> uncompromising model who runs the risk of getting lost the better to
> hold us. So much the better, so much the worse, for it is he who lays
> himself open to danger ... for our sake.
>
> (Kristeva, 1993:72-3)

References

1. In the 1979 general election, Thatcher had been famously photographed cuddling a new-born calf with husband Denis muttering about its imminent demise if the photographers didn't get their picture quickly.

2. On 23 April 1981, unemployment passed 2.5 million. This news was preceded by scenes of urban violence as images of the Brixton riots filled the newspapers and TV screens (10 April to 12 April). July saw further riots in Toxteth, Liverpool and Moss Side, Manchester. Inflation was at 20 per cent. In January 1982, unemployment reached 3 million (Butler and Kavanagh, 1984; Gamble, 1988).

3. Polls indicated that 64 per cent of respondents were dissatisfied with her leadership (*Guardian*, 14 April 1982:5).

4. Christopher Lawson was formerly the director of the company that made *Mars* chocolate bars and applied his experience of marketing Mars's products to promoting the Conservative Party (Cockerell, 1983:1-2).

5. See Brian McNair (1989:124-142) for details of the television news coverage of the nuclear debate in the election campaign. McNair illustrates how television news coverage largely bypassed the substantive issues of nuclear debate and focused on Labour's policy and clashes between former premier Jim Callaghan, Denis Healey and Michael Foot over Labour's non-nuclear policy.

6. At its 1982 conference Labour, by a two thirds majority, endorsed the

principle of unilateral disarmament and this principle was included in the 1983 manifesto although splits in the party over the retention of Polaris featured as major news items during the campaign. The *Economist*, just prior to the general election campaign, outlined the Labour Party's ambiguous relationship to anti-nuclear sentiments and pointed out that Conservative governments, on entering office after Labour governments, had frequently found fully developed nuclear projects. In 1951, Winston Churchill took over a British atom bomb project moving towards its first test. In 1970, Edward Heath found an active research programme and a completed Polaris submarine. In 1979, Margaret Thatcher found that Labour, despite its great cost, had constructed the new Chevaline warhead for the Polaris missiles and 'had laid the groundwork for buying Trident' (*Economist*, 2-8 April 1983:31-4).

7. NATO's 'dual-track' policy maintained that the central aim was to negotiate for a reduction in European nuclear weapons. However, the scheduled deployment of Cruise and Pershing II missiles in Europe would not be halted, as it would place pressure on the USSR to negotiate (McNair, 1989:141 footnote 5).

8. These figures were compiled from a sample of eight days of Conservative ministers campaign speeches from 17 May 1983 to 24 May 1983. In this period, 36 speeches, 15 official statements and 3 official letters to the party are recorded in the Conservative Party Archive 'Ministers/Election' files (April/May 1983). Of these, 16 texts were on the subject of defence, CND, the Falklands, arms control or the dangers of the USSR.

9. Michael Heseltine had taken over Defence from John Nott in January 1983 in a Cabinet reshuffle.

10. In a survey conducted for the BBC by Gallup, 38 per cent of respondents chose defence policy as important to their voting choice. This compared with only 2 per cent in 1979 (Crewe in Curtice, 1989:145).

11. Butler and Kavanagh's (1984: 201) in-depth study of the 1983 general election provides valuable breakdowns of campaign and newspaper contents. Table 9.6 reveals the highest scoring lead story to be that of defence with sixteen entries throughout the campaign, closely followed by fourteen lead stories on opinion polls and twelve on party strategies.

12. Lucy Noakes's research, based on Mass Observation responses by women and men to the Falklands conflict, reveals complex, and often gender-divided, uses of the images of the Second World War which appeared in political discourses and media representations at the time. Even respondents who opposed the Government's policy during the conflict frequently drew upon the Second World War to articulate an anti-war narrative (Noakes, 1996).

13. For alternative analyses of media coverage of the Falklands conflict see Harris (1983) and Hastings and Jenkins (1983).

14. The Cheltenham Address is reprinted in entirety at the back of Barnett (1982).

15. In January 1983 a MORI poll found that 54 per cent of respondents disapproved of Cruise missiles in Britain, while a Marplan poll found 61 per cent did not agree with Cruise on British soil (Taylor, 1986:211).

16. This emphasis contrasted with their previous emphasis on disarmament in the 1950s and 1960s when Britain's exemplary moral standpoint was underlined. Such an approach by CND chimed with the then prevalent popular sense that Britain was a world power.

17. See Alison Young for an account of the alleged relationship between DS19 and the popular press (1990: 29ff).

18. See Campbell (1987:123-38) for an account of the opposition to the movement Lady Maitland met within the Conservative Party.

19. Lady Olga Maitland's father, Lord Lauderdale, was a Conservative MP and foreign correspondent for the *Times* who gave the group considerable coverage (Young, 1990:132).

20. In an interesting aside Freud indicated that the strategies of fetishism were called upon to disavow the loss of treasured national institutions which he compared to the panic of feared castration: 'In later life a grown man may perhaps experience a similar panic when the cry goes up that Throne and Altar are in danger, and similar illogical consequences will ensue' (Freud, 1927:352).

21. In January 1983, following the appointment of Michael Heseltine as Minister of Defence, Defence ministers were advised to lose the phrase 'unilateral disarmament'. There was an explicit adoption of the preferred phrase, 'one-sided disarmament', in the newspapers, particularly the tabloid press, alongside the technique of casting doubt on the ideological motivations of nuclear protestors by placing inverted commas around 'peace' when referring to the aims of Greenham protesters or CND (Young, 1990:133-5).

22. The transcript of this speech is only seven pages of double-spaced type, the extracts I have selected form about an eighth of the speech as a whole but capture the tone and language of all of it.

23. In some respects this process anticipated the emphasis on 'hi-tech precision bombing' in much American and British political and media coverage of the Gulf War following the Iraqi invasion of Kuwait in early August 1990 (Kellner, 1995:Ch.6).

24. Neil Hamilton and his wife Christine achieved infamy in the mid-1990s for alleged financial misdemeanours. Hamilton lost his Tatton seat in the

May 1997 general election to former journalist Martin Bell. In his final speech to his constituency, TV cameras captured Hamilton with a delegate for the 'transvestite party' on stilts, towering behind him. Two large mock pointy breasts with red flashing lights on their tips seemed to ensconce Hamilton as he made his speech. The image seemed to encapsulate the symbolism of 'sleaze' which had been attached to the Conservative Party in the media intermittently since John Major's ill-fated 'Back to Basics' campaign, launched in late 1993.

25. Attempts by Thatcher's opponents to mobilise the same rhetoric of soldierly honour and political dishonour through military misdeed were invariably turned against them. Michael Foot was widely attacked in the newspapers for his criticism of Lord Chancellor Hailsham's alleged role in the appeasement of Hitler in the 1930s (*Mail*, 19 May 1983:9). When Denis Healey rounded on Thatcher and accused her of 'glorying' in the Falklands slaughter, the tabloids responded with full fury (*Sun*, 3 June 1983:6; *Express*, 24 May:1).

CHAPTER SIX:

Thatcher and the Haunting of Politics Present

In the 1990s, Margaret Thatcher continued to be a prominent icon, signifying in diverse ways the moral, political and cultural tone of the previous decade. After her fall from power she figured as motif in contemporary artworks and fringe theatre, fictional television drama, contemporary literature, advertisements and as fashion detail in designer clothing.[1] Thatcher kitsch, mass-produced in the 1980s, has undergone new popularity since her fall from power. At auction, in the mid-1990s, Thatcher memorabilia (from satirical teapots to keyrings to toilet tissue bearing her face) outstripped more sober lots featuring Disraeli and Lloyd George. Dealers predicted she would soon exceed Churchill as highest-yielding political figure in the commemorative market (no doubt critics would take some recompense from the marketing of such memorabilia under the category 'derogatory junk').[2] The proliferation of her image and the elevation of Thatcher to an emblem of an epoch illustrate how she captured the cultural imagination but also how a complex phenomenon can become condensed into a humorous, celebratory or derogatory icon. More significantly, she became firmly embedded in grander narratives of nation and institution. She can be encountered as waxwork figure at Madame Tussauds, reciting Aaron Copland's *Lincoln Address* at the *BBC Experience,* and as an attraction of Oxford's 'heritage' culture.

In this conclusion, I will signal attempts to 'fix' political history and Thatcher's role within that history. I will also point up how Thatcher's adversarial persona persisted after her fall from power in November 1990. While she memorably described her own departure in mythic terms as political colleagues' 'treachery with a smile on its face', she did not dwell long on her enforced resignation.[3] Her ability to adapt and transform her political rhetoric to the unstable condition of the Middle East and former Yugoslavia revealed her ongoing ability to orchestrate narratives of aggression and mastery to match the changing political times.

History, memory, myth

> Like history, memory is inherently revisionist and never more chameleon than when it appears to stay the same.
>
> (Samuel, 1994:x)

> The faithful were awed and orgasmic
> When the wraith rover pulled up outside
> And spectrally white, ectoplasmic
> She strolled in as bold as a bride
> A trick of a shadow disguised as a shade –
> The Downing Street dowager!
>   Would she had stayed!
>
> (Greenwell in *New Statesman* 30 May 1997:29)

On 12 June 1998, Reuters predicted a momentous supernatural event: 'Britain's Thatcher to speak from the grave' (Griffiths, 1998:1). Margaret Thatcher had just given the go-ahead for an authorised biography to be published after her death and the book's author, Charles Moore, long-term friend of Thatcher and editor of the *Daily Telegraph*, would be allowed full access to her, her friends and her private papers. Andrew Rosenheim, managing director of the prospective publishers Penguin Press, anticipated the text as 'among the most important political biographies to appear in the next century' (Griffiths: 1). The news release predicted the posthumous 'definitive account' as revelatory: 'As for secrets ... few would expect the outspoken Thatcher to go quietly' and suggested that, like her own two-volume memoirs this would be a certain 'hit' (p1).

This release illustrated elements of much media and political representation of Thatcher since her resignation in November 1990. Thatcher's formidable presence at the centre of British political life has left a distinct political legacy, perhaps foremost in the debate about continuation or adaptation of her political doctrine by Conservative and New Labour successors. Of equal importance, though, has been her frequent representation as an uncanny and potentially dangerous presence. Throughout the 1990s it was commonplace for Thatcher to appear in political commentary as an intrusion from the political past upon the present, rising up in turn to trouble or advise her successors John Major and William Hague, as well as the New Labour leader Tony Blair. In numerous cartoons she murderously attacked John Major. Gerald Scarfe sketched her in edgy lines as an axe splitting Major completely in half (*The Sunday Times*, 14 January 1996:7). She was drawn as a giant menacing shadow about to handbag Major in an alley and appeared as a red-eyed, slathering dinosaur about to feed on cavemen Michael Howard and Major as they hunched over a square stone wheel (*Sun*, 22 May 1995:6; *Guardian Weekend Supplement*, 20 November 1993:20). There were frequent press references to her imminent savaging of former colleagues, and journalists anticipated her 'sinking her teeth' into them or erupting into the Conservative Party's midst. The accompanying imagery was of Thatcher as the 'Great Blue Shark' trawling under the Conservative Party to enact 'another-all-too-familiar bloodbath' or as killer 'Maggie the Knife' (*Guardian*, 15 June 1996:3; *Daily Mail*, 8 June 1993:12). John Major's successor, William Hague, was intermittently hailed and then attacked by her at Conservative Party Conferences, which were presented as a spectacle worthy of a Hollywood 'freak show' in which Thatcher appeared at Blackpool like a 'gruesome creature from the grave' (*Mail on Sunday*, *Review*, 10 October 1996:57; *Evening Standard*, 7 October 1999:13).

In disturbing imagery she often appeared as the uncanny madwoman: a political revenant returning unhinged and vengeful from the outskirts of power. In 1995 her entrance to the party conference was captioned as 'The Ghost of Conferences Past', making 'her annual earthly visit' (*Today*, 13 October 1995:5). Similarly, George Urban's diary extract in *The Times* recalled that when he met her in 1993 she appeared psychologically unable to cope with her loss of power: 'I was distressed. Was this great lady entertaining false ideas about her place in the universe? Was she lapsing into a phantom world, waiting for the bugle to sound, summoning her back to the field of action?' (*The Times*, 24 September 1996:18-19). Numerous journalistic and political responses to her influence on the 1990s involved fantasies of potential aggression wrought upon the Conservatives who ousted her or upon her contemporary political detractors.

On one level, the presentation of Thatcher as a wraith, fiend or mad harridan preying upon her male successors is a (too easy) way to discount the politics of the 1980s. Her current rumblings from the political sidelines are as a vaguely disturbing or humorous insurrection of the dead. Furthermore, the representation of Thatcher as a violent or disturbed presence reveals the process of projection. The troubling aspects of a political decade – greed, war, selfishness, chauvinism – are lodged firmly with Thatcher alone and then drawn upon for vicarious fantasies of the disturbed woman publicly enacting violence and revenge. On another level, Thatcher's persistent presence enables the media's repeated discussion of the Conservative Party or Parliament's inconsistency and potential ministerial dissent.

In the first of Peter York's six-part TV series *The Eighties* (1996), he signalled the fantasmatic status of such recollection: 'People are still dreaming eighties' dreams'.[4] Thatcher appeared as a signifier of the decade – rarely a whole image – but a flash of blue cloth, a harsh close-up of her mouth or as waxwork image in Madam Tussauds. She appeared as emblem of the excesses of the decade: power, lust, greed, heady success, self-indulgence, egotism, attributes that were simultaneously disparaged and admired throughout the series. In the dramatised documentary *Timewatch: Memo from Machiavelli – How to succeed in British Politics* (1994) sixteenth century political theorist Niccolo Machiavelli's harsh words[5] on necessary cunning, deception and utter ruthlessness in politics were intercut with footage of Thatcher from her years as Prime Minister. Ian Richardson, who has appeared in numerous political dramas, read Machiavelli's words. In the four-part *Final Cut* (1995), the last of the *House of Cards* series, Richardson appeared as Francis Urquhart, Conservative Prime Minister, a man haunted by Thatcher's record time as Prime Minister. The first programme began with Thatcher's fictionalised state funeral and the third episode featured the construction of Thatcher's huge monument outside the Houses of Parliament.[6] Both examples imbued her with a particular malign overweening presence and illustrate a broader cultural attempt to articulate the disturbing sense of unrelenting ruthless power in 1980s politics and its continuation in her iconic form.

On Thatcher's part, the Reuters announcement of her posthumous political voice reveals her maintenance of a public profile since 1990 and simultaneously her attempt to 'fix' political history as empirical fact. Thatcher's masquerade as 'Iron Lady' involved an emphasis on her consistency of vision and a denial of any disparity between her version and the reality of any political event. Thatcher's spokesman stressed that Moore, the author, would be 'objective' in his Penguin biography, while Moore stated that his work would be no 'hagiography' but 'a full and proper history' (Griffiths, 1998:1). Similarly, HarperCollins's promotional copy for *The Downing Street Years* (1993)[7] stressed

Thatcher's eleven-and-a-half-year premiership as 'one of the most significant eras in twentieth century British political, economic and social history' and that 'history' had validated Thatcher as 'one of the outstanding leaders of our time'. Hugh Scully, executive producer of the tie-in television series *Thatcher: The Downing Street Years* (1993), informed the press in pre-broadcast publicity that Thatcher had put no restrictions on the programme-makers: 'We had total freedom, complete access and no-holds barred. We aim to be totally impartial and that is something [Thatcher] has accepted all along. She had no rights to veto or view the programmes' (*Evening Standard*, 3 August 1993:17).[8] Scully spent fifteen three-hour sessions with his subject, and these interviews formed the basis of the TV series. Denys Blakeway, the series writer/producer, commented: 'People will be astonished at how frankly and openly she talks', whilst Alan Yentob, BBC1 Controller, described the series as 'stunningly frank and a unique and riveting portrait of a political colossus' (*Guardian*, 4 August 1993: 6).

As authenticity in the world of political affairs appears increasingly illusive, the expression of emotion and confessional openness provides an apparent route to documentary truth about Thatcher's experience of political power. Scully claimed: 'it is almost as if [Thatcher] has total recall' of her 'last intimate meeting' with ministers (*Evening Standard*, 3 August 1993:17). The memoir was set up as an objective account in which the evidence of the foremost character spoke for itself; her testimony was validated as true by the programme-makers. Alongside this was the sense of her as a political subject who determined history and who continued to unsettle present political incumbents of lesser stature. The TV series followed soon after the Conservative Party conference. As the *Guardian* characterised her TV broadcast: 'Thatcher to judge PM in "frank" series' (4 August 1993:6). Personal witnesses of the Thatcher years, including Mikhail Gorbachev, Ronald Reagan, Nigel Lawson and Geoffrey Howe, were contributors to the programmes. Yet it was Thatcher's account of her colleagues' perfidy that was accorded most evidential weight. On television Thatcher appeared in medium close-up, perfectly groomed, almost immobile with her eyes staring frequently just to the side of the picture's frame, as though in reverie or concentrated recollection. When political colleagues – Francis Pym, Ian Gilmour, Lord Carrington, William Whitelaw, Jim Prior – sometimes expressed carefully modulated doubt about Thatcherite policies or convictions, the camera then invariably cut to her unstinting justification of each political action taken while in office. There was a refusal on her part to brook any criticism or acknowledge any failure. The authorial voice-over, plus the use of stills of newspaper front page headlines to recall moments of political crisis, attempted to close down other versions of Thatcher's past and to underline the historical veracity of her account.

In previews, the personal and visceral aspects of public office were foregrounded by Hugh Scully: 'She [Thatcher] is emotional about the circumstances of her resignation ... She used the word treachery, but I can't say about who' (*Guardian*, 4 August 1993:6). The emotion and 'treachery' of political events, of 'flesh and blood' conflict were drawn upon to underwrite *The Downing Street Years's* superior status as an archive of the era. The cover notes for the series' BBC video claimed it as a 'new form of historical document. A record of our time for future generations to study'.[9] Beneath this a puff by London University's Professor of Contemporary History Peter Hennessy states: 'I won't let any of my students down to the Public Record Office in 2010 ... until they have sat through every moment at least twice ... They are the nearest thing to flesh and blood that remain.' In contrast, Stephen Glover, in the *Evening Standard*, cleverly pinpointed much contemporary media fascination with Thatcher's memoirs as something more than a desire for personalised historical veracity, but rather: 'a fascination not unlike that generated by an old-fashioned murder story. We want to know *from the victim herself* whose hand was on the knife that was plunged into her back during her last days as Prime Minister' (*Evening Standard*, 2 September 1993:9, his emphasis).

The televised memoir represented a very public act of recollection. It was, in many respects, a perpetuation of the 'Iron Lady' masquerade. In the four programmes she figured as preferred point of identification. Even while appearing to acquiesce to her political rivals and peers in acknowledging their opinions of and contributions to her political project, she was presented as an absolute, conviction-led, certain political subject. Despite the promotional publicity's promises of emotional revelation, the series denied a glimpse of the politician's interior self; it was a refusal of intimacy or privacy, the personal or confessional. In structure and sequencing of events the memoir set up politics as largely motivated by personality. Complex economic, social and international policy decisions and debates presented as counter to, or deviation from, her perspective were reduced to acts of weakness, moral failure or spite on the part of Thatcher's 'rivals' in the Cabinet and Whitehall. But, I would stress, *The Downing Street Years*, as televised memoir, was refused the function of memory: memory as transitory, flawed, subjective and open to dispute. Stuart Hall, speaking of Thatcher's performance in the series, expressed my own personal frustration at watching an authorised account of her political past that allowed no new insight into her role in the Conservative politics of the 1980s. He spoke of her 'playing her mythical self' on the small screen as 'a magisterial exercise in self caricature' (Hall, 1993:2).

The planned Penguin biography, like Thatcher's memoirs, is already constructed as sanctioned site, presented as a forthcoming memorial that marks the power of a woman who determined history. Violence is once again attached to her persona in imagery of the refusal to go quietly, of her stridency. In addition, an abstract notion of 'history' is added as a weighty judge of biographies' cultural value. In late 1997, the Margaret Thatcher Foundation (formed after her resignation) announced to the media that it was donating a grant of £1.9 million to Cambridge University to finance a professorship to research Thatcher's 'very own brand of free enterprise economics.' A Thatcher aide informed the *Sunday Times* that, in contrast to the 'capitalism of the cowboy' exemplified by the post-Cold War practices of Russia and 'large parts of China', the Cambridge Chair was designed to teach that 'capitalism does have a moral and legal basis' (BBC 1997:1). The University endowment, as with the political memoirs, was not about opening up of Conservative policy and practice to academic or public scrutiny, but was an underwriting of Thatcher's continuing political significance. Thatcher's founding of academic chairs and bequeathing of memoirs points up her attempted control of public memory. But equally important is the way that media accounts of her almost compulsively repeat the images of violent adversity that were an integral part of her persona in the 1980s. Revisiting these events through the linear and convention-bound structures of political biography, documentary, news journalism or televised memoir reveals the difficulty of acknowledging ambiguity, fantasy or elusive memory within such forms.

More broadly, the publication of Thatcher's written memoir and its TV tie-in was a media event that was interpreted as part of a wider Thatcherite attack on John Major's Conservative government. The memoirs became public in a particularly volatile year for Major. Speculation about his likely consolidation of, or alternatively his fall from, political power was accompanied by imaginary spectacles of Thatcher's anger, plotting or violence against her hapless successor. The media depicted 1993 as a 'crisis' year for Major's government. It is worth charting briefly the key events and their press coverage in order to understand the volatile situation into which Thatcher's memoirs were inserted as a motif of political revenge.

Central to John Major's alleged loss of control over his party and its much-publicised schism was the passage of the Maastricht Treaty Bill which wedded Britain firmly to future European economic, social and political policy. On the 8 March 1993 the Conservative government was defeated by 314 to 292 votes on an amendment to the Treaty Bill, with 26 rebel Conservative MPs voting against them; a result that forced a report stage and delayed ratification of the Treaty. The defeat was interpreted as part of a broader attack on the Prime Minister by the 'Euro-sceptics' who had 'harried and humiliated him' since the general election in April 1992 (*Guardian*, 24 July 1993:21). Behind these Euro-sceptics, political pundits frequently imagined the vengeful machinations of Thatcher herself. These fractures within the Conservative Party were humorously captured in a 'JAK' cartoon of Smith Square, SW1. Here, Conservative Central Office nestled alongside the makeshift revolutionary banners of the 'Provisional Conservative Party', the 'Alternative Conservative Party' and 'Baroness Thatcher's Conservative Party' with Euro-sceptic 'Lord Rees-Mogg C. Party' tucked in her attic (*Evening Standard*, 3 June 1993).

The Maastricht result fuelled fantasies of Major's political demise or, more positively, of his rejuvenation as the 'New Major': 'sharper in cabinet, funnier at City dinners and more brutal at the Dispatch Box' (*Guardian*, 24 July 1993:21). On the 22 July 1993, a Government motion on the ratification of the Treaty was defeated by 8 votes, with the 'Noes' again including 26 Conservative MPs. Major immediately announced a vote of confidence for the following day, forcing rebel MPs, together with Ulster Unionist support, to carry the vote by 399 to 299 votes. The anti-Maastricht rebellion was strongly linked by political pundits to Thatcher who, in her new arena of the House of Lords, had during the previous weeks warned against the diminution of Parliament's power, authority and prestige in Europe. Under the headline 'Maggie the Knife', *Daily Mail* political correspondent John Deans reported her 25-minute speech in early June as 'a scathing assault on her successor's judgement and policy'. Thatcher's call for a public referendum on the Treaty was described as twisting the knife into 'Major's deepening wounds' (*Daily Mail*, 8 June 1993:12). John Wells, reporting on the final debate in the House of Lords on 14 July, employed the predictable device of describing the 'other place' as an ensemble of harmless and near lunatic English eccentrics amidst which Thatcher sat 'muttering and scribbling like a woman possessed'. Thatcher and anti-European ally Norman Tebbit were depicted as virulently xenophobic, their adversarial streak floundering in the 'terri-fying politeness' of the Lords, their Little England doctrine ultimately confining them to the political backwoods (*Evening Standard*, 14 July 1993: 9; see also Bell cartoon, *Guardian*, 27 July 1993:17). The follow-ing day, Michael White in the *Guardian* recalled Thatcher's 'final doomed charge last night' and her 'apocalyptic warning' against European integration and Maastricht as a 'treaty too far'. Despite the call for a referendum being defeated in the Lords by 445 votes to 176, White portrayed the conflict as a 'civil war which has split the British political establishment for a generation' and 'could yet bring down Major's administration' (*Guardian*, 15 July 1993:1).

The whole process led to clichéd Shakespearean declarations in the press. Major was depicted as melancholy Hamlet staring at death's skull and 'Bearing the whips and scorns of time' (*Guardian*, 15 July 1993:21). Under the headline 'It's time to call off the dogs of war', he became Caesar undermined by the political crisis gripping the nation (*London Evening Standard*, 10 May 1993:9). The *Evening Standard* linked Major's failure to handle Europe within his party to the disas-trous Newbury by-election of 6 May, which epitomised broader Conservative loss of a thousand Tory council seats in the local county council elections. These articles exemplified broader media discussion throughout the year in which Major's leadership crisis was located in the wider spectrum of Conservative failure. Here, diverse political events were assembled as evidence of emasculated leadership: the belea-guered economy, debates about the financial viability of the Welfare State, a 'crisis in crime', rail privatisation, the imposition of the Social Chapter by the TUC and the conflict in Bosnia. Frequently, images of Thatcher as a rigorously determined premier were set against this litany of incompetence.

Thatcher was depicted as the infuriated former premier persistently haunting and recriminating Major for letting down the nation through weak government. A structure of riposte and counter-riposte framed the largely mythic battle between former and present party leader. On 13 April 1993 she appealed on television for direct military help for Bosnian Moslems. The press reported on Thatcher's intervention in the Bosnian crisis, claiming it as an 'instinctive' sense of 'the people's' outrage at systematic oppression.[10] In response, Defence Secretary Malcolm Rifkind stressed the government's opposition to the use of interventionist force and derided Thatcher for talking 'emotional nonsense', and shadow Foreign Secretary Dr Jack Cunningham simi-larly described Thatcher's comments as 'emotional claptrap' (*Evening*

Standard, 15 April 1993:9). In a thinly veiled attack on Thatcher, a senior minister was quoted as saying: 'It is time some of the elderly loose cannons on the deck were pitched overboard and shut up' (*Evening Standard*, 20 April 1993:13). But such comments were largely overwhelmed by cartoons, political commentary or published letters from the general public. These either vindicated Thatcher's stand or, if censorious, still frequently represented her as a strong, powerful or even maniacally aggressive woman who stood out from the weaker images of a lesser masculinity that captured Major's alleged ineffectualness and poor leadership.[11]

This onslaught against Major came only one year after his success in the 1992 general election when his 'homely style of campaigning' from a 'soapbox' was interpreted by some commentators as a 'backlash' against the 'sophisticated image management' and 'presidential' techniques of his predecessor (McNair, 1995: 126). The Conservatives' public relations strategy was to portray Major as youthful, of modest social background, 'ordinary', mild-mannered and courteous: a persona intended as an unadorned and realistic development of Thatcherism for the 1990s. Major was promoted as an 'updated product': 'Thatcherism with a *human* face' (McNair: 126-7, my emphasis). Significantly, one year on, Thatcher's contrasting assertive impatience was frequently represented through violent images of *inhuman* femininity. In numerous media representations, Thatcher as vampire, voodoo witch, murderous strangler and tidal wave erupted like the return of the Conservative repressed to stab, throttle, drown, shoot or haunt the nightmares of ineffectual Major. Mid-year, as the publication of her memoirs approached and debates over Major's political future continued, motifs of Thatcher as uncanny or violent were commonplace. A *Guardian* cartoon portrayed her as bloodthirsty Goddess Kali, her six arms brandishing scimitars as she danced on a tomb inscribed 'Goddess of the Golden Age' while nearby her acolyte Michael Portillo set fire to Major and the bound corpse of Thatcherism on a funeral pyre (27 July 1993:17). In the *Evening Standard*, Thatcher, a towering figure with blazing eyes, pursued Major, brandishing a placard bearing the word 'SHAME!' (20 April 1993:19). Cummings, in the *Sunday Express*, sketched Thatcher as a massive tidal wave looming over a frightened John Major on the shoreline clutching a banner 'Please observe High Tide mark' (19 September 1993:23).

Inevitably, Thatcher's memoirs were linked in the press to this broader 'crisis' of Major and his party and, in retrospect, the anticipated damage her revelations would do far outweighed the result once they were published and screened. In July 1993, immediately following the confidence vote for Major, journalist Michael White anticipated Thatcher as a mad Mrs Rochester, burning down the forthcoming Conservative Party Conference by applying a match to her 'highly-inflammable autobiographies': 'whoosh – there goes Blackpool' (*Guardian Outlook*, 24 July 1993:21). A fortnight later, the BBC's damaging leak of Major's off-the-air dismissal of party opponents as 'bastards' was linked to the forthcoming Thatcher TV series. The *Daily Mirror*, which had published the transcript of Major's comments, created further furore in October prior to the party conference. Lawyers for Thatcher, publishers HarperCollins and the *Sunday Times* (who were due to publish serialised extracts from Thatcher's memoirs) failed to prevent the *Mirror*'s advance publication of extracts of *The Downing Street Years* (1993). In the extracts Thatcher attacked former political colleagues Richard Ryder, Michael Heseltine, Malcolm Rifkind and Jeffrey Archer. The front page of the *Mirror* (7 October 1993) reported how she stuck 'the knife in Major's men' while over the page, journalist David Bradshaw presented the previous night's party conference as a political coup. He warned that Major's political authority was on the verge of collapse after 'the Right went on the rampage under the shadow of Lady Thatcher'. He claimed that Thatcher 'stormed' Blackpool aided by Cabinet right-wingers happy to exploit 'the weakness at the top' and 'to push for a return to hard-line Thatcherism'. The party, it was claimed, was faced with an imminent 'future leadership battle' (*Mirror*, 7 October 1993:2).

Writing his last political column for the *Evening Standard*, Simon Heffer reflected that Major's crisis-ridden government was emblematic of the cultural and political instability that had plagued the post-Thatcher period. Even detractors had conceded Thatcher's premiership was characterised by her sense of motivation and direction. Thatcher's memoirs provided a 'salutary yardstick against which to measure Major' (*Evening Standard*, 26 October 1993:13). Seen positively, her memoirs were read as revelation and affirmation: the political past rising up to discredit the present. In contrast, for a more sceptical commentator such as the *Guardian's* Martin Kettle, her memoirs and the hullabaloo surrounding them were examples of 'phoney nostalgia ... implanted right at the corrosive centre of the present'. The inflated recollection of Thatcherism was a 'self-deluding series of myths' born of an absence of power (*Guardian*, 4 September 1993:21).[12] On one level these responses to Thatcher's memoirs reveal the difficulty in establishing any consensus about the past, since each analysis or evaluation brings with it the analyst's own investments and political partialities. They also underline the commonplace observation that political biography and the critical response to it inevitably involves the fictional.

The mild masculinity of Major was supposed to signify a sea-change in the Conservative Party: in contrast to the bombast and battle he offered himself as emblem of a more restrained and everyday form of Conservatism cast in the idiom of 'English' self-effacement, decency and accommodation. But his party was Janus-faced. It was split by the desire for consensus and a new forward-looking identity that would seize the popular imagination, and a longing backward glance that sought to re-instil Thatcherite values in present practices. The representation of Thatcher as madwoman, axe-murderer or vengeful ghost are deeply gendered forms of imagining political violence and of translating frustration with Major into the return of repressed female fury. As images of political dissent they reveal a fascination with, and hystericisation of, violence and the authoritarian persona. Furthermore, they are an easy way to siphon off the undesirable or uncomfortable aspects of Thatcherism, to locate them in the dispossessed woman whose violent potential was rendered safe through humour or supernatural imagery. Such fantasies of Thatcher as the Conservative's undead sat side-by-side with fantasies of the clarity and force her return to power would bring.

The preoccupation with Thatcher's opinion and return was overtaken, in the mid-1990s, by media focus on the disintegrating Conservative Party which became associated in the popular imagination with 'sleaze', cynicism and loss of direction. The electorate's ousting of the Conservatives in May 1997 for Tony Blair and New Labour constituted a huge repudiation of them and signalled the public's distance from and disavowal of the Thatcher regime and its discredited successors. The polarisation of human and inhuman, humane and inhumane took another unexpected turn as Thatcher was again resurrected in political commentary on the 'feminisation' of politics following the death of Princess Diana in a car crash outside Paris at the end of August. In the 1980s Margaret Thatcher vied with Princess Diana as 'most photographed woman' and often they appeared in succession in the tabloid press, women's magazines and on TV. In the aftermath of Diana's death they were reconfigured in popular political commentary to celebrate the new feminised political times and to secure Tony Blair's credentials as a humane force in British politics.[13]

In September 1997, the month after the fatal crash, Diana figured in much media coverage as the idealised fantasy of Britain's humanisation:

a sign of modern times. Her consummate range of feminine public personae – the fairy-tale Princess, the mother, the wronged wife, the modern woman experimenting with New Age therapies, psychotherapy and fashion, the political activist cast as nurse or Samaritan – were repeated continually across TV screens and in the press. In obituaries and tributes, Diana's compassionate persona was contrasted with the stilted emotion of the Royal Family, but more importantly with Thatcher as emblem of Britain's now rejected excesses of phallic power. Diana stood for a radical identification with those 'outcasts and rejects of Thatcherite Britain': the poor, people with Aids, immigrants blighted by racism, deserted and battered women.[14] Thatcher's phrase 'one of us', a common signal of acceptance of her creed of masculine self-dependence and atomised responsibility, was rearticulated as evidence of Diana's commonalty: she was 'on our side', 'one of us' and not 'one of them'. It became the slogan for a new form of popular civic interconnectedness. The effusive public response to Diana's death could be understood partly as an extension of Diana's own public strategy: the mobilisation of a feminine stereotype in self-defence. It enabled the collective retrieval of the attributes of vulnerability, indecision and care that Thatcher had evicted from her image as 'conviction politician' and her vision of national and individual self-sufficiency. Imagery of 1980s greed, exorbitant City salaries, boardroom profiteers and consumer excess were contrasted with fantasies of a charitable, caring society in which identification with Diana offered the British atonement and severance from their political past.

Tony Blair opportunistically coined the phrase 'the People's Princess' as he publicly acknowledged Diana's death from his constituency, thereby signalling the transformation of his 'people's party' into a softer, feminised New Labour Party. It was an astute attempt to conflate popular feeling for Diana with popular support for Labour. Journalists across the board from the once largely pro-Thatcher *Spectator* to the anti-Thatcherite *New Statesman* spoke of Blair being attuned to the people's new mood and of his readiness to revitalise politics with a new empathetic, demotic modern agenda. At their October 1997 party conference, the Conservatives desperately scrambled to capture the feminised attributes that had been grafted onto Blair. The media reported Michael Portillo's conversion at a lecture for the Centre of Policy Studies, where he called for a 'reinvigorated Conservatism' of tolerance, feeling and a 'self-enlightened capitalism'. In the post-conference party political broadcast, the new Conservative Leader William Hague stressed that 'compassion' was not a 'bolt-on-extra' for the party, but at its very heart. Diana's death provided the means by which a break with Thatcher could be underlined. Temporarily, violence, aggressive politics and national might were shifted from the cultural imagination. The narcissistic fantasy of an intimate humane community fleetingly washed over the potent spectres of violence that Thatcher had continued to represent.

An unlaid ghost

> No wonder that 'historical memory' should sometimes seem to slip out of kilter with the present, continuously raising ghosts and anxiously holding old answers up against the disorientating light of new questions.
> (Wright, 1985:16)

This research is not exempt from personal investment. My own personal history as an adult has been marked by Thatcher's presence. In 1979, the first general election for which I had the right to vote, I voted for Margaret Thatcher, not for the Conservative Party, but for her. The reasons were complex and in retrospect assure me that voting is much more than rational investment: it is also a diffuse set of desires about what the vote might make of you, about who one might want to be. On a rational level, one key influence on my vote, coming as I did from a traditionally Labour-voting family, was that she was a woman and that her accession to power might empower other women, including myself. In the mid-1980s I worked in the City of London for the bastions of finance and venture: Lloyd's Register and The Stock Exchange. I witnessed first-hand Thatcherism's influence in the processes of deregulation, the opportunities offered to some hard-working individuals, the consumerist excess, the widespread support, admiration, indeed adulation that Thatcher enjoyed in 'the square mile'.

This book has been in part an attempt to understand the position Thatcher occupied for over a decade, as well to interpret crucial aspects of her allure. As Jacqueline Rose has astutely commented, Thatcher was, and is, 'both a fantasy and a real event' (Rose, 1988:71). The difficulty remains that any analysis of the power she exerted prompts a slippage between Thatcher as constructed persona and Thatcher as real woman. To locate the symbolic violence that Thatcher invoked purely in the real woman is to ignore the continuing force of the themes that girded her persona and animate political culture, individual and collective imagination. Mainstream party political discourses still address the conditions of political success that Thatcher put centre stage in the

1980s: adversity, competition, self-responsibility, clarity of purpose, strong leadership and magisterial might. The metaphor of haunting perhaps accurately captures the intrusion and relevance of things past to things present. It refuses to put a firm line between then and now. I have argued throughout this book that one crucial route into understanding the ties and oppositions of collective life is through the analysis of fantasy and the way fantasies weave through and shape political texts. The processes of self-definition, of identifying and trying to cast out the enemy, which characterised the appeal of Thatcherism, still remain. I wish to conclude with a suggestion that Freud delivered at the beginning of the last century. He urged others to consider the psychic compulsion to repeat: 'a thing which has not been understood inevitably reappears; like an unlaid ghost, it cannot rest until the mystery has been solved and the spell broken' (Freud, 1909:122).

References

1. Contemporary fictions in which Thatcher features include Patrick Skene Catling's *Harrassment* (1993), Jonathan Coe's *What A Carve Up!* (1995), Hilary Mantel's *An Experiment in Love* (1995) and Philip Hensher's excellent *Kitchen Venom* (1996). Thatcher's image appeared on a video screen over a medical couch in a surgical room in Richard Hamilton's installation 'The Treatment Room' at the Venice Bienalle 1993. In April 1995 old footage of Thatcher appeared in a British Telecom television advertisement broadcast on commercial channels. In May 1995, Thatcher appeared alongside Elizabeth I and Queen Victoria on a poster in the London Underground advertising Madam Tussauds. In October 1995, following the London Fashion Show preview of her spring/summer collection 'Beautiful is Painful' (for which the design theme was plastic surgery), the young feminist fashion designer Karen Savage was considering drawing on Baroness Thatcher for her next collection. See Savage's interview with Lorna Russell in 'Wear your heart on your sleeve' (*Independent on Sunday*, *Real Life* section, 29 October 1995:5). In September 1997, a fringe theatre production of *The Wasp Factory* at the Lyric Theatre, Hammersmith featured Thatcher's face on video screens at either side of the stage during the production. Her face appeared amidst flickering images of wasps, clocks, shadowed mechanisms, overlaid with uncanny sounds. This visual imagery signified the disturbed mind of one of the protagonists.
2. On 15 March 1995, a Thatcher teapot with elongated nose, on sale in 1990 for around £25, was sold at Phillips auction house for £207. John Pym, the

manager of *Hope and Glory*, a London shop specialising in memorabilia, reported heavy demand for Thatcher memorabilia and noted that prices for objects like Thatcher teapots were fetching up to four times the price asked for just 18 months before in mid-1993 . For further details on Thatcher memorabilia see Marie Woolf's article 'Lady Thatcher springs eternal' in *Independent on Sunday* (19 March 1995:5).

3. In *Thatcher: The Downing Street Years*, broadcast on BBC1, 20 October 1993.

4. Broadcast on BBC2, 6 January 1996.

5. *Timewatch: Memo from Machiavelli* was broadcast on BBC2, 11 December 1994.

6. The series was broadcast throughout November 1995, the first and third episodes appeared on BBC1 on 5 and 12 November.

7. Thatcher's memoir *The Downing Street Years* (1993) was publicly released on 18 October 1993. It has been suggested that HarperCollins, owned by media mogul Rupert Murdoch, paid £3.5 million for the rights to this text and the prequel *The Path to Power* (1995). The memoir was largely ghost-written by two of Thatcher's speechwriters, Robin Harris and John O'Sullivan with Thatcher's editorial intervention.

8. *The Downing Street Years* was broadcast in four parts on consecutive weeks on BBC1 during October and November 1993.

9. The TV series was packaged and sold as a double video by BBC Enterprises Ltd. in 1994.

10. See for example Stephen Glover's commentary 'Over the top with Maggie' (*Evening Standard*, 15 April 1993: 9) and Sarah Baxter's political notebook 'Beaten up by the big bad Baroness' (*Evening Standard*, 20 April 1993:13).

11. After Thatcher's call for intervention in Bosnia, the Thatcher Foundation received 9000 letters from the public (ten to one in support) and her Maastricht speeches attracted a large response. The average day brought around 1000 letters (*Guardian 2*, 11 May 1993:2-3).

12. See for example Martin Kettle's 'Myths that form inside the well of nostalgia' (*Guardian*, 4 September 1993:21).

13. For a fuller discussion of this see my article 'Violence and the Sacred: the Iron Lady, the princess and the people's PM' in *New Formations*, No.36, 1999.

14. See David Cannadine 'The making of the myth of Saint Diana', Special Diana Section, (*Guardian*, 16 September 1997).

Bibliography

Abbott, P. and Wallace, C. (1992) *The Family and the New Right*, London: Pluto.

Abse, L. (1989) *Margaret, Daughter of Beatrice*, London: Jonathan Cape.

Adonis, A. and Pollard, S. (1997/1998) *A Class Act: The Myth of Britain's Classless Society*, Harmondsworth: Penguin.

Alexander, S. (1984) 'Women, Class and Sexual Difference', in S. Alexander (1994).

Alexander, S. (1989) 'Becoming a Woman in London in the 1920s and '30s', in S. Alexander (1994).

Alexander, S. (1994) *Becoming A Woman and Other Essays in 19th and 20th Century Feminist History*, London: Virago.

Anderson, B. (1983) *Imagined Communities*, London: Verso.

Anderson, D. and Dawson, G. (eds) (1986) *Family Portraits*, London: Social Affairs Unit.

Appignanesi, L. and Forrester, J. (1992) *Freud's Women*, London: Weidenfeld and Nicolson.

Ariès, P. (1960/1962) *Centuries of Childhood*, Harmondsworth: Penguin.

Atkinson, M. (1984) *Our Masters' Voices: The Language and Body Language of Politics*, London: Methuen.

Auchlich, J. (1992) 'Wildlife in the South Atlantic; Graphic Satire, Patriotism and the Fourth Estate', in J. Auchlich (ed), *Framing the Falklands War: Nationhood, Culture and Identity*, Buckingham: Open University Press.

Baker, K. (1993) *The Turbulent Years: My Life in Politics*, London: Faber and Faber.

Ball, S. (1995) *The Conservative Party and British Politics 1902-1951*, Harlow: Longman.

Barker, M. (1984) *The Video Nasties: Freedom and Censorship in the Arts*, London: Pluto Press.

Barker, M. and Petley, J. (eds) (1997) *Ill Effects: The Media/Violence Debate*, London: Routledge.

Barnett, A. (1982) *Iron Britannia*, London: Allison and Busby.

Barnett, A. (1989) 'After Nationalism', in R. Samuel (ed) (1989).

Barthes, R. (1973) 'Photography and Electoral Appeal', in *Mythologies*, London: Paladin.

Barthes, R. (1977/1984) 'The Rhetoric of the Image', in *Image, Music, Text*, London: Fontana .

BBC (1997) 'Thatcher Funds Free Market', www.bbc.co.uk/politics97/news/07/0720/thatcher.shtml>.

Behrens, R. (1980) *The Conservative Party from Heath to Thatcher*, London: Saxon House.

Benjamin, J. (1988/1990) *The Bonds of Love: Psychoanalysis, Feminism, and the Problem of Domination*, London: Virago.

Benton, S. (1986) 'Cosmopolitics: Tax and feminism but no sex and violence', in *New Statesman*, 28 November, p16.

Benton, S. (1987) 'The Triumph of the Spirit of War', in *New Statesman*, 29 May, pp12-14.

Benton, S. (1996) 'Knights against the nightmares', in *Soundings*, Issue 2, Spring, London: Lawrence and Wishart, pp16-31.

Berman, M. (1982/1983) *All That Is Solid Melts Into Air: The Experience of Modernity*, London: Verso.

Bhabha, H. (1994) 'DissemiNation: Time, narrative and the margins of the modern nation', in *The Location of Culture,* London: Routledge.

Billig, M. (1995) *Banal Nationalism*, London: Sage.

Blackstone, T. (1990) *Prisons and Penal Reform*, Chatto Counterblasts No.11, London: Chatto and Windus.

Blake, R. (1982) 'Disraeli's Descendants', *Guardian*, 4 October 1982, p7.

Blake, R. (1985) *The Conservative Party from Peel to Thatcher*, London: Fontana.

Bocock, R. (1992) 'The Cultural Formations of Modern Society', in S. Hall and B. Gieben (eds) (1992).

Boorstin, D.J. (1962) *The Image*, London: Weidenfeld and Nicolson.

Boxer, A. (1996) *The Conservative Governments 1951-1964*, Harlow: Addison Wesley Longman.

Braudy, L. (1986) *The Frenzy of Renown: Fame and its History*, New York: Oxford University Press.

Bromley, R. (1988) *Lost Narratives*, London: Routledge.

Brunt, R. (1987) 'Thatcher Uses her Woman's Touch', in *Marxism Today*, June, pp22-4.

Budge, L. (1987/1988) '"The Salisbury Review": A Study in the Discourse of Neo-Conservatism', in *Block*, 13, pp69-78.

Burgin, V., Donald, J. and Kaplan, C. (eds) (1986) *Formations of Fantasy*, London: Methuen.

Butler, D. and Kavanagh, D. (1984) *The British General Election of 1983*, Basingstoke: Macmillan.

Butler, D. and Kavanagh, D. (1988) *The British General Election of 1987*, Basingstoke: Macmillan.

Butler, D. and Pinto-Duschinsky, M. (1980) 'The Conservative Elite 1918-78: Does Unrepresentativeness Matter?', in Z. Layton-Henry (ed) (1980).

Butler, J. (1990) *Gender Trouble: Feminism and the Subversion of Identity*, London: Routledge.

Callaghan, J. (1987) *Time and Chance*, London: Collins.

Campbell, B. (1987) *The Iron Ladies: Why Do Women Vote Tory?*, London: Virago.

Campbell, B. (1988) *Unofficial Secrets: Child Sexual Abuse, the Cleveland Case*, London: Virago.

Campbell, B. (1993) *Goliath: Britain's Dangerous Places*, London: Methuen.

Carter, E., Donald, J. and Squires, J. (eds) (1995) *Cultural Remix: Theories of Politics and the Popular*, London: Lawrence and Wishart.

Cashmore, E. and McCaughlin, E. (eds) (1991) *Out of Order? Policing Black People*, London: Routledge.

Cecil, Lord H. (1912) *Conservatism*, in S. Ball (1995).

Cixous, H. (1976/1981) 'Castration or decapitation?', in *Signs*, 7: 1, pp41-55.

Clarke, P. (1996/1997) *Hope and Glory: Britain 1900-1990*, London: Penguin.

Cockburn, C. (1987) *Women, Trade Unions and Political Parties*, Fabian Research Series 349, London: the Fabian Society.

Cockerell, M. (1983) 'The marketing of Margaret', in *The Listener*, 16 June, pp2-4, 22.

Cockerell, M. (1988) *Live From Number 10: The Inside Story of Prime Ministers and Television*, London: Faber and Faber.

Cole, J. (1987) *The Thatcher Years: A Decade of Revolution in British Politics*, London: BBC.

Colley, L. (1992/1994) *Britons: Forging the Nation 1707-1837*, London: Pimlico.

Collings, R. (ed) (1991/1992) *Reflections: Selected Writings and Speeches of Enoch Powell*, abridged version, London: Bellew.

Conservative Party, (1970) *A Better Tomorrow: The Conservative Programme for the Next Five Years*, London: Conservative Political Centre.

CPC (1980) *Going Places: Women in the Conservative Party*, London: Conservative Political Centre.

Cook, A. and Kirk, G. (1983) *Greenham Women Everywhere*, London: Pluto.

Cooke, A. (ed) (1989) *Margaret Thatcher: The Revival of Britain Speeches on Home and European Affairs 1975-1988*, London: Aurum Press.

Coote, A., Harman, H. and Hewitt, P. (1990) *The Family Way*, London: Institute for Public Policy Research.

Coote, A. and Pattullo, P. (1990) *Power and Prejudice: Women and Politics*, London: Weidenfeld and Nicolson.

Copjec, J. (1989) 'The Sartorial Super Ego', in *October* 50, pp58-72.

Copjec, J. (1995) 'The *Unvermögender* Other: Hysteria and Democracy in America', in E. Carter, J. Donald, J. Squires (eds), *Cultural Remix: Theories of Politics and the Popular*, London: Lawrence and Wishart.

Coveney, P. (1967) *The Image of Childhood: The Individual and Society: A Study of the Theme in English Literature*, Harmondsworth: Penguin.

Cowling, M. (ed) (1978) *Conservative Essays*, London: Cassell.

Crewe, I. (1988) 'Has the Electorate Become More Thatcherite?', in R. Skidelsky (ed) (1988).

Crewe, I. and Harrop, M. (eds) (1986) *Political Communications: The General Election Campaign of 1983*, Cambridge: Cambridge University Press.

Critchley, J. (1985/1986) *Westminster Blues*, London: Futura Publications.

Cunningham, H. (1995) *Children and Childhood in Western Society Since 1500*, London: Longman.

Currie, E. (1989/1990) *Lifelines*, London: Pan.

Curtice, J. (1989) 'The 1983 Election and the Nuclear Debate', in Marsh and Fraser (eds) (1989).

Davidoff, L. and Hall, C. (1987) *Family Fortunes: Men and Women of the English Middle Class 1780-1850*, London: Hutchinson.

Dawson, G. (1994) *Soldier Heroes: British Adventure, Empire and the Imagining of Masculinity*, London: Routledge.

Department of Social Security (1996) *Households Below Average Income: A Statistical Analysis, 1979-1993/4*, London: HMSO.

Derbyshire, J. and Derbyshire, I. (1990) *Politics in Britain From Callaghan to Thatcher*, Edinburgh: W. and R. Chambers.

Doane, M.A. (1991) *Femmes Fatale: Feminism, Film Theory, Psychoanalysis*, London: Routledge.

Dobson, C. and Payne, R. (1984) *The Dictionary of Espionage*, London: Harrop.

Dolar, M. (1995) 'The Legacy of the Enlightenment: Foucault and Lacan', in E. Carter, J. Donald and J. Squires (eds) (1995).

Donald, J. (1992) *Sentimental Education: Schooling, Popular Culture and the Regulation of Liberty*, London: Verso.

Donald, J. and Hall, S. (eds) (1986) *Politics and Ideology*, Milton Keynes: Open University Press.

Dowell, S. and Williams, J. (1994) *Bread, Wine and Women: The Ordination Debate in the Church of England*, London: Virago.

Dorfman, A. and Mattelart, A. (1972) *How to Read Donald Duck: Imperialist Ideology in the Disney Comic*, New York: International General.

Dunleavy, P., Gamble, A. and Peele, G. (eds) (1990) *Developments in British Politics, iii*, London: Macmillan.

Durham, M. (1991) *Sex and Politics: The Family and Morality in the Thatcher Years*, Basingstoke: Macmillan Education.

Dyer, R. (1991) 'Charisma', in *Stardom: Industry of Desire*, C. Gledhill (ed) London: Routledge.

Edgar, D. (1986) 'The Free or the Good', in R. Levitas (ed) (1986).

Elliott, A. (1996) *Subject to Ourselves Social Theory, Psychoanalysis and Postmodernity*, Cambridge: Polity Press.

Evans, H. (1981) *Downing Street Diary 1957-63*, London: Hodder and Stoughton.

Evans, J. (ed) (1986) *Feminism and Political Theory*, London: Sage.

Evans, D. (1996) *An Introductory Dictionary of Lacanian Psychoanalysis*, London: Routledge.

Fletcher, J. (1988) 'Versions of Masquerade', in *Screen*, Vol. 29. No.3, pp43-70.

Foley, M. (1993) *The Rise of the British Presidency*, Manchester: Manchester University Press.

Foot, M. (1984) *Another Heart and Other Pulses: The Alternative to the Thatcher Society*, London: Collins.

Franklin, B. (1994) *Packaging Politics: Political Communication in Britain's Media Democracy*, London: Edward Arnold.

Franklin, S., Lury, C. and Stacey, J. (eds) (1991) *Off-Centre: Feminism and Cultural Studies*, London: HarperCollins.

Fraser, A. (1988) *Boadicea's Chariot: The Warrior Queens*, London: Weidenfeld and Nicolson.

Freud, S. (1908) 'Family Romances', in P. Gay (ed) (1995).

Freud, S. (1909) 'Analysis of a Phobia in a Five-Year-Old Boy', in J. Strachey (ed), *The Standard Edition of the Complete Psychological Works of Sigmund Freud*, Vol. X, London: Hogarth Press and The Institute of Psycho-Analysis.

Freud, S. (1911) 'Formulations of the Two Principles of Mental Functioning', in P. Gay (ed) (1995).

Freud, S. (1915) 'Thoughts for the times on war and death', in A. Dickson (ed), *Civilization, Society and Religion: Group Psychology, Civilization and its Discontents and Other Works*, Pelican Freud Library Vol.12, Harmondsworth: Pelican.

Freud, S. (1919) 'A Child is Being Beaten', in J. Strachey (ed), *The Standard Edition of the Complete Psychological Works of Sigmund Freud*, Vol. XVII, London: Hogarth Press and The Institute of Psycho-Analysis.

Freud, S. (1920) 'Beyond the Pleasure Principle', in P. Gay (ed) (1995).

Freud, S. (1921/1991) 'Group Psychology and the Analysis of the Ego', in A. Dickson (ed), *Civilization, Society and Religion*, The Penguin Freud Library Vol. 12, Harmondsworth: Penguin.

Freud, S. (1924) 'A Note upon the "Mystic Writing Pad"', in J. Strachey (ed), *The Standard Edition of the Complete Psychological Works of Sigmund Freud*, Vol. XIX, London: Hogarth Press and The Institute of Psycho-Analysis.

Freud, S. (1925/1984) 'On Negation', in A. Richards (ed), *On Metapsychology: The Theory of Psychoanalysis*, Pelican Freud Library Vol. 11, Harmondsworth: Penguin.

Freud, S. (1927/1991) 'Fetishism', in A. Richards (ed), *On Sexuality*, Pelican Freud Library Vol. 17, Harmondsworth: Penguin.

Freud, S. (1930) 'Civilization and its Discontents', in A. Richards (ed), *Civilization, Society and Religion*, The Penguin Freud Library Vol. 12, Harmondsworth: Penguin.

Friedman, M. (1977) *Inflation and Unemployment*, London: IEA.

Frosch, S. (1987) *The Politics of Psychoanalysis: An Introduction to Freudian and Post-Freudian Theory*, New Haven: Yale University Press.

Gamble, A. (1974) *The Conservative Nation*, London: Routledge and Kegan Paul.

Gamble, A. (1988/1994) *The Free Economy and the Strong State*, Second Edition, Basingstoke: Macmillan.

Gamble, A. (1990) 'The Thatcher Decade in Perspective', in P. Dunleavy, A. Gamble and G. Peele (eds) (1990).

Gardiner, G. (1975) *Margaret Thatcher: From Childhood to Leadership*, London: Kimber.

Gardiner, J. (1983) 'Women, Recession and the Tories', in S. Hall and M. Jacques (eds) (1983).

Gay, P. (ed) (1995) *The Freud Reader*, London: Vintage.

Gellner, E. (1983) *Nations and Nationalism*, Oxford: Basil Blackwell.

Gerth, H.H. and Mills, C.W. (eds) (1972) *From Max Weber*, New York: Oxford University Press.

Giddens, A. (1985) *The Nation-State and Violence*, Cambridge: Polity Press.

Giddens, A. (1987) *Social Theory and Modern Sociology*, Cambridge: Polity Press.

Giddens, A. (1990) *The Consequences of Modernity*, Cambridge: Polity Press.

Gilbert, M. (1981) *Churchill's Political Philosophy*, Oxford: Oxford University Press.

Gilmour, I. (1977/1978) *Inside Right: A Study of Conservatism*, London: Quartet Books.

Gilmour, I. (1992) *Dancing with Dogma: Britain under Thatcherism*, London: Simon and Schuster.

Gilroy, P. (1987) *'There Ain't No Black in the Union Jack': The Cultural Politics of Race and Nation*, London: Hutchinson.

Gittins, D. (1998) *The Child in Question*, Basingstoke: Macmillan.

Glasgow University Media Group (1985/1995) 'The Falklands War: 'the home front', in G. Philo (ed) (1995).

Gray, R. (1982) 'The Falklands Factor', in *Marxism Today*, July, pp8-12.

Green, E.H.H. (1995) *The Crisis of Conservatism: The Politics, Economics and Ideology of the British Conservative Party 1880-1914*, London: Routledge.

Griffiths, L. (1998) 'Britain's Thatcher to Speak from the Grave', Reuters, UK and Ireland, <http://www.yahoo.co.uk/head-lines/980612/news/897684240-0000006529.html>.

Gummer, J., Heffer, E. and Beith, A. (1987) *Faith in Politics*, London: SPK.

Halevy, E. (1971) *The Birth of Methodism in England*, Chicago: University of Chicago Press.

Hall, S., Critcher, C., Jefferson, T., Clarke, J. and Roberts, B. (1978) *Policing the Crisis: Mugging, the State, and Law and Order*, London: Macmillan.

Hall, S. (1979) 'The Great Moving Right Show', in S. Hall and M. Jacques (eds) (1983).

Hall, S. (1988) *The Hard Road To Renewal: Thatcherism and the Crisis of the Left*, London: Verso.

Hall, S. (1993) *Moving On*, London: Democratic Left.

Hall, S. and Gieben, B. (eds) (1992) *Formations of Modernity*, Cambridge: Polity Press and Open University.

Hall, S. and Jacques, M. (eds) (1983) *The Politics of Thatcherism*, London: Lawrence and Wishart.

Hall, S. and Jacques, M. (eds) (1989) *New Times: The Changing Face of Politics in the 1990's*, London: Lawrence and Wishart.

Halloran, P. and Hollingsworth, M. 'How Mark Thatcher Made His Millions', in *Night and Day*, *Mail on Sunday Review*, 9 April 1995, pp14-22.

Hartley, J. (1992) *The Politics of Pictures: The Creation of the Public in the Age of Popular Media*, London: Routledge.

Harris, K. (1988/1989) *Thatcher*, London: Weidenfeld and Nicolson.

Harris, R. (1983) *Gotcha! The Media, the Government and the Falklands Crisis*, London: Faber and Faber Ltd.

Harris, R. (1990/1991) *Good and Faithful Servant: The Unauthorized Biography of Bernard Ingham*, London: Faber and Faber.

Harvey, D. (1980/1989) *The Condition of Postmodernity: An Enquiry into the Origins of Cultural Change*, Oxford: Basil Blackwell.

Hastings, M. and Jenkins, S. (1983) *The Battle for the Falklands*, London: Book Club Associates.

Hayek, F. A. (1944) *The Road to Serfdom*, London: Routledge.

Heath, S. (1986) 'Joan Riviere and the Masquerade', V. Burgin, J. Donald and C. Kaplan (eds), *Formations of Fantasy*.

Heffer, E. (1983) 'Turbulent Priests', in *New Statesman*, 4 February, pp12-13.

Heywood, A. (1992) *Political Ideologies*, London: Macmillan.

Hillyard, P. and Percy-Smith, J. (1988) *The Coercive State: The Decline of Democracy*, London: Fontana.

Hirst, P. (1989) *After Thatcher*, London: Collins.

Hobsbawm, E. (1996) 'The Nation is Labour's for the Taking', in *New Statesman*, 3 May, pp14-15.

Hobsbawm, E. (1994/1995) *Age of Extremes: The Short History of the Twentieth Century 1914-1991*, London: Abacus.

Hofstadter, R. (1967) *The Paranoid Style in American Politics and Other Essays*, New York: Vintage Books.

Hogg, Q. (1959) *The Conservative Case*, Revised Edition,

Harmondsworth: Penguin.

Holland, P. (1992) *What is a Child? Popular Images of Childhood*, London: Virago.

Holland, P. (1997) 'Living for libido; or, *Child's Play IV*: the imagery of childhood and the call for censorship', in M. Barker and J. Petley (eds) (1997).

Holmes, M. (1982) *Political Pressure and Economic Policy: British Government 1970-1974*, London: Butterworth.

Holmes, M. (1989) *Thatcherism: Scope and Limits, 1983-7*, Basingstoke: Macmillan.

Hutton, W. (1995) *The State We're In*, Revised Edition, London: Vintage.

Ignatieff, M.(1993) *Blood and Belonging: Journeys into the New Nationalism*, London: Chatto and Windus.

Ivy, M. (1995) 'Have You Seen Me? Recovering the Inner Child in Late Twentieth-Century America', in S. Stephens (ed) (1995a).

James, B. (1983) 'Paris in the Spring', in *Daily Mail*, 13 May, pp18-19.

Jenkins, P. (1987/1989) *Mrs Thatcher's Revolution*, London: Pan Books.

Jessop, B., Bonnett, K., Bromley, S. and Ling, T. (1988) *Thatcherism*, Cambridge: Polity Press.

John, M. (1995) 'Children's Rights in a Free-Market Culture', in S. Stephens (1995a).

Johnson, R.W. (1985) *The Politics of Recession*, London: Macmillan.

Johnston, L. (1992) *The Rebirth of Private Policing*, London: Routledge.

Junor, P. (1983) *Margaret Thatcher: Wife, Mother, Politician*, London: Sidgwick and Jackson.

Kaplan, C. (1986) '*The Thorn Birds*: fiction, fantasy, femininity', in V. Burgin, J. Donald and C. Kaplan (eds) (1986).

Kavanagh, D. (1987) *Thatcherism and British Politics: The End of Consensus?*, Oxford: Oxford University Press.

Keane, J. (1996) *Reflections on Violence*, London: Verso.

Keay, D. (1982) '"Whatever I Go Through Now, Can't Be As Terrible": Exclusive interview with Margaret Thatcher', *Woman's Own*, 28 August 1982, pp8-10, 34.

Keegan, W. (1984) *Mrs Thatcher's Economic Experiment*, London: Allen Lane.

Keeton, G.W. and Schwarzenburger, G. (1960) *The Yearbook of World Affairs*, London: Stevens and Sons Ltd/London Institute of World Affairs.

Keith, M. (1991) 'Policing a perplexed society?: No-go areas and the mystification of police-Black conflict', in E. Cashmore and E. McCaughlin (eds) (1991).

Keith, M. (1993) *Race, Riots and Policing: Lore and Order in a Multiracist Society*, London: UCL.

Kellner, D. (1995) *Media Culture: Cultural Studies, Identity and Politics Between the Modern and the Postmodern*, London: Routledge.

Kennard, D. and Small, N. (eds) (1997) *Living Together*, London: Quartet.

Kennedy Martin, T. (1990) BFI Extracts from Introduction to *Edge of Darkness*, London: Faber and Faber.

King, A. (1985) 'Margaret Thatcher: The style of a Prime Minister', in A. King (ed), *The British Prime Minister*, Revised Edition, Basingstoke: Macmillan.

King, A. (1988) 'Margaret Thatcher as a Political Leader', in R. Skidelsky (ed) (1988).

Kristeva, J. (1980/1982) *Powers of Horror: An Essay on Abjection*, L.S. Roudiez (trans), New York: Columbia University Press.

Kristeva, J. (1993) *Nations Without Nationalism*, L.S. Roudiez (trans), New York: Columbia University Press.

Lacan, J. (1953-4/1988) *The Seminar: Book I. Freud's Papers on Technique 1953-4*, J. Forrester (trans), Cambridge: Cambridge University Press.

Lacan, J. (1964/1977) *The Seminar: Book XI. The Four Fundamental Concepts of Psychoanalysis*, A. Sheridan (trans), London: Hogarth Press and Institute of Psycho-Analysis.

Lacan, J. (1973/1986) *The Four Fundamental Concepts of Psycho-Analysis*, A. Sheridan (trans), Harmondsworth: Penguin.

Lacan, J. (1977) *Écrits: A Selection*, A. Sheridan (trans), London: Tavistock Publications.

Lacan, J. (1977) 'The line and the light', in *The Four Fundamental Concepts of Psychoanalysis*, A. Sheridan (trans), London: Hogarth Press and Institute of Psycho-Analysis.

Lacan, J. (1982) *Feminine Sexuality*, J. Mitchell and J. Rose (eds), J. Rose (trans), London: W.W. Norton.

Laplanche, J. and Pontalis, J.B. (1973/1988) *The Language of Psychoanalysis*, London: Karnac Books.

Laplanche, J. and Pontalis, J.B. (1968/1986) 'Fantasy and the Origins of Sexuality', in V. Burgin, J. Donald and C. Kaplan (eds) (1986).

Layton-Henry, Z. (1980) *Conservative Party Politics*, London: Macmillan.

Lechte, J. (1990) *Julia Kristeva*, London: Routledge.

Letwin, S.R. (1992) *The Anatomy of Thatcherism*, London: Fontana.

Levitas, R. (1985) 'New Right Utopias', in *Radical Philosophy*, No.39, Spring, pp2-9.

Levitas, R. (ed) (1986) *The Ideology of the New Right*, Cambridge: Polity Press.

Levitas, R. (1986a) 'Competition and Compliance: The Utopias of the New Right', in R. Levitas (1986).

Leys, C. (1989) *Politics in Britain: From Labourism to Thatcherism*, London: Verso.

Liddington, J. (1989) *The Long Road to Greenham: Feminism and Anti-Militarism in Britain Since 1820*, London: Virago.

Light, A. (1991) *Forever England: Femininity Literature and Conservatism Between the Wars*, London: Routledge.

Loach, L. (1987) 'Can Feminism Survive a Third Term?', in *Feminist Review*, No 27, September, pp23-35.

Lovenduski, J. and Randall, V. (1993) *Contemporary Feminist Politics: Women and Power in Britain*, Oxford: Oxford University Press.

Lumsden, A. and Forbes, P. (1986) 'The War of the Agencies', in *New Statesman*, 22 August, pp5-8.

MacDonald, S. (1987) 'Boadicea, Warrior, Mother, Myth', in S. Macdonald et al (eds) (1987).

MacDonald, S., Holden, P. and Ardener, S. (eds) (1987) *Images of Women in Peace and War*, Basingstoke: Macmillan.

Malone, A. and Cohen, H. (1994) 'Satire rampant over Thatcher coat of arms', in *Sunday Times*, 20 November, p9.

Mann, M. (1986) *The Sources of Social Power*, Vol.1, Cambridge: Cambridge University Press.

Marsh, C. and Fraser, C. (eds) (1989) *Public Opinion and Nuclear Weapons*, Basingstoke: Macmillan.

Massey, D. (1987) 'Heartlands of Defeat', in *Marxism Today*, July, p23.

Mayer, A.J. (1979) *Madam Prime Minister: Margaret Thatcher*, USA: Newsweek Books.

McAlpine, A. (1992) *The Servant: A New Machiavelli*, London: Faber and Faber.

McEwan, I. (1987/1988) *The Child in Time*, London: Picador/ Pan.

McFadyean, M. and Renn, M. (1984) *Thatcher's Reign: A Bad Case of the Blues*, London: Chatto and Windus.

McGuigan, J. (1996) *Culture and The Public Sphere*, London: Routledge.

McNair, B. (1989) 'Television News and the 1983 Election', in C. Marsh and C. Fraser (eds) (1989).

McNair, B. (1995) *An Introduction to Political Communication*, London: Routledge.

McNeil, M. (1991) 'Making and not making the difference: the gender politics of Thatcherism', in S. Franklin et al (eds) (1991).

McRobbie, A. (1987) 'Parent power at the chalkface', in *Marxism Today*, May, pp24-7.

Mercer, K. (1990) 'Welcome to the Jungle: Identity and Diversity in Postmodern Politics', in J. Rutherford (ed) (1990).

Miles, R. (1985) *Women and Power*, London: Paladin.

Miles, R. (1988/1989) *The Women's History of the World*, London: Paladin.

Minford, P. (1988) 'Mrs Thatcher's Economic Reform Programme', in R. Skidelsky (ed) (1988).

Moi, T. (1985) *Sexual/Textual Politics*, London: Methuen.

Money, E. (1975) *Margaret Thatcher: First Lady of the House*, London: Leslie Frewin.

Moore, K. (1978) *She for God: Aspects of Women and Christianity*, London: Allison and Busby.

Mosse, G.L. (1985) *Nationalism and Sexuality: Respectability and Abnormal Sexuality in Modern Europe*, New York: Howard Fertig.

Mount, F. (1982/1983) *The Subversive Family: The Alternative History of Love and Marriage*, Hemel Hempstead: Unwin.

Muncie, J. and Wetherall, M. (1995) 'Family Policy and Political Discourse', in J. Muncie, M. Wetherall, R. Dallos and A. Cochrane (eds) (1995).

Muncie, J., Wetherall, M., Dallos, R. and Cochrane, A. (eds) (1995) *Understanding the Family*, London: Open University/Sage Publications.

Murray, T. (1978) *Margaret Thatcher*, London: W.H.Allen.

Murray, R. (1988) 'Fordism and Post Fordism', in Hall and Jacques (eds) (1989).

Nairn, T. (1977/ 1981) *The Break-Up of Britain*, 2nd Edition, London: Verso.

Nava, M. (1988) 'Outrage and Anxiety in the Reporting of Child Sexual Abuse: Cleveland and the Press', in M. Nava (1992).

Nava, M. (1992) *Changing Cultures: Feminism, Youth and Consumerism*, London: Sage Publications.

Nava, M. and O'Shea, A. (eds) (1996) *Modern Times: Reflections on a Century of English Modernity*, London: Routledge.

Negrine, R. (1989/1994) *Politics and the Mass Media in Britain*, Second Edition, London: Routledge.

Noakes, L. (1996) *Mass-Observation, Gender and Nationhood: Britain in the Falklands War*, Mass-Observation Occasional Paper No.5, University of Sussex Library.

Nunn, H. (1999) 'Violence and the Sacred: the Iron Lady, the Princess and the People's PM', in *New Formations*, London: Lawrence and Wishart, No.36, pp92-110.

O'Gorman, F. (ed) (1986) *British Conservatism: Conservative Thought from Burke to Thatcher*, London: Longman.

O'Shea, A. (1984) 'Trusting the People: How Does Thatcherism Work?', in *Formations of Nation and People*, London: Routledge and Kegan Paul.

O'Shea, A. (1996) 'English Subjects of Modernity', in M. Nava and A. O'Shea (eds) (1996).

Parker, I. (1997) *Psychoanalytic Culture: Psychoanalytic Discourse in Western Society*, London: Sage.

Parton, N. (1996) 'The New Politics of Child Protection', in J. Pilcher, and S. Wagg (eds) (1996).

Peters, P. (1978) 'The Tidy Mind of Margaret Thatcher', *Sunday Times*, 20 August, p1, pp8-14.

Philo, G. (ed) (1995) *Glasgow Media Group Reader: Vol. 2 Industry, Economy, War and Politics*, London: Routledge.

Pilcher, J. and Wagg, S. (eds) (1996) *Thatcher's Children: Politics, Childhood and Society in the 1980s and 1990s*, London: Falmer Press.

Pimlott, B. (1985) *Fabian Essays in Socialist Thought*, London: Heinemann.

Pimlott, B. (1993) *Harold Wilson*, London: HarperCollins.

Powell, E. (1968) 'Annual General Meeting of the West Midlands Area, Birmingham Conservative Political Centre, 20 April', in R. Collings (ed) (1991).

Powell, E. (1968) 'Speech to the London Rotary Club, Eastbourne, 16 November', in E. Powell (1969).

Powell, E. (1969) *Freedom and Reality*, London: B.T. Batsford.

Powell, E. (1977) *Wrestling With The Angel*, London: Sheldon Press.

Prior, J. (1986) *A Balance of Power*, London: Hamish Hamilton.

Public Information Office, House of Commons (1995) *Factsheet: Women in the House of Commons*, No. 5, Revised June 1995, London: House of Commons Library.

Pugh, M. (1985) *The Tories and the People 1880-1935*, London: Blackwell.

Pym, F. (1984) *The Politics of Consent*, London: Hamish Hamilton.

Raban, J. (1989) *God, Man and Mrs Thatcher*, London: Chatto and Windus.

Rawlings, P. (1999) *Crime and Power: A History of Criminal Justice 1688-1998*, Harlow: Addison Wesley Longman.

Richards, B. (1997) 'Popular Culture', in D. Kennard and N. Small (eds) (1997).

Riddell, P. (1983/1985) *The Thatcher Government*, London: Basil Blackwell.

Riddell, P. (1991) *The Thatcher Era and its Legacy*, Oxford: Basil Blackwell.

Riley, D. (1983) *War in the Nursery*, London: Virago.

Riviere, J. (1929) 'Womanliness As A Masquerade', in V. Burgin, J. Donald and C. Kaplan (eds) (1986).

Robertson, P. (1996) *Guilty Pleasures: Feminist Camp from Mae West to Madonna*, London: I.B. Tauris.

Rogers, B. (1988) *Men Only: An Investigation into Men's Organisations*, London: Pandora.

Rootes, C.A. (1989) 'The Campaign for Nuclear Disarmament: from Moral Crusade to Mobilisation of Anxiety?', in Marsh and Fraser (eds) (1989).

Rose, J. (1984) *The Case of Peter Pan or the Impossibility of Children's Fiction*, London: Macmillan.

Rose, J. (1986) *Sexuality in the Field of Vision*, London: Verso.

Rose, J. (1988/1993) 'Margaret Thatcher and Ruth Ellis', in J. Rose (1993).

Rose, J. (1993) *Why War?: Psychoanalysis, Politics, and the Return to Melanie Klein*, Oxford: Blackwell.

Rose, J. (1993a) 'An Interview with Jacqueline Rose', in J. Rose (1993).

Russel, T. (1978) *The Tory Party*, Harmondsworth: Penguin.

Rutherford, J. (ed) (1990) *Identity, Community, Culture, Difference*, London: Lawrence and Wishart.

Salecl, R. (1994) *The Spoils of Freedom: Psychoanalysis and Feminism After the Fall of Socialism*, London: Routledge.

Samuel, R. (1983) 'The Tory Party at Prayer', in *New Statesman*, 28 January, pp8-10.

Samuel, R. (ed) (1989) *Patriotism: The Making and Unmaking of British National Identity*, Vol. 1: History and Politics, London: Routledge.

Schoen, D. (1977) *Enoch Powell and the Powellites*, London: Macmillan.

Schwarz, B. (1986) 'Conservatism, Nationalism and Imperialism', in J. Donald and S. Hall (eds) (1986).

Schwarz, B. (1987) 'Conservatives and Corporatism', in *New Left Review*, Nov-December, pp107-128.

Schwarz, B. (1996) 'Ancestral citizens. Reflections on British Conservatism', pre-publication manuscript, (published in *New Formations*, 28, London: Lawrence and Wishart).

Schwarz, B. (1998) 'Politics and Rhetoric in the Age of Mass Culture', in *History Workshop Journal*, Issue 46, pp129-159.

Scott, A. (1996) *Real Events Revisited: Fantasy, Memory and Psychoanalysis*, London: Virago.

Scott, J. (1988) *Gender and the Politics of History*, Cambridge: Cambridge University Press.

Scraton, P. (1999) *Hillsborough*, Edinburgh: Mainstream Publishing Projects Ltd.

Scruton, R. (1980) *The Meaning of Conservatism*, London: Penguin.

Scruton, R. (1986) *Sexual Desire*, London: Weidenfeld and Nicolson.

Seldon, A. and Ball, S. (eds) (1994) *Conservative Century: The Conservative Party Since 1900*, Oxford: Oxford University Press.

Seyd, P. (1975) 'Democracy within the Conservative Party', in *Government and Opposition*, 10, pp219-37.

Sennett, R. (1986) *The Fall of Public Man*, London: Faber and Faber.

Sharpe, J.A. (1990) *Judicial Punishment in England*, London: Faber and Faber.

Sheehy, G. (1989) 'What Makes Maggie Run?', in *New Woman*, August.

Shingler, M. (1995) 'Masquerade or Drag? Bette Davis and the Ambiguities of Gender', in *Screen*, Vol. 36, No 3, pp179-92.

Shorter, E. (1975) *The Making of the Modern Family*, London: Fontana/Collins.

Skidelsky, R. (ed) (1988) *Thatcherism*, London: Chatto and Windus.

Smith, A.M. (1994) *New Right Discourse on Race and Sexuality: Britain 1968-1990*, Cambridge: Cambridge University Press.

Stallybrass, P. and White, A. (1986) *The Politics and Poetics of Transgression*, London: Methuen.

Strachey, A. (1957) *The Unconscious Motives of War: A Psycho-analytical Contribution*, London: Unwin Brothers.

Strachey, A. (1960) 'The Psychological Problems of Nationhood', in G.W. Keeton and G. Schwarzenberger (eds) (1960).

Steedman, C. (1986) *Landscape for a Good Woman: A Story of Two Lives*, London: Virago.

Steedman, C. (1990) *Childhood, Culture and Class in Britain, Margaret McMillan, 1860-1931*, London: Virago.

Stephens, S. (1995) 'Introduction: Children and the Politics of Culture in "Late Capitalism"', in S. Stephens (ed) (1995a).

Stephens, S. (ed) (1995a) *Children and the Politics of Culture*, Princeton, N.J.: Princeton University Press.

Strachey, A. (1957) *The Unconscious Motives of War*, London: Unwin Bros Ltd.

Strachey, A. (1960) 'Psychological Problems of Nationhood', in G.W. Keeton and G. Schwarzenberger (eds) (1960).

Taylor, R. (1986) 'CND and the 1983 election', in Crewe and Harrop (eds) (1986).

Thatcher, C. (1995) 'I've made colossal changes. That is why I am an "ism"', in *Daily Mail*, 13 October, p9.

Thatcher, M. (1968) 'What's Wrong With Politics?', in N. Wapshott and G. Brock (eds) (1983).

Thatcher, M. (1975) 'Conservative Party Conference', in A. Cooke (ed) (1989).

Thatcher, M. (1975a) 'Let the Children Grow Tall', in A. Cooke (ed) (1989).

Thatcher, M. (1977) 'The Dimensions of Conservatism: The Iain Macleod Memorial Lecture', in A. Cooke (ed) (1989).

Thatcher, M. (1977a) *Let Our Children Grow Tall: Selected Speeches 1975-7*, London: Centre for Policy Studies.

Thatcher, M. (1978) 'St. Lawrence Jewry, City of London', in A. Cooke (ed) (1989).

Thatcher, M. (1979) 'The Renewal of Britain', in A. Cooke (ed) (1989).

Thatcher, M. (1979a) 'Conservative Party Conference', in A. Cooke (ed) (1989).

Thatcher, M. (1981) 'St. Lawrence Jewry, City of London', in A. Cooke (ed) (1989).

Thatcher, M. (1984) 'Conservative Party Conference', in A. Cooke (ed) (1989).

Thatcher, M. (1984a) 'The Carlton Lecture', in A. Cooke (ed) (1989).

Thatcher, M. (1986) 'Conservative Women's Conference', in A. Cooke (ed) (1989).

Thatcher, M. (1987) 'Conservative Party Conference', in A. Cooke (ed) (1989).

Thatcher (1988) 'The College of Europe', in A. Cooke (ed) (1989).

Thatcher, M. (1988a) 'General Assembly of the Church of Scotland, Edinburgh', in A. Cooke (ed) (1989).

Thatcher, M. (1993/1995) *The Downing Street Years*, London: HarperCollins.

Thatcher, M. (1995) *The Path To Power*, London: HarperCollins.

Thatcher, M. (1995a) 'The Path To Power' extract in *The Sunday Times*, Section 3, 28 May, pp1-3.

Thomas, S.J. (1992) *Margaret Thatcher, Religion and Morality*, M.Phil. thesis, University of Sheffield, April.

Thompson, E.P. (1963) *The Making of the English Working Class*, London: Victor Gollancz.

Thomson, A. (1989) *Margaret Thatcher: The Woman Within*, London: W.H. Allen.

Tusscher, T. (1986) 'Patriarchy, capitalism and the New Right' in J. Evans (1986).

Utley, T.E. (1968) *Enoch Powell: The Man and His Thinking*, London: William Kimber.

Waddington, D. (1992) *Contemporary Issues in Public Disorder*, London: Routledge.

Wagg, S. (1996) '"Don't Try to Understand Them": Politics, Childhood and the New Education Market', in J. Pilcher and S. Wagg (eds) (1996).

Wapshott, N. and Brock, G. (1983) *Thatcher*, London: Macdonald and Co.

Warner, M. (1985) *Monuments and Maidens: The Allegory of the Female Form*, London: Weidenfeld and Nicolson.

Watkins, A. (1991/1992) *A Conservative Coup: The Fall of Margaret Thatcher*, Second Edition, London: Gerald Duckworth.

Weber, M. (1904-5/1985) *The Protestant Ethic and the Spirit of Capitalism*, Trans. T. Parsons, London: Counterpoint/Unwin Paperbacks.

Webster, D. (1988) *Looka Yonder! The Imaginary America of Populist Culture*, London: Comedia/Routledge.

Webster, W. (1990) *Not A Man To Match Her*, London: The Women's Press.

Weeks, J. (1981/1989) *Sex, Politics and Society: The Regulation of Sexuality Since 1800*, Second Edition, Harlow: Longman.

Whiteley, P., Seyd, P. and Richardson, J. (1994) *True Blues: The Politics of Conservative Party Membership*, Oxford: Oxford University Press.

Williams, V. (1994) *Who's Looking at the Family?*, London: Barbican Art Gallery.

Wilson, E. (1977) *Women and the Welfare State*, London: Tavistock.

Winship, J. (1987) *Inside Women's Magazines*, London: Pandora Press.

Winter, D. (1988) *Battered Bride? The Body of Faith in an Age of*

Doubt, Eastbourne: Monarch Publications.

Winter, K. and Connolly, P. (1996) '"Keeping it in the Family": Thatcherism and the Children Act 1989', in J. Pilcher and S. Wagg (eds) (1996).

Wolpe, A. and Donald, J. (eds) (1983) *Is Anyone Here From Education?*, London, Pluto Press.

Wright, P. (1985) *On Living in an Old Country*, London: Verso.

Young, A. (1990) *Femininity in Dissent*, London: Routledge.

Young, H. (1989/1990) *One of Us*, Revised Edition, London: Pan Books.

Young, H. and Sloman, A. (1986) *The Thatcher Phenomenon*, London: BBC Publications.

Žižek, S. (1991) *For They Know Not What They Do: Enjoyment as a Political Factor*, London: Verso.

Žižek, S. (1994) *The Metastases of Enjoyment: Six Essays on Woman and Causality*, London: Verso.

Archive Source List

Key

CPA: GE	General Election Folders, Conservative Party Archives, Bodleian Library, Oxford.
CPA: PEB	Party Election Broadcasts (transcripts), Conservative Party Archives, Bodleian Library, Oxford.
CPA: PPB	Party Political Broadcasts (transcripts), Conservative Party Archives, Bodleian Library, Oxford.
CPA: TS	Thatcher Speeches Folders, Conservative Party Archives, Bodleian Library, Oxford.
CPPA	Conservative Party Poster Archive, Conservative Party Archives, Bodleian Library, Oxford.
NSA	National Sound Archives, British Library, London.

Conservative Party Archives

CPA: PPB 79	Transmission Transcript, *On The Record*, BBC 2, 24 March 1979, 21.30pm.
CPA: TS 11/79	Margaret Thatcher, speech to The Lord Mayor's Banquet, Guildhall, 12 November 1979.
CPA: TS 174/80	Margaret Thatcher, speech to the First Airey Neave Memorial Lecture, 3 March 1980.
CPA: TS 445/81	Margaret Thatcher, speech to the 51st Annual Conservative Women's Conference, 20 May 1981.
CPA: 405/82	Margaret Thatcher, speech to the 52nd Annual Conservative Women's Conference, 26 May 1982.
CPA: 73/83	Margaret Thatcher, speech to the 23 National Young Conservative Conference, 12 February 1983.

CPA: GE 357/83 — Michael Heseltine, Secretary for Defence, letter to candidates on CND in marginal constituencies, 17 May 1983.

CPA: GE 367/83 — Michael Heseltine, Secretary for Defence, speech to Watford Party Workers, 17 May 1983.

CPA: PEB 17/5/83 — Conservative Party Election Broadcast, transmitted on BBC1, BBC2, ITV and Channel 4, 17 May 1983.

CPA: GE 387/83 — Conservative Party Election Broadcast, transmitted on BBC1, BBC2, ITV and Channel 4, 20 May 1983.

CPA: GE 363/83 — Douglas Hurd, speech to Royal United Services Institute, 18 May 1983.

CPA: GE 393/83 — Douglas Hurd, speech to Littleborough and Saddleworth constituency, 23 May 1983.

CPA: GE 394/83 — Dr Rhodes Boyson, Parliamentary Under Secretary for Education and Science, speech to Ealing North Party Workers, 23 May 1983.

CPA: GE 404/83 — Edward Heath, speech to Darlington party workers, 23 May 1983.

CPA: GE 347/83 — Margaret Thatcher, speech to the Scottish Conservative Conference, Perth, 13 May 1983.

CPA: GE 438/83 — Margaret Thatcher, speech to the Royal Hall, Harrogate, 26 May 1983.

CPA: GE 583/83 — Margaret Thatcher, speech at the Flyde Coast Rally, Fleetwood, 7 June 1983.

CPA: GE 539/83 — Margaret Thatcher, speech to the West Midlands Rally, Birmingham, 3 June 1983.

CPA: GE 554/83 — Margaret Thatcher, speech to the Youth Rally, Wembley, 5 June 1983.

CPA: 376/84 — Margaret Thatcher, speech to the 54 Conservative Women's Conference, 23 May 1984.

CPA: TS 229/88 — Margaret Thatcher, speech to 58 Conservative Women's National Conference, 25 May 1988.

CPA: TS 8/88 — Margaret Thatcher, speech to the Press Association, Savoy Hotel, London, 8 June 1988.

CPA: TS 7/90 — Margaret Thatcher, speech to The 300 Group, 18 July 1990.

CPA: TS 11/90 — Margaret Thatcher, Prime Minister's speech to Central Office Workers, 26 November 1990.

CPPA: GE 1970 — General Election Posters 1970.

National Sound Archives

NSA: LP36969	Margaret Thatcher Speech to Finchley constituency, 31 July 1976.
NSA: P1261	*Desert Island Discs* (off air recording), BBC Radio 4, 18 February 1978.
NSA: LP38518	*The Jimmy Young Show*, BBC Radio 2, 31 January 1979.
NSA: LP40788	*Pete Murray Late Show*, BBC Radio 1, 7 March 1982.
NSA: B1154	*The Jimmy Young Show*, BBC Radio 2, 26 January 1986.
NSA: B2075	*Woman's Hour*, BBC Radio 4, 11 December 1986.

Index

INDEX